UPSET:
Australia Wins the America's Cup

UPSET:

AUSTRALIA WINS THE AMERICA'S CUP

By Michael Levitt & Barbara Lloyd
Color Photography by Dan Nerney

A NAUTICAL QUARTERLY BOOK
WORKMAN PUBLISHING, NEW YORK

ACKNOWLEDGMENTS

The authors wish to thank more than a few people who made this project possible. This list includes yacht designers Ben Lexcen, Johan Valentijn, Bruce Kirby, Bill Langan, and David Pedrick for their candid appraisals of the summer of 1983; William H. Dyer Jones and Victor Romagna, members of the New York Yacht Club, who were willing to discuss what went right and what went wrong; *Freedom* Campaign '83 officials George F. (Fritz) Jewett, Jr., Edward du Moulin, and Jack Sutphen; *Liberty*'s sailtrimmer John Marshall for his dispassionate view of the summer and his unmatched view of the action on the race course; *Defender/Courageous* officials and sailors Charles Kirsch, Dave Vietor, Tom Blackaller, Gary Jobson, John Kolius, and John Bertrand; Alan Bond, head of the *Australian II* syndicate, who gave a private interview and his very candid thoughts on the summer; *Australia II* crewman/manager John Longley, for an inside look at the *Australia II* camp; Donald C. McGraw, Jr., publisher of *Nautical Quarterly;* Joe Gribbins, editor of *Nautical Quarterly* and the editor of this book; Marilyn Rose, designer of *Nautical Quarterly* and the designer of this book; Laura Riegel and Bud Lovelace of the *Nautical Quarterly* staff; the people at Workman Publishing, especially Suzanne Rafer, Alexandra Halsey, Lynn Strong, Jennifer Rogers, Wayne Kirn, and Douglass Grimmett; Dan Nerney, who contributed much more to this project than just his extraordinary photographs; Bob Blumenstock, former measurer for the New York Yacht Club and USYRU; Jeff Spranger, associate editor of *America's Cup Report;* Sohei Hohri, New York Yacht Club librarian, for his cheerful willingness to check a fact; Eileen Slocum, for her human insights; Monique Panaggio, Newport Preservation Society; Lois Muessel, director of the America's Cup office; Len Panaggio, America's Cup press liaison; Mark Smith, who provided the race drawings in Chapter 12; Robert Hopkins, whose writings on John Bertrand of *Australia II* were helpful; and Jay Broze, Keith Taylor, Bob MacDonald, and Joanne Fishman.

On a more personal level the authors wish to thank Herb McCormick, Isabel Coyle, Linda Murray, Christopher Lloyd, and the Whittemores: Sally, Lisa, Katie, and Liz—who will be missed.

Library of Congress Cataloging in Publication Data
Levitt, Michael.
 Upset: Australia wins the America's Cup.
 "A Nautical Quarterly book."
 1. America's Cup races. 2. Australia II (Boat)
3. America's Cup races—History. I. Lloyd,
Barbara.
II. Title.
GV830 1983.L48 1983   797.1'4   83-21910
ISBN 0-89480-674-2

A Nautical Quarterly Book
Cover and Book Design: Marilyn Rose
Photographs: Dan Nerney
America's Cup course diagrams by Mark Smith
Editor: Joseph Gribbins

Workman Publishing Company, Inc.
1 West 39 Street
New York, NY 10018

Manufactured in the United States of America
First printing November 1983
10 9 8 7 6 5 4 3 2 1

CONTENTS

UPSET:
Australia Wins the America's Cup

"God smiled on us."
—DENNIS CONNER, AFTER WINNING THE SECOND
AMERICA'S CUP RACE

CHAPTER 1
The Race of the Century

On Monday, September 26, 1983, Dennis Conner seemed poised to take his place in history. It was the seventh and final race of the 25th defense of the America's Cup, and one small measure of this extraordinary series of sea battles waged off Newport's Brenton Reef was the fact that there had never been a seventh race in 132 years of this competition. Since the switch to 12-Meter boats in 1958, there had never been a sixth race for what amounts to sailing's Holy Grail. But momentum and history aside, Dennis Conner and his painfully obsolete 12-Meter *Liberty,* representing the prestigious New York Yacht Club—but, more to the point, representing America—were dying out there, and had been for nearly a week.

It had been six days since Conner had won a race, and six days since he had truly savored a breeze untainted by the white Australian boat with the trick keel, the challenger that the New York Yacht Club had fought so tenaciously to oust from the competition. Now Conner had time—if only a second—to look back at *Australia II,* the challenger, and perhaps to think about what lay ahead: a victory in this seventh and deciding race against what seemed like impossible odds. It was within his grasp.

At the start of the final race—Conner had been consistently brilliant and aggressive at the starts—he led his rival, John Bertrand, skipper of *Australia II,* by eight seconds. Traditionally, eight seconds at the start of an America's Cup race is an eternity; but this boat from Down Under was no traditional boat. As the two 12 Meters worked their way slowly up the weather leg, *Australia II* crossed ahead; once again she seemed powered by something other than the wind. The New York Yacht Club, in its efforts to get rid of this boat, had called her a 12.45 Meter when she was heeled at 20 degrees. That aspersion seemed conservative now, and had for a week. On this day, *Australia II* seemed a 14 Meter.

Then Conner, who hadn't been able to buy a wind shift in a week, found one, and led at the first mark by 29 seconds. On the reaching leg—the only point of sail in which *Liberty* seemed the least bit faster than *Australia II*—

Conner stretched his lead to 45 seconds. They jibed for the second reaching leg, and with the wind a little squarer, *Australia II*, which was reputed to be so slow downwind, cut *Liberty*'s lead to 23 seconds. Another upwind leg and the ruby-hulled *Liberty* led by 57 seconds. Nearly a minute! Only once before in the series had Conner and *Liberty* led *Australia II* by more than that. At this moment, Dennis Conner—this man of action, this man of destiny, this man of few words—seemed poised to do the impossible: win the seventh race of the America's Cup over a boat that appeared to be from another planet. Only 8.8 miles of sailing as the crow flies—two legs—stood between Conner and a successful defense of the 25th America's Cup. It seemed like fate—for Dennis Conner, for the New York Yacht Club, and for America. For a moment on this beautiful fall afternoon, all was right with the world; what had been secure for 132 years looked safe—until the next competition.

Even for Conner, a man who doesn't express joy easily, this must have been a heady moment, one of the most sublime moments in his life. He was going to do it. Not because American technology was better (it had been shown to be wholly inadequate this time), not because America had 132 years of momentum on its side in what had become the longest winning streak in sports, not because the New York Yacht Club was better—but simply because Dennis Conner, the husky skipper from San Diego, was better. He simply willed his slow red boat to win; and, by God, she seemed about to grant him his wish.

The Almighty's name had been much invoked in this contest. When Dennis Conner won his second race on Thursday, September 15, to lead the contest 2–0, he took his victory lap past a heavily loaded ferry boat. This was *East Chop*, which in ordinary life ferries passengers from Hyannis to Martha's Vineyard. Her mission this week was different; *East Chop* was a spectator boat for the America's Cup. As 420 passengers, who had paid $45 each, lined the port rail to catch a glimpse of the victorious Conner and his boat, *East Chop* leaned ominously toward the water and toward what seemed imminent disaster. Nevertheless, the spectators broke into a heartfelt rendition of "God Bless America." It was spontaneous and wonderful, a patriotism that seemed to come from another century. Conner, enjoying it all, flashed his sunny All-American smile and waved as he sailed past. At the press conference following the race, Conner was asked how he won the contest. His answer was to the point. "God smiled on us," he said. The comment was innocent—as we like to think America used to be—and totally without self-reference. This man who seemed such a stranger to words had delivered the perfect line.

On Saturday, September 17, in winds under 10 knots and growing ever lighter, *Liberty* trailed *Australia II* by 5 minutes and 57 seconds on the fifth leg. But the time limit* expired with *Australia II* two miles from the finish line and two miles from delivering the most crushing defeat of a defender in America's Cup history. Thankful for the reprieve, Conner decided that, this day, God "must be an American."

On Sunday, September 18, the Australians finally won a race by a huge 3 minutes and 14 seconds—a record margin for a challenger. Conner would win the next day; but then the Australians, with their backs against the bulkhead, won two races to tie the score at three races. Before the seventh and final race, Conner called it "the race of the century" and claimed to be glad to be part of it, although his expression belied his words. One had seen it to lesser degrees for a week; Dennis Conner, the best 12-Meter sailor America had to offer, doubted he would win. That day the doubt was written clearly on his face.

Monday, September 26, was *the* day; it was the biggest day in Dennis Conner's life, the day when an historical judgment on his towering career would likely be written. As the two yachts rounded the second weather mark and started downwind, *Liberty*, ahead by 57 seconds, went left, away from the troubled waters churned by the spectator fleet. *Australia II* went right, in search of her destiny. *Australia II*, which was supposed to be so slow downwind, ate up acres of water on her run into history. Perhaps Conner should have covered her—and this is a question that is likely to be debated for years—but what seemed more apparent, more frightening, was the fact that *Australia II* was sailing lower and faster than the red boat. When your rival is sailing lower *and* faster on a downwind leg, the only thing you can cover her with is a howitzer. In 4.3 miles of sailing, *Australia II* gained one minute and 18 seconds to lead *Liberty* at the bottom mark by 21 seconds.

Conner, making his last stand on the last leg, started tacking. Before the weather leg was over, both boats tacked a gut-busting 47 times. You could nearly smell the blood in the winch grinders' cockpits as they fought for feet and then inches of heavily loaded jib sheets; you could sense the tension on both boats as everyone knew that one sheet override, one late or early castoff, one overly anxious tack, could change the course of history. Forty-seven times they tacked, and 47 times the 11 men on each boat had to do more than 11 men can possibly do well. And this was the final leg in the final race for the America's Cup in the closest and most demanding series sailed in 132 years. There was not one mistake. *Liberty* couldn't take an inch back from the stubborn *Australia II*.

At 5:20 P.M. on Monday, September 26, as the sun settled over Block Island and the chill of fall returned to the air, *Australia II* crossed the finish

---

*The time limit for the race is 5 hours and 15 minutes.

line between the elegant *Black Knight* and an orange buoy to win the race by 41 seconds. The America's Cup belonged to the Australians, after belonging to the Americans—or, to be perfectly accurate, to the New York Yacht Club—since before the Civil War. Conner had called it "the race of the century." It was more than that: it was the most sublime sailboat race ever sailed. This was the race that caused the world to discover sailboat racing, and this was one of those rare days when there was something weighty in the air, a day when a mere sporting event transcended the usual considerations of who won and who lost. Wherever one looked, there were lessons about life, about the pursuit of excellence for its own sake, about tradition, about nationalism, about commerce, about arrogance, about hubris, and about the deeper meanings of victory and defeat.

Understanding the victory and defeat were easier. America lost the America's Cup because *Australia II* was faster, thanks primarily to the inspired keel and hull shape that her designer, Ben Lexcen, gave her. But faster challengers have been known to lose in this game before. In 1934, T. O. M. Sopwith's British J-Boat *Endeavour* gave every evidence of being faster than the New York Yacht Club's *Rainbow;* but victory for the British was not to be. More recently, *Gretel II*, the Australian challenger in 1970, was judged to be faster than a redesigned *Intrepid;* but again it was not to be. A more complex answer to the events of September, 1983, is that *Australia II* was significantly faster than *Liberty*—faster than a challenger had ever been relative to a defender. *Australia II* was the biggest breakthrough in the 77-year history of 12-Meter design, perhaps in the history of yacht design.

To win, Dennis Conner had to be perfect. And he was perfect for three of seven races. It was one extraordinary man—unquestionably this country's most brilliant performer in this type of racing—versus a perfect machine. And the man came close to beating the inspired machine. But for Conner the absolute need to maintain this extreme level of perfection—knowing that one mental mistake in a thousand small and large decisions in the typical sailboat race, or one physical mistake by the 11 men on *Liberty*, would lose the Cup—began to wear. Small cracks began to appear, and John Bertrand skillfully sailed *Australia II* through them to win the most important contest there ever was in sailing.

And what of those lessons about life, about the pursuit of excellence for its own sake, about tradition, about nationalism, about commerce, about arrogance, about hubris, and about the deeper meanings of victory and defeat? That brings us to the rest of this book.

"If she is right, then we are all wrong."

—THE MARQUIS OF ANGLESEY, UPON VISITING
THE SCHOONER *AMERICA* IN 1851

CHAPTER 2
America: There Is No Second

I t might have been called the Maria Cup rather than the America's Cup. Had New York Yacht Club Commodore John Cox Stevens taken his brother's yacht *Maria* to England for the Race of All Nations, one wonders if the Maria Cup would have become the most sought-after prize in yachting. Would the Maria Cup have launched a hundred little ships, and would men like Sir Thomas Lipton, Baron Marcel Bich, and Alan Bond have spent scores of millions of dollars in an effort to displace the Maria Cup from its place of honor at the New York Yacht Club? One doubts it.

Tied up in that wonderful name, the America's Cup, is the pride of nations and the pride of some of the world's most successful men. The America's Cup has become sailing's Holy Grail over 132 years of history—sought after with a dedication, a tunnel vision, a compulsive need to spend that defies rational understanding. That is, unless one understands excellence for its own sake and the need of a very few to measure themselves against standards of excellence that have existed since the middle of the last century. The America's Cup is about excellence; it is about tradition; it is about the New York Yacht Club; it is about arrogance and power and money; it is about competitive dreams; it is about tilting at windmills. The America's Cup is also rather ugly.

If a rose in name, the America's Cup is less so in appearance. The Cup, with its rather overwrought Victorian curves and flourishes, stands 27 inches high and is made of 8.4 pounds of silver. When it was struck in 1848 by London silversmith Robert Garrard, for Britain's Royal Yacht Squadron, its value was "100 guineas." The value of the silver in the Hundred Guineas Cup, as it was then called, has ebbed and flowed in 132 years, and today it is worth perhaps $1,500.

In 1851, England and its far-flung Empire celebrated its place in the world—at the head of the queue—and invited the world to bring to London the very best of its goods, arts, wonders, and inventions. Prince Albert's Great London Exposition of 1851 was what we call today a world's fair.

America sent such wonders as a threshing machine, Colt revolvers, printing presses, pianos, sculptures, and a New Yorker named Briggs who was the world's best lockpicker. Mr. Briggs, it was said with some humor, stole the show. He also confirmed, as did some other Yankee exhibits, a stereotype of America as a rude land populated by clever peasants.

America—or, to be more precise, John Cox Stevens, commodore of the New York Yacht Club—sent the schooner *America* to England in that festive summer of 1851 as a nautical accompaniment to the exhibits in the Crystal Palace, and she, too, would steal the show. Commodore Stevens, very much a man of his world, had two aims for his schooner: she was to win races and to win wagers in a time when men raced yachts for more than just silver trophies.

The New York Yacht Club was started on another Stevens yacht, *Gimcrack*, in July of 1844. Stevens was the club's first commodore, and he and his three brothers were prominent and wealthy New Yorkers with interests in real estate, shipping, and America's first railroad. When Stevens learned through his maritime connections that the British were interested in having an example of the excellent New York pilot schooners, he and a syndicate of fellow New York Yacht Club members—all men of sporting blood—commissioned *America* from designer George Steers, who had pioneered the clipper model of the deservedly famous New York pilot boat, as well as fast boats of other types. *America* was built at the yard of William H. Brown on the East River in Manhattan, and she was built in a hurry. The syndicate was willing to pay $30,000 for her, *provided* she proved "faster than any vessel in the United States brought to compete with her." When *America* was delivered 10 weeks later than the contract specified, Stevens was not pleased, a sentiment that would continue when he first raced her.

Stevens raced his then gray-painted new schooner against his brother Edward's *Maria*, a big but cranky sloop designed by another Stevens brother, Robert. *America* was beaten, and the commodore, very much a man of his world and his word, paid $20,000 for her. Despite her less than auspicious debut, *America* sailed for England. Stevens and his syndicate believed she was fast enough to acquit herself well across the pond, and they also concluded that she was sturdy enough to make the passage. *Maria*, a shallow-bodied racing yacht with a cloud of sail, was not a sea boat. *America*, under the command of the famous Captain Dick Brown, crossed the Atlantic in an uneventful 20 days. The crew's impression of her performance on the crossing? "She is the best sea boat that ever went out of [Sandy] Hook," wrote James Steers, brother of her designer, in his log of the adventure. "The way we have passed everything we have seen must be witnessed to be believed."

Before his yacht left for Europe on June 21, Stevens initiated correspondence with the commodore of England's Royal Yacht Squadron, the eminent British yacht club that began in Cowes on the Isle of Wight in 1815 and is considered to this day the *ne plus ultra* of such clubs. Stevens wrote from one commodore to another and announced his intention of coming to Cowes for a summer of socializing and perhaps some racing. The Royal Yacht Squadron, the first club in England honored with the "royal" prefix, must have been amused to discover that there was a yacht club in the New World. Nevertheless, they responded with civility, welcoming Stevens and the New York yacht that was then expected only as an example of American shipbuilding skill. Wrote the Earl of Wilton, commodore of the Royal Yacht Squadron: "For myself I may be permitted to say that I shall have great pleasure in extending to your countrymen any civility that lies in my power and shall be glad to avail myself of any improvements in shipbuilding that the industry and skill of your nation have enabled you to elaborate."

Stevens' reply was in kind: "We propose to avail ourselves of your friendly bidding and take with good grace the sound thrashing we are likely to get by venturing our 'longshore craft on your rough waters." For Commodore Stevens, at least, the ante was up.

Captain Brown took *America* to Le Havre, France, where she received a coat of black paint and fresh supplies. Waiting for her there were John Cox Stevens, his brother Edwin, and Alexander Hamilton's son, Colonel James A. Hamilton. While in France, Cox met William C. Rives, the American minister to Paris, and the famous Horace Greeley, who, as the world knows, liked to deliver global statements. (One of them was not "Go west, young man," however. That was said by John L. Soule, a newspaper reporter from Terre Haute, Indiana.) What Greeley said this day was, "The eyes of the world are on you. You will be beaten, and the country will be abused, as it has been in connection with the Exposition." He urged Stevens and his party not to race any British yachts, and so did Ambassador Rives.

America arrived in the Solent, the channel between the Isle of Wight and the mainland, the first day of August. There she encountered the British yacht *Lavrock*, considered one of the fastest cutters of her type. *America* was floating five inches down on her lines, due to her recent provisioning with the best of French wines and viands for the lavish entertaining that Stevens planned when he anchored his schooner off the Royal Yacht Squadron at Cowes. Stevens, never one to resist a little sport, engaged *Lavrock* in an ad-hoc race. He described the engagement as high drama: "In the morning early, the tide was against us, and it was a dead calm. At nine o'clock a gentle breeze sprang up, and with it came gliding down the *Lavrock,* one of the newest and fastest cutters of her class. The news spread like lightning that the Yankee clipper had arrived, and that the *Lavrock* had gone to show her the way. . . . The yachts and vessels in the harbor, the wharves and windows of all the houses bordering on them, were filled with thousands of spectators, watching with eager eyes the eventful trial they saw we could not escape.''

The wind had built to five or six knots and the course was upwind, a direction much to the liking of Captain Brown and his crew. ''After waiting until we were ashamed to wait longer,'' continued Stevens, ''we let her get about two hundred yards ahead and then started in her wake. During the first five minutes not a sound was heard, save, perhaps, the beating of our hearts, or the slight ripple of the water upon her sword-like stem.'' Stevens' words were more dramatic than the action. Captain Brown worked the rakish schooner to weather of *Lavrock,* and easily beat her to the anchorage at Cowes. An hour later, the Earl of Wilton and a welcoming party were aboard *America.* Some of the French champagne was poured, and words poured forth at Cowes that the Yankee yacht had arrived and was not to be taken lightly.

It was a good beginning, but not if one's aims included the winning of wagers. Stevens issued a low-key challenge to any number of ''schooners of the Old World'' for a race in a breeze of not less than six knots. The British responded politely to Stevens and his party; they made them honorary members of the Royal Yacht Squadron, but they also politely ignored his invitation to a contest. When there were no takers, Stevens boldly issued a challenge to race any British vessel ''for any sum from one to ten-thousand guineas.'' (The latter figure would represent something like $500,000 today.) Stevens' only condition was that the wind be above a zephyrous six knots. Again there were no takers from this nation that considered itself the ruler of the waves.

While this was pending, interest in the mysterious American yacht intensified. The *Illustrated London News* dismissed her as ''a rakish, piratical-looking craft'' and commented that she ''seemed rather a violation of the old established ideas of naval architecture.'' The Marquis of Anglesey, who had an opportunity to visit her, remarked, ''If she is right, then we are all wrong.'' The Marquis, then governor of the Isle of Wight, was perhaps the most eminent member of the Squadron in 1851, and his judgment would prove correct. If the schooner *America* was very different from anything ever seen at Cowes, she was more familiar to the British Admiralty. In its self-appointed role as the sea's policeman, the Admiralty knew her type well after several decades of chasing American slavers designed along the same lines as George Steers' New York pilot boats.

The London *Times'* "Own Correspondent at Cowes" was less xenophobic and professed to be delighted by her clean, straightforward hull lines and the way she seemed rigged "without an extra rope." She was, he reported, "the *beau idéal* of what one is accustomed to read about in [James Fenimore] Cooper's novels." He was also amused by the stir *America* created:

> Day after day, gentlemen in most wonderful costumes, ranging in style from Dirck Hatterick to Wright in an Adelphi farce, sit at the windows or in the porch of the clubhouse with telescope to eye, staring at the phenomenon, or they row around her in grotesque little punts, or go on board and have a chat with the Commodore, his brother, and Colonel Hamilton, three very cautious and gentlemanly persons—as downright 'cute and keen as the smartest in the States, but who can hardly disguise, nevertheless, their pleasure at John Bull's astonishment and evident perturbation, owning, as he does, a fleet of about 800 yachts of all sizes—from nearly 400 tons down to three tons.

And not one of them was willing to meet the black schooner. Meanwhile, things weren't grim aboard *America,* not for the gentlemen, not for the crew. Captain Brown and the crew enjoyed their new roles as guides to a nautical curiosity. According to Colonel Hamilton: "There was at one time a very great impression among the lower classes of the people about the docks at Cowes that *America* had a propeller which was ingeniously concealed; and our crew amused themselves by saying to the boatmen who came alongside with visitors (there were thousands, as people of all classes were permitted to examine the vessel), 'In the stern sheets, under the gangway, there is a grating which the commodore does not allow any person to open.' "

Propeller or no, the ordinary watermen around Cowes were embarrassed and disgusted that the gentry had ignored the American challenge. One of them offered to man a crack cutter with the best of his mates if some gentlemen would put up the wager to race *America* out to Cape Clear and back in the worst weather that turned up, and "to crack on till the masts went to Hell."

America took an occasional afternoon sail if the wind piped up. Although Stevens stayed at anchor when the Ryde Regatta started on August 15, because the morning's breeze was barely perceptible, he took an unofficial turn on the course that afternoon. The London *Times* was impressed. As the paper reported:

> She went along very steadily and well up to Ryde but did not show any great superiority till she was off the pier, about 3:20, when she seemed as if she had put a screw into her stern, hoisted her fore and aft foresail, and began "to fly" through the water. She passed schooners and cutters one after the other just as a Derby winner passes the "ruck," and as the breeze freshened slid with the speed of an arrow out towards the Nab, standing upright as a ramrod under her canvas, while the schooners were staggering under every stitch

they could set, and the cutters were heeling over under gaff topsails and balloon jibs. She went about in splendid style, a little short of the Nab, spinning around like a top, and came bowling away toward Cowes as fast if not faster than ever. As if to let our best craft see she did not care about them, the *America* went up to each in succession, ran to leeward of every one of them as close as she could, and shot before them in succession, coming to anchor at Ryde at least two miles, as it seemed to me, ahead of any of the craft she had been running against.

This was a performance to make Commodore Stevens wish he had challenged the Squadron that morning, and his success this day may have influenced his decision to sail for the Hundred Guineas Cup a week later in a race with no time allowance. His biggest worry must have been the idiosyncratic course, with tricky tides and currents that would favor those who knew them best.* For their part, the Squadron considered the August 22 free-for-all around the Isle of Wight their best chance for redeeming their reputation with the press and public. They must have been pleased that their so-called Race of All Nations was not to be a race for money, and they must have hoped for a light breeze that would favor their fleet of heavily canvased cutters.

"The anxiety attending this race is deep and earnest," wrote the Special Correspondent of the London *Times* on August 20, two days before the race was to sail. The old salts of Cowes were predicting disaster, and the town was crowded from the beaches to the rooftops on the morning of the contest. Anxiety was equally deep and earnest aboard *America*. Several British crewmen had been signed aboard, and a pilot had been hired to advise Captain Brown on local conditions. The Americans had been warned not to trust any English pilot, and even this one, guaranteed honest by the admiral of the Portsmouth Dockyard, had been damned as a liar in an anonymous letter written to Commodore Stevens. The commodore had other problems: he was wishing for a breeze of at least six knots, if not a full gale.

"No one not present can realize the anxieties of that contest," Colonel Hamilton recalled years later, "for we knew the ground was most unfavorable for us. When the yachts got off, while the wind was fresh, we got away easily, but twice the wind failed us, and, with a strong head tide, we were actually drifting back, while lighter vessels with a greater and loftier spread of canvas, taking advantage of small draught of water and eddies known to them, were gradually overhauling us."

America had hoisted her sails before raising her anchor, and she slewed

---

*Much of the Admiral's Cup, the world's preeminent team ocean-racing series, is sailed today off Cowes; in fact, the races often start on a line off the porch of the Royal Yacht Squadron's castle. To this day, the area's idiosyncratic tides, and the premium put on local knowledge, have generated much criticism of the venue of this series.

around in some confusion before starting the course around the Isle of Wight in last place. "We got off before the wind," recalled Commodore Stevens, "and in the midst of a crowd that we could not get rid of for the first eight or nine miles." The Squadron fleet, their sails boomed out before a growing breeze, bunched up to keep the schooner at bay on the run to the Nab, and Captain Brown was forced to maneuver in ways that risked collision or an all-standing jibe. At one point, Captain Brown asked Stevens, "Shall I put her bowsprit through that fellow's sail?"

Captain Brown worked her carefully through the first dozen boats of the fleet, and when she passed the Noman's Land buoy, she was only two minutes behind *Volante,* the leader, with *Freak, Aurora,* and *Gipsy Queen* between. *Volante* and *Aurora* had stood out to round the Nab light while most of the rest of the fleet, including *America,* turned the corner inshore. In the two circulars issued for the race, one had put the course inside the Nab, the other outside. As a result, *Bacchante, Arrow, Volante, Constance,* and *Aurora* rounded the light and returned on a course nearly dead to windward. There would be protests from all five yachts.

America was, it was said, unbeatable going to windward, and when she came around the corner and headed upwind, she left them all behind. "Her canvas," wrote the ever-admiring Special Correspondent, "was as flat as a sheet of paper." He continued: "While the cutters were thrashing through the water, sending the spray over their bows, and the schooners were wet up to the foot of the foremast, the *America* was as dry as a bone."

America broke her jib boom at 12:58 powering against the wind and current, but her lead was already substantial enough that the delay was of no consequence. Hard on the wind and heeling, she beat down the back of the Isle of Wight and increased her lead by miles. "At 5:40 the *Aurora,* the nearest yacht, was fully 7½ miles astern, the *Freak* being about a mile more distant, and the rest being 'nowhere,'" reported the *Times.* The steamers anchored at Alum Bay gave three cheers as *America,* now under the lee of the land, ghosted past them on a slow run. As *America* neared the royal yacht *Victoria and Albert,* Queen Victoria supposedly asked one of her attendants, "Who is first?" When informed that it was *America,* she asked who was second. "There is no second," was the reply.

Whether that story is apocryphal or not, the well-connected or highly mobile Special Correspondent reported that, when *America* passed *Victoria and Albert,* "The commodore took off his hat, and all the crew, following his order and example, remained with uncovered heads for some minutes till they had passed the yacht—a mark of respect to the Queen not the less becoming because it was bestowed by republicans."

America ghosted to the finish at 8:37, as night was falling over the island. *Aurora,* under a cloud of sail, had gained in the zephyrous breezes of the evening and finished eight minutes later. It was all over, as they say, but the shouting.

The shouting began with the five protests. *America's* crew stayed awake much of the night to await their fate. They were told before morning that they had survived the protests and had won the ornate silver urn which would come to be known as the America's Cup.

The next day, Queen Victoria asked that *America* sail down to Osborne House, her summer cottage, to receive a royal visit. The Queen, Prince Albert, and a retinue of ladies and gentlemen in waiting came aboard. It was an unprecedented gesture, and it became the subject of a week's gossip. The royal party took a complete tour, during which Captain Brown reminded Prince Albert to wipe his feet before going below. The Prince, a trifle astonished, stood still at the top of the companionway. "I know who you are," said Captain Brown, an unabashed republican, "but you'll have to wipe your feet." Victoria asked to see the bilges and the way the ballast was stowed. The fastidious Queen ran a royal handkerchief over the shelves of the galley and found no dust. Back on deck, she presented each member of the crew of *America* with a gold sovereign. The next day Captain Brown received from a representative of the Crown a package containing a gold pocket compass and a note that said Her Majesty hoped he might keep it as bright as he kept his ship.

A few days later, *America* was visited by the peg-legged Marquis of Anglesey, in his official capacity as governor of the Isle of Wight. Refusing to accept even now that *America* was right, he peered long and hard over *America's* transom, looking for her fabled propeller. Beginning to succumb to the pull of gravity, he was yanked back aboard the yacht with his good leg by Commodore Stevens.

America's victory was literally staggering to the British yachting establishment, and its implications of American prowess at sea and elsewhere were unacceptable to much of the British public in that summer of the Great Exposition, when the Crystal Palace stood in Hyde Park as a symbol of the Empire's greatness. Weeks of correspondence and comment in British newspapers showed both a tough realism and a blind arrogance in British response, with hardly any sentiments in between.

"It is a remarkable incident, and not satisfactory to the national pride," wrote the London *Spectator,* which decided that the schooner's superiority was due to an accidental discovery by her designer, George Steers, of the efficiency of the sharp, clipper type of hull form. The more realistic—indeed, pessimistic—London *Merchant* wrote: "We write to record our opinion that the empire of the seas must before long be ceded to America; its persevering enterprise, its great commerce, are certain to secure this prize; nor will England be in a condition to dispute it with her. America, as mistress of the ocean, must overstride the civilized world.''

As letters pro and con appeared daily in the press, Colonel Hamilton received a gushing note of congratulation from the formerly cautious Rives, the American minister in Paris. Crowed the minister, ''To beat Britannia, 'whose flag has braved a thousand years the battle and the breeze,' to beat her in her own native seas, in the presence of her Queen, and contending against a fleet of seventeen sail of her picked models of naval architecture, owned and personally directed by the proudest names of her nobility—her Marlboroughs and her Angleseys—is something that may well encourage us in the race of maritime competition which is set before us.''

Commodore Stevens brought the Cup back to America, but left his famous yacht in Britain. He unsentimentally sold her at a $1,750 profit after his expenses, which were not inconsiderable.

Members of Stevens' original syndicate passed the Cup around from house to house, and after six years the Cup was given to the New York Yacht Club as the prize for an international competition. The Deed of Gift specified: ''It is to be distinctly understood that the Cup is to be the property of the club, and not of the members thereof, or owners of the vessel winning it in the match.'' The yacht club informed seven yacht clubs in seven countries of their new competition and promised ''a liberal, hearty welcome, and the strictest fair play.''

"The New York Yacht Club was the only game in town. That's not the case anymore . . ."

—W. H. DYER JONES,
CHAIRMAN OF THE NYYC AMERICA'S CUP RACE COMMITTEE

CHAPTER 3
The Keepers of the Cup

The America's Cup belonged to the New York Yacht Club. And the New York Yacht Club had no intention of losing it. Not in the summer of '83. Not ever. It was called the America's Cup not because it was a national sailing trophy to be shared by all Americans, but simply because the yacht that won the trophy in 1851 was named *America.*

With the increasing media fascination that developed over this ultimate in sporting trophies, more Americans than ever learned about the Cup. Some became defensive about it—even patriotic. Others became cynical— disturbed that America, represented by the NYYC, once again seemed to be making things difficult for other nations who had come here to wage a fair-and-square battle for this prize. Television for the first time carried live coverage of the final races. News reports chronicled events leading up to the climax of the summer on a regular basis. National magazines were filled with descriptive pieces. Newspapers couldn't write enough. The result was an ever-widening awareness of the America's Cup, and something of a nationalistic fervor over it. Here was a trophy that America had won fair and square and had miraculously held on to for 132 years. Yet it wasn't America's trophy. It was the New York Yacht Club's. Its founder won it in 1851 and brought it home, and finally one of his friends and syndicate partners—George L. Schuyler—gave it to the club.

Since that day when Schuyler delivered it in 1857, the NYYC has determined the rules under which other clubs could challenge for the Cup. They were the keepers of the Cup, and they kept it. Few challengers understood this better than Alan Bond. As he said this summer when the storm of controversy raged around the legality of the keel of his *Australia II,* "The New York Yacht Club wants you to challenge for the America's Cup; they just won't let you win it." That realization no doubt contributed to the fact that Alan Bond—or, to be precise, his yacht club in Western Australia—is now the keeper of the Cup.

What Bond said in 1983 has always been true. From the beginning, America's Cup rules were drawn to favor defenders rather than challengers. This state of affairs was modified through the years—however grudgingly—but never sufficiently that one might characterize this contest as a display of "the strictest fair play," as promised by the NYYC's 1857 invitation to the world. This is yachting, after all, not everyman's baseball.

Yachting didn't start out to be democratic. Rules in sailing were established by wealthy members of exclusive yacht clubs who valued tradition more than equal opportunity. From its pantheon, the New York Yacht Club set the rules for this competition, if not for the entire sport. (To briefly illustrate the power of this club and some of its members, the International Yacht Racing Rules—which govern the America's Cup series and nearly every other sailing competition in the world—were written by New York Yacht Club commodore Harold "Mike" Vanderbilt.) Some might complain about an apparent lack of sportsmanship displayed by the NYYC in America's Cup competition, but they were lonely voices sounded in the desert. The club's answer—when it deigned to give one—was that these things are traditional. For decades, that seemed sufficient.

"If clubs don't stand up for tradition, pretty soon it will be wiped out," NYYC commodore Robert Stone, Jr., remarked recently. It may, in fact, have been the club's inability to function outside the constraints of tradition that finally caused the America's Cup pedestal to crack and then crumble. Members maintained proper decorum as the upheavals of the 1983 America's Cup summer swirled around them. The club was remote and unapproachable—still running the show, but from afar. And it tried to pull strings and bring fine interpretations to rules, as it had learned to do so well when turn-of-the-century tycoons ruled the waves. The likes of J. Pierpont Morgan, William and Cornelius Vanderbilt, and August Belmont—all members of the NYYC—were powerful figures who ran their businesses and their sport with affirmative nods and with nearly unassailable assumptions about how games of finance or sailing would be played. The NYYC evolved a tradition of rule-making and competition that was characterized by boardroom tactics mixed with gentlemanly savoir faire. They never learned to tangle because they never had to.

The NYYC in 1983, cowering under its historical umbrella, tried to behave in the same way. But it didn't work. Jeff Spranger, a yachting journalist long associated with the Cup scene, summed it up this way in the *America's Cup Report,* a weekly newsletter on the races:

> While their contenders brawled and snarled, the NYYC America's Cup Committee let itself get sidetracked by controversy and ambushed by Australian public relations. The Aussies did not answer their questions; they mocked them. The club wrote legal briefs; the Australians replied with

eminently quotable one-liners. After the recent years of dealing with the likes of Frank Packer, Peter de Savary, Baron Marcel Bich and Alan Bond, the NYYC still used tactics more appropriate to the likes of Sir Thomas Lipton and T. O. M. Sopwith.

Ever since the yacht *America* won its epic battle around the Isle of Wight, other clubs have had designs on the Cup. The first challenge, in 1870, came from the Royal Thames Yacht Club of Great Britain in a vain attempt to win back the lost trophy. Six subsequent attempts by various clubs within Great Britain failed. The Canadians tried twice and also failed. By the time Sir Thomas Lipton came along in 1899, the Deed of Gift, which the NYYC signed in taking ownership of the Cup, had been modified twice, mostly to assuage complaints from challengers of unfair advantages taken by the NYYC.

In the first challenge, in 1880, the club sent out a fleet of 17 schooners to race against James Ashbury's *Cambria*. The NYYC maintained that this was only fair, since their *America* had to compete against a fleet of 17 British yachts in 1851. When Ashbury challenged again in 1871, the club limited itself to one defender; but it still reserved the right to choose a different boat each day, depending on the weather. Ashbury was not amused.

The NYYC found itself embroiled in controversy again during challenges from an Irish peer, Windham-Thomas Wyndham-Quin, fourth Earl of Dunraven, between 1893 and 1895. The Deed of Gift had been changed in 1887 to require challengers to send dimensions of their boats 10 months before the first race. The NYYC established such a rule, they said, to ensure that racing would take place between similar yachts; but Dunraven opposed it with Irish ire, knowing that supplying such vital information so far in advance gave the defense plenty of time to design a strong defending yacht. He sent only the load waterline length of his *Valkyrie II*. In the summer of 1893, Dunraven arrived with his 133-foot *Valkyrie II*, and the NYYC met the challenge with the 128-foot *Vigilant*, which had been commissioned from that genius of racing-yacht design, Nathanael Herreshoff. *Vigilant* beat *Valkyrie II* in three straight 30-mile races, sailed off New York's Sandy Hook.

Lord Dunraven tried again in 1895, this time with *Valkyrie III*. The American contender was another Herreshoff design, the 123-foot *Defender*. Dunraven's yacht won the first race. But he complained that the spectator fleet got in his way and that the American boat had illegally taken on more ballast overnight. The boats were then remeasured and raced a second time. *Valkyrie III* won on the water, but lost the race in a protest over a small collision with *Defender* at the start. Dunraven pulled his boat out of the third race, angered again over an infringing spectator fleet.

When James Ashbury complained of unfair treatment in 1871, the NYYC returned several of the trophies he had donated and sent a letter of defense to his sponsoring yacht club. With Dunraven, the NYYC called for a special panel to investigate charges of cheating that Dunraven renewed after abandoning that third race in 1895. On the panel were Edward J. Phelps, a former ambassador to Great Britain; George L. Rives, a former assistant secretary of state; Captain Alfred T. Mahan, the famous theorist of naval strategy; William Whitney, a former secretary of the navy; and, as chairman, J. P. Morgan, the most powerful banker in the world. This impressive—indeed, all but omnipotent—panel found no merit in Lord Dunraven's case. Dunraven's Royal Yacht Squadron smoldered for years over what it considered to be the unfairness of the NYYC, and much of the British yachting establishment believed in the 1890s that the Americans were sharp businessmen rather than sportsmen.

The Lipton challenges between 1899 and 1930 were a relatively tranquil time for the America's Cup Races. But they were not without their disagreements—the principal difficulty being the requirement that a challenging yacht cross the Atlantic on her own bottom. The British yachting journal *Land and Water* explained the inherent unfairness of such a rule: "To sail a boat that must be seaworthy to cross the Atlantic and compete in the light, fleecy airs off Sandy Hook against a volatile cockleshell kind of racing machine built with all the foreknowledge of a rival's plans and lines of construction must obviously be a stupendous obstacle to a challenger's success."

Lipton spent years negotiating—in gentlemanly fashion—for a more structured basis to the design and engineering of America's Cup yachts. With success. The J-Boat era of the 1930s was a result of his continued pressure. The "Js" were an international class of unhandicapped yachts built to a specific design rule. While the J-Boats were not the largest vessels to contend for the America's Cup, they were the most powerful and the most sophisticated yachts of their time. To those who still remember them, they were also the most exciting sailing machines that ever charged around a match-racing course. More so, even, than 12 Meters.

Harold "Mike" Vanderbilt, the great-grandson of Commodore Cornelius Vanderbilt, defended the Cup with *Enterprise* in 1930. She was a high-tech J-Boat designed by Starling Burgess, a scientific man who had built aircraft under license to the Wright brothers before World War I, and an eccentric genius who was said to be able to do complex calculus in his head. Vanderbilt and Burgess's *Enterprise* beat *Shamrock V,* the last of Lipton's America's Cup challengers, in four straight races. It was a fair contest, with both boats designed to the same international rule, and *Enterprise* humbled *Shamrock V* simply because she was a far superior racing machine. The venue of the America's Cup by this time had shifted from New York to Newport, Rhode Island, mostly because wind and water conditions were more reliable—and fairer—in Rhode Island Sound than in "the light, fleecy airs off Sandy Hook" cited by *Land and Water*.

When Lipton lost that final race, he was an old man. He is recorded in *The History of the New York Yacht Club* as saying publicly that day: "I canna' win, I canna' win." A journalist at the time wrote that "there was hardly a dry eye in an American speakeasy."

Lipton had lost; but he had lost a fair contest. Proof of the relative "fairness" of things in the J-Boat era was the 1934 America's Cup contest, which the NYYC nearly lost. In probably the closest match in Cup history until 1983, Vanderbilt and designer Starling Burgess teamed up a second time. Vanderbilt, the racing-rule giver and heir to part of the family fortune, was an accomplished helmsman aboard big yachts and another scientific thinker who had invented contract bridge in 1925 for his own amusement. Burgess and Vanderbilt were a perfect team.

They needed all of their skills and more in 1934 when Burgess designed *Rainbow*. The challenger, British aircraft magnate T. O. M. Sopwith, was a new player in the game; but his boat was ominously familiar. His *Endeavour*, like *Enterprise* and *Rainbow*, was a "mechanical boat," a superb synthesis of fresh technology. She was feared to be faster than *Rainbow* before the 1934 Cup series, and known to be faster after. She would have captured the Cup if her crew had been better prepared and if C. Sherman Hoyt had been anywhere except at *Rainbow*'s helm in the third Cup race of 1934. Vanderbilt later described the series as a "constantly changing panorama of breaks and mistakes."

Sopwith's *Endeavour* won the first two races, and it looked even to Mike Vanderbilt that the Cup could be lost. In the third race, *Endeavour* was ahead by 6 minutes and 39 seconds at the first mark of a 30-mile up-and-back course, and Vanderbilt gave up the helm to Hoyt, resigning himself to the fact that *Endeavour* was the likely winner. Hoyt was his light-air expert, and he hoped for a miracle. "Maybe you can make the darned thing go," Vanderbilt told Hoyt, then retired below so as not to watch it. Hoyt did better than that. He made Sopwith's boat almost stop by luring him into making two tacks—maneuvers that not only slowed *Endeavour* down, but allowed *Rainbow* to pass to leeward. In the fourth race, Sopwith cried foul over two separate tactical situations, but his voice was never heard in the protest room. The NYYC race committee declined to hear either protest, citing a U.S. racing rule that requires a protest flag to be shown as soon as possible after an alleged foul. Sopwith was incensed, and Sherman Hoyt felt that his pique impaired his sailing ability in the final two races. He lost both.

Sopwith challenged again in 1937 with an even faster boat—*Endeavour*

II. Vanderbilt, however, appeared with *Ranger,* a vastly improved J-Boat. She represented the combined efforts of Burgess and a young designer who would later make history in the sport—Olin Stephens. The boat was the fastest J-Boat ever designed, and she beat *Endeavour II* with ease in what turned out to be an uneven contest. The 1937 America's Cup series came at the end of the J-Boat era. The Js afforded perhaps the greatest racing in America's Cup history, but their prominence ended with World War II. In fact, most of the world's Js, magnificent machines though they were, went to scrap yards to provide vital metals for the war effort. Aesthetically and competitively, the Js were racehorses, the best of their breed. But economically they were dinosaurs, too costly and specialized to survive. Harold Vanderbilt had borne the total cost of *Ranger*'s 1937 campaign, and there were few other men whose means and will were equal to such a challenge. After the Depression, and after a war that changed much of the world, the contest for this Cup which had gathered the magic of years and deeds would need to be different. In 1938, Harold Vanderbilt commissioned a yacht named *Vim* from Olin Stephens, designed to the worldwide 12-Meter rule. She would be a portent for the America's Cup in the postwar era.

After a 21-year hiatus, America's Cup racing was resumed in 1958 using the smaller, 67-foot 12 Meters as vehicles. The Twelves, like the Js, were an international class of relatively similar boats, and with them the America's Cup series was fairer, but it still wasn't baseball. Since 1958, the NYYC has increasingly eased the restrictions under which challengers race. Resolutions adopted in 1958, 1980, and 1982 clarified the rules in the Deed of Gift, and made them fairer. But this issue of "fairness" needs to be seen in the context of a sport that has always brought complex rules and understandings to competition. As a case in point: before the Australians departed these shores, with the America's Cup tucked safely under their arms, their legal bill was a reported $75,000.

The NYYC today remains a haven for the wealthy and powerful, but sailing is its common ground. When John Cox Stevens, original owner of the yacht *America,* held the club's first meeting, it was on a boat—his 51-foot schooner *Gimcrack,* which was anchored off the Battery in New York City. It was July 30, 1844, at 5 P.M., and nine men were present. "An original founding member recorded that it was a very simple affair at which the assembled gentlemen were told they were members of a yacht club, a statement which seems to have suited them well," writes John Parkinson, Jr., in the club's history book.

All nine of the men of 1844 owned yachts. Membership today does not exclude people without yachts, but they must show an interest in yachting or maritime pursuits to become a member. Only yacht owners can vote on club business. Of the club's 2,563 members, 1,200 own yachts. Members are required to pay an annual fee of $450. Belonging to the NYYC means being nominated and seconded by club members, then having three other members write letters of recommendation. About 200 new members are accepted each year.

The NYYC is one of the world's remaining bastions of yesteryear. Although women are allowed to join, only 36 are members. There are still places within the club where women are not welcome—specifically, the dining room and bar at lunchtime. But their status is improving. Until about 15 years ago, women were not allowed into the club at all in the evening.

The prestigious America's Cup Committee of the NYYC includes former 12-Meter sailors Robert McCullough, chairman; Victor Romagna, secretary; Robert Bavier, Jr.; Briggs Cunningham; Stanley Livingston, Jr.; and Emil (Bus) Mosbacher, Jr., club vice-commodore.

Briggs Cunningham was the skipper aboard *Columbia,* the 12 Meter that defended the America's Cup in 1958. He, more than most members of the committee, represents the "Old Guard" of the NYYC. Briggs Cunningham is a gentleman to the core and a yachtsman to the bone.

Bus Mosbacher was helmsman on two Cup defenders—*Weatherly,* in 1962, and *Intrepid,* in 1967. Mosbacher was known for his aggressive tactics at the helm and for leading his team with the dedication and discipline of a nautical Vince Lombardi. He was—and is to this day—considered among the best of American skippers. *Weatherly* was a slower boat than *Gretel I,* the Australian challenger in 1962. But Mosbacher won the series through determination and skill. "This is no democracy," he said to his crew during that campaign. "However, I do like to hear any well thought out, reasonable suggestion. Once." They loved him for his toughness.

Mosbacher was equally at home on the revolutionary *Intrepid,* a breakthrough in 12-Meter design. Mosbacher and Vic Romagna contributed their ideas to the boat's deck layout and interior. Mosbacher then was able to take what was considered to be a radical Olin Stephens design and sail it to its best advantage in 1967.

Bob Bavier was helmsman of the U.S. defender *Constellation,* which won the Cup series in 1964. Ten years later, he became skipper of *Courageous,* only to lose that spot to Ted Hood and Dennis Conner just before the end of the summer's trial racing.

These, then, were the men who fought the battles of the summer of '83 on and off Rhode Island Sound. They were the new keepers of the Cup. The 1983 America's Cup Committee (sometimes referred to as the selection committee) was responsible for choosing an American defender in a summer-long series of trial races among the 12-Meters *Liberty,*

Courageous, and *Defender.* The committee members were—as were the men of Cup committees before them—steeped in the traditions of the sport: racing fouls are handled in the protest room, but political battles are won in private. That attitude worked with the likes of Lipton and Sopwith, and even to a large extent with the contentious Lord Dunraven. But the 1970s and 1980s brought another breed of challenger to the America's Cup arena—wealthy businessmen who knew sailing as sport, but also knew that involvement with the America's Cup could reap great commercial rewards. They were hard-nosed businessmen, and egotists, men who would go to great lengths to see things their way. They were never compliant competitors.

Most were newly minted millionaires who amassed fortunes on their own. Even Baron Marcel Bich, the French pen magnate who challenged from 1970 to 1980, was not always a baron. Bich once sold lamps door to door. The late Sir Frank Packer, the Australian who bankrolled the *Dame Pattie* and the *Gretel I* and *II* challenges, was a wealthy newspaper executive who achieved knighthood status through his enormous media influence. Packer, flamboyant and often crass, bucked the NYYC as a matter of course. "Protesting the New York Yacht Club is like complaining about your wife to your mother-in-law," he once said. Peter de Savary, the British multimillionaire who brought the *Victory* team to Newport in 1983, once sold encyclopedias. And Alan Bond painted signs for a living before his fortunes changed.

This is not to say that all previous challengers came from noble or wealthy circumstances. Sir Thomas Lipton, in fact, was a one-store grocer before he made his millions with 500 stores. But the likes of de Savary and Bond were schooled in a hard world where amassing a fortune depended on aggressive behavior and a no-nonsense approach. They represent 1950s and 1960s money to which the value of public exposure and international connections is greater than tradition or family lineage. For the most part, the money that paid for America's Cup challenges in the past two decades was new money, and it bought nearly everything it wanted. It couldn't buy the America's Cup, but it could buy the public image that made pursuing the America's Cup a worthwhile venture.

The keepers of the Cup failed to keep it in the summer of '83; but within a month of Australia's victory in the 1983 America's Cup series, there was talk of other challenges. Several U.S. syndicates expressed an interest in going to Perth to win the America's Cup back. But the NYYC was remaining quiet, almost as if it had turned inside itself. Commodore Robert Stone, Jr., announced with great fanfare at the America's Cup presentation ceremony that there would be another U.S. challenge, but he never mentioned what club would sponsor the boat. The way the Deed of Gift is written, it is the sponsoring club that takes title to the America's Cup. "It is distinctly understood that the Cup is to be the property of the Club, subject to the provisions of this deed, and not the property of the owner or owners of any vessel winning a match," the Deed of Gift states.

For the Australians, this clause means that the Royal Perth Yacht Club is the new owner of the Cup, not Alan Bond's *Australia II* syndicate. As for the NYYC, it remains to be seen whether members will choose to challenge the Australians. "The New York Yacht Club was the only game in town," says W. H. Dyer Jones, the America's Cup race committee chairman. "That's not the case anymore. The NYYC could launch a very viable challenge in 1987. But there's considerable sentiment within the club that the club should not. Members feel that the America's Cup used to stand for all the best there was in sailing. After this summer, they don't feel that way anymore."

*"He [Conner] takes himself and what
is going on here [in Newport] so
seriously that it is repulsive. If the
guys in the Pentagon took themselves
as seriously as Dennis does—and
those guys are dealing with the lives
of everyone—I'd still think it was
wrong. You have to see some humor
in this, and to relax now and then."*

—TOM BLACKALLER,
SKIPPER OF DEFENDER

CHAPTER 4
The Defenders of the Cup

or Dennis Conner, actions speak louder and more eloquently than
words. Since 1974, when this earnest young man from San Diego
entered the highly visible America's Cup arena, he was determined—
some would say grimly determined—to take his place in the history of the
sport. He has.

In 1974, after a less than auspicious start with the awful 12-Meter
Mariner, a 31-year-old Dennis Conner was invited into the cockpit of the
struggling *Courageous* to be starting-line helmsman. In this role—as on
Mariner—his aggressiveness and brilliance were noted.

That summer a former America's Cup sailor said of Conner, "In match
racing, there are only so many moves as the aggressor and only so many
countermoves. Dennis Conner knows them all. Most guys go for clear air,
while Conner goes for the controlling position." Bob McCullough, then
head of the *Courageous* syndicate, and a man we would come to know
better 10 years later as head of an embattled America's Cup Committee,
gave young Conner a simple mandate when he came aboard *Courageous.*
"Young man," said McCullough, "I don't want you to feel as though
we're putting any undue pressure on you. I don't want you to feel as
though you have to dominate them at the start. Just as long as you're
comfortably ahead."

With Conner as starting helmsmen, and with Ted Hood, the taciturn

Marblehead sailmaker and sailor as skipper, *Courageous* won the defense trials by one thin race over the very game *Intrepid,* a two-time America's Cup defender. Then they went on to face the Australians in the form of *Southern Cross,* whose syndicate was controlled by a combative man from Down Under named Alan Bond. Again Conner's aggressiveness at the starting line did not go unrecognized. Said Bond after the first race, "Conner was yelling and screaming and calling false luffs. If he continues to do so, we will have no alternative but to protest."

Dennis Conner was raised in San Diego, a city dominated by freeways and the Pacific Ocean. The San Diego Yacht Club, where he will become commodore this year, was, he says, the pool hall of his youth. It was the place where he found spiritual sustenance, where he developed a sense of who he was and where he was going. Whether he sensed it then or not, he would go far. Conner said in his autobiography, entitled *No Excuse to Lose,* that as a youth he suffered from an inferiority complex. It was important for him to do well at something, and sailing was it.

Unable to afford a boat in those early days, he crewed for anyone who would have him. Among those who would were Jim Kilroy, America's so-called "maxi man," who has owned a series of maximum-sized (and -rated) yachts all named *Kialoa.* Conner also raced on Lightnings, a popular Olin Stephens–designed 19-footer. (Stephens, the dean of naval architecture, would ultimately design two America's Cup 12 Meters for Dennis Conner, and with one of them, *Freedom,* he would defend the America's Cup in 1980.) Through Lightning sailing, he met Alan Raffee, who hired Conner out of San Diego State College to work in his drapery business. Raffee was killed in a plane crash in 1979, and Conner took over the drapery business.

In the small world of yacht racing, success on the race course typically leads to a career in sailmaking. A cursory look at 1983's America's Cup sailors provides ample proof of this: John Marshall, who sailed with Conner in both the 1980 and 1983 America's Cup defenses, is the president of North Sails; Tom Blackaller, the skipper of *Defender* and Conner's long-time bête noire, runs the San Francisco loft of North Sails; Tom Whidden, who sailed with Conner as tactician in the last two Cup years, is the president of Sobstad Sails; John Kolius, who sailed *Courageous* so brilliantly in the summer of '83, ran the Houston loft for Ulmer Sails. He is now president of Ulmer, and the name has been changed to Ulmer & Kolius; and John Bertrand, skipper of *Australia II,* ran the North Sails loft in Melbourne. His territory is now all of Australia.

Asked why he never became a sailmaker, Conner said, "It has often been tempting, but I feel that it would be hard to mix both [business and pleasure] . . . When I am sailing against someone, I don't feel that kindly toward them. I've just never relished the idea of having to walk down the dock and have someone say, 'Hey! What's wrong with the leech of my sail?' when I'm thinking about how I want to beat them, not help them. I felt that if I mixed my sport with my vocation, it might ruin my sport.''

Conner has beaten more than a few people in his time: he has won two Star World Championships, an Olympic Bronze medal in the Tempest class and two Congressional Cups—the world championship of match racing—as well as any number of victories in the competitive Southern Ocean Racing Conference and membership on two U.S. Admiral's Cup teams. And he successfully defended the America's Cup in 1974, as starting helmsman, and in 1980 as skipper.

Yet, despite his lack of actual employment in the sport, Conner has, according to more than a few observers, turned the America's Cup into a full-time job. When he was handed *Freedom* and her trial horse *Enterprise* on April 12, 1979, he logged 180 days at sea on both coasts and tested 120 potential crew members before going on to beat Alan Bond's Australians 4-1. A similar—if not greater—effort was made for the America's Cup campaign of 1983. Not only did he put in the days, weeks, months, and years of boat time, but for 1983 he built three new 12 Meters (*Liberty, Magic,* and *Spirit of America*) at a cost of about $300,000 apiece. This determination, this unwavering focus on goals, this prodigious spending, this no-stone-left-unturned approach to the sport—all of which are summarized in the title of his book, *No Excuse to Lose*—has brought Conner some criticism. In 1980, he refused to apologize for working harder than his competitors. Said Conner, ''I certainly don't apologize for having a more all-out effort than the other groups.''

The more loquacious John Marshall, the president of North Sails and Conner's sail trimmer on *Freedom* and *Liberty,* put it this way: ''Dennis was right. In 1980, he had not sailed 12 Meters very much. He set out starting with very little experience, knowing he would race against Ted Turner, who had a great deal of experience. He set out, as his first priority, to make himself a better 12 Meter racer than anyone else. He spent hours and hours changing himself, doing the hard job of taking raw talent and turning it into a powerful performer.''

Tom Blackaller, skipper of *Defender* this year and a world-class sailor who predicted for two years that he was the only man in America who could beat Dennis Conner, sees it differently. Said the very loquacious Blackaller, ''He [Conner] takes himself and what is going on here [in Newport] so seriously that it is repulsive. If the guys in the Pentagon took themselves as seriously as Dennis does—and those guys are dealing with the lives of everyone—I'd still think it was wrong. You have to see some humor in this, and to relax now and then.'' Humor and charisma didn't help Blackaller this summer, as Conner and his near-perfect organization walked all over the fast-talking Blackaller and his slow-moving *Defender*.

As good as Dennis Conner unquestionably is, he is not a popular hero. In a world where there are so many words they are now "processed," Conner doles them out sparingly, as if using words stole away his strength. His contrast to the likes of Ted Turner, his rival in 1980 and a man who is all sound and fury (it was the charismatic Turner who turned the America's Cup into a media event), or Blackaller, a man who talks generously and well, was stark. Some days that separation from the people—or that separation from the words with which to reach them—seemed to weigh on Conner. As he said from his fenced compound at Newport's Williams & Manchester Shipyard in late July, before disappearing into his silver trailer (nicknamed the Oval Office), "We're all in this together against a foreign challenger. Some people are behind the other boats now; but if we're selected to defend the America's Cup, we'll have 300 million American supporters on our side. I think when it comes down to the short strokes, everyone will come behind us."

The 43-year-old Tom Blackaller is cut from very different cloth. Blackaller is movie-star handsome, with a full head of silver curls, and is a self-professed free spirit who at this stage of his life seems to prefer driving his race cars (presently he owns a Formula Atlantic, "really an amazing machine," says Blackaller) to driving more ponderous sailboats. Blackaller is no stranger to words. He delivers patter nearly as quotable and as outrageous as the nonstop gab of Ted Turner, head of the two Cable News networks, owner of the Atlanta Braves, and the man who defended the America's Cup in 1977.

Blackaller was born in Seattle in 1940 and raised in the San Francisco Bay area. He started sailing when he was 10. Some boys grow up wanting to be major-league baseball players; others want to be firemen; today maybe they want to design video games or make a music video for MTV; but Blackaller's life's ambition, he says, "was to win the Star World Championship." (The Star class has always attracted the sport's best and brightest dinghy sailors.) This he accomplished in 1974 and again in 1980.

Blackaller studied mechanical engineering at Berkeley. And then, in a progression as typical and as wonderful as the American dream, he married, had two children, and became vice-president of marketing for a small company that manufactured electric generating equipment. Through Star sailing he came to know Lowell North, the sailmaker, who opened his first sail loft in 1958. North, says Blackaller, often invited him to join the business, but the young vice-president couldn't see trading a $40,000-a-year salary in the real world to become a $10,000-a-year sailmaker.

Through the Star class, Blackaller also encountered Dennis Conner. At the Star Western Hemisphere Championship in New Orleans in 1967, Conner was crewing for Alan Raffee. Blackaller remembers the meeting. "I didn't know Dennis at all. He came up to me before the regatta and said, 'Well, you're the favorite.' I said, 'Oh?' Because I really didn't consider myself as that. Lowell North was there; a lot of people were there who I had been racing against for years and hadn't handled too easily. I was on the way up, but I didn't think I was going to win it. I had a new boat and good crew; I was organized and perhaps was one of five guys who could win it. But Dennis says, 'Oh, you're the favorite.' And he said, 'I've studied it and watched it.' He told me all about what I'd been doing. He knew more about what I'd been doing than I did. And, sure enough, I won the regatta. I beat Lowell [North] by a point. It impressed me that Dennis would know that."

Asked if Conner's statement seemed curious, Blackaller responded, "It did seem curious that anybody would take the time to study it. It was funny because, at that time, I was only a weekend sailor. I mean, I didn't study what I was doing. I did it because I loved doing it, and I did it because it was fun. But here was someone who seemingly had studied it; you know, it was like he stayed awake nights figuring this stuff out. Now that I know him better, I suppose he did."

In 1970, Blackaller was divorced. "I decided what I really wanted to do with my life was race sailboats. The business thing wasn't the most important thing in my life anymore. The most important thing in my life was winning sailboat races." Blackaller joined North Sails in 1973, reopening the moribund San Francisco loft.

In 1980, Blackaller trained for the Olympics in the Star class, until President Jimmy Carter declined this country's invitation to the Moscow Games. With nothing better to do, Blackaller sailed the Newport to Bermuda Race on *Williwaw,* and won. He thinks it was this victory in a prestigious East Coast event that brought him to the attention of young Russell Long, who with *Clipper* and his kiddy corps was being overwhelmed by Dennis Conner in the Cup-defense trials. The median age of the crew on *Clipper* was 24, the age of the skipper, who was a recent graduate of Harvard. This inspired a rival crew member to comment, "I've owned dogs that have lived longer than most of those guys."

The 40-year-old Blackaller was invited aboard *Clipper* to be tactician and perhaps to provide a small measure of maturity. Blackaller remembers that "Russell said to me, 'Look, you're not going to steer this boat, period.' I said that I understood that. 'That's not why I'm here. I'm here to see what's going on.' The real reason I was there was because I had nothing else to do." In addition to being tactician, Blackaller also concentrated on sails—surreptitiously, at least. "We sort of stole some stuff that they'd been developing over in Dennis's camp. Dennis isn't into sharing anything that he develops with anybody. He thinks it's his property, and he doesn't want anybody else in the sport to benefit from it.''

Clipper continued to "get hammered" (Blackaller's words) in July. Then, between the July and August trials, the crew scrimmaged with *Courageous,* sailed by Ted Turner, who that summer seemed to be just going through the motions. After defending the Cup in 1977, Turner's interest seemed more in business than in boats; he had just started his first Cable News network, which was then losing a reported $1 million a month. Russell Long let Blackaller start the boat against Turner. "I slammed him," recalls Blackaller. "Turner's easy to start against, because he never really did understand starting." Long was impressed. He asked Blackaller to start *Clipper* in the August trials.

Blackaller claims to be confused by Russell Long. As he says, "I don't know what Russell was trying to prove with his operation. If you're in the 12-Meter game, and you're trying to prove anything other than to do your best, you're doing the wrong thing. You're not going to make a good reputation here; if anything, it is a good place to lose one.''

If Blackaller was puzzled about Long's motivation, he knew someone who might be able to sort it out—Werner Erhard, the founder of est. He invited Erhard to conduct Erhard Seminar Training sessions for the *Clipper* crew. Dave Vietor, the other senior citizen on *Clipper*—he then was 38—doubted that Blackaller believed fervently in Erhard's message. "I think Tom just wanted to sell him a suit of sails," Vietor says. Vietor described the session. "We got into this room and Werner Erhard and his disciples are there. He says to start meditating on your little toe. It's all dark; we've cracked a few beers; we'd just lost to Dennis Conner by 10 minutes, and Erhard is going through this patter. He has this really good, mellow voice. So soon you hear Jack Crane, a grinder, start to snore in the background. Seemingly untroubled by this lack of attention, Erhard says, 'Tell me your deep, dark secrets.' Well, these guys aren't going to say anything; I mean these are tough guys. He isn't getting anywhere. So finally he says, 'Why do you think you guys are losing to Dennis Conner?' And at that point, Jack Crane wakes up from this deep, dark sleep and shouts, 'Because he's f—— better than us.' ''

There were three public complaints against Dennis Conner this summer, sounded primarily by Tom Blackaller and his tactician, Gary Jobson, the latter being the sport's most visible—and presumably most highly paid—spokesman. Jobson is the nautical version of football's O. J. Simpson, except that Jobson sails through life rather than running through airports. In June, Dennis Conner was accused of "sandbagging"—that is, not showing what he had in terms of boat speed and sail development—

supposedly to depress the learning curves of *Defender* and *Courageous*. Said Jobson, who in two previous Cup campaigns had been Ted Turner's tactician and, in that role, had learned the powerful magic of words, "I believe that Dennis Conner feels his chances of winning are better by not showing his cards until the last possible instant. The problem with that is, I don't believe, in any sporting competition, you make real progress until you are forced to compete at your highest level, against as many people as you can, for long periods. If we are to lose the Cup in 1983, I feel the fault would belong to Dennis Conner . . . for taking a very selfish approach to the defense. It is selfish because he is trying to enhance his chances of winning, which could be a detriment to successfully defending the Cup. It is a real tragedy."

Asked about the charges of sandbagging, Conner came right to the point: "That's my business." When the question was reintroduced, Conner, who does not seem to appreciate follow-up questions, or often questions at all, said ominously, "We do what we have to, to win."

The second complaint was that Conner entered only one boat (*Liberty*) in the competition, despite the fact that his *Freedom* syndicate owned three others: *Freedom, Magic,* and *Spirit of America.* (Of these three, *Freedom* was in Newport and ready to be sailed; that was true at least until the boat was mistakenly changed in such a way that she was no longer a legal 12 Meter. [See Chapter 10: "The Cream Rises to the Top."]) An odd number of boats meant that one Twelve was sitting idle every day, so there was less racing for all.

"The trials would have been better on the American side—more competitive—if he had entered both *Freedom* and *Liberty*," says Black-aller. "We would have been able to race every day; likewise, when we were training in California this past March, and we had four 12 Meters out there within 80 miles of each other, we begged him to have a competition with us—to let both camps see where they were. Well, he wouldn't have anything to do with that. His theory was that we could not possibly teach him anything. He could teach us, however, and thus his chances of winning would be diminished. What he totally neglected, however, was that the American defense effort would be better served if he competed with us. But he didn't care about that."

Jobson put it this way: "For the defense of the Cup, it would be really good to have four boats out there racing. If you took the boat that defended twice [*Courageous*], and the boat that defended most recently [*Freedom*], and two brand-new boats [*Defender* and *Liberty*], I think the American effort would be better for it. The reason it upsets me is because *Australia II* is looking pretty tough. I think we'd all be better if there were more racing. To sit out one of every three days doesn't make sense. We only had eight days of racing in June, and we only had 12 days of racing in July, so that's 20 days of racing. The foreign guys were racing 40 days during that time. Also, we only race two other boats, so our style can't be as well-rounded as theirs. They have to race all kinds of boats. I'm sure racing *Advance* is different than racing *Azzurra*; I'm sure racing *Australia II* is different than racing *Victory*..."

Asked whether it would be a stronger U.S. effort with four boats in competition, Conner said, with some depth of feeling, "If we thought so, we would have four of them out there. Last time Ted Turner and Russell Long said the same thing that you're hearing from those guys [Blackaller and Jobson, or "Tommy Terrific" and "Gary Glitter," as Conner would disparagingly call them by the end of the summer]. The proof of that theory was that Ted Turner won one race and lost 18 in a row; Long and *Clipper* didn't do much better. I think the best thing for the America's Cup is to win 47 races and lose four—as we did last time—and defend the Cup. So I'll just let the results stand in the record book, and let you all judge for yourself as to who has the best program."

The third complaint, though less public, was that Conner locks up talent. In his afterguard were the two best sailmakers in the country, if not the world (Tom Whidden and John Marshall), and he had the two best 12-Meter designers in this country (Johan Valentijn and Sparkman & Stephens), until Machiavellian politics saw S&S cashiered from the program (see Chapter 6: "America's Cup Yacht Design"). Blackaller put it this way: "That's another thing Dennis does; he tries to eliminate all the competition. He invites everyone he can think of to come with him, so no one else can have anyone. I've seen that in the Southern Ocean Racing Conference [SORC]. I've been organizing crew for the SORC, and he would ask all the same guys I would ask. I would come across 50 people that had been invited on his boat, and there were only 10 spaces. It's obvious what is happening. He is trying to lock everybody up. He sees that as part of the game. He sees it as a fair way of doing it. I don't see that as fair at all."

Jobson offered this example of Conner's need to control people and resources. When Jobson was struggling to raise money for the Twelve that finally became *Defender,* Conner offered Jobson an undefined spot on his boat. "I think," said Jobson, "that he's a guy who feels he gets an edge by having exclusives with people and equipment. Personally, I don't feel the sport of sailing should have exclusives. Having been a sailing coach, I'm always trying to help people and share information."

Gary Jobson, who endorses products ranging from beer to deck shoes, was not born with a silver spoon in his mouth. He grew up on the New Jersey shore, sailing sneakboxes, prams, and scows. "In high school," said Jobson, "I started sailing all the time—when I say all the time, I mean winter, spring, summer, and fall. That was sort of unusual at the time, particularly in this part of the country." In college at the New York State Maritime Academy, he met Graham Hall, a gifted teacher, who was the sailing coach there. Remembered Jobson, "Graham was the first person to say to me, 'You can win.' I mean, I used to win some and lose some, but he said, 'You can win; but you're disorganized on the race course. You've got a nice touch; you've obviously got a lot of time in boats; but we've got to get you organized.' He just broke down a race into logical sequences: there are the same parts to a race, whether you're sailing a 12 Meter or an Interclub dinghy." While under Hall's tutelage, Jobson raced 2,000 times in four years of college, was a three-time college All-American and was twice named College Sailor of the Year. After college, he started coaching at the U.S. Merchant Marine Academy, at Kings Point, New York. "When I got out of college, I went into coaching because I was broke. I guess everyone is when they get out of school. I coached for four years. But, at the same time, I also sailed a lot and continued to study the sport full-time. In 1976, Turner asked me to sail with him as tactician on *Courageous*. By this time I thought I was good enough to handle the job. Turner said to me, 'You know, there's a lot more to the world than sailing.' That was different than what Graham Hall said to me. Turner said, 'There's a big-business world out there, and you'll enjoy that, too. I'm going to show you a lot about that and a lot about sailing, too.' "

Jobson takes credit—and rightfully so—for elevating the role of the tactician in America's Cup racing. As he said, "It wasn't too many years ago that all you heard about were skippers and navigators. Now every magazine I read mentions skipper and tactician. I think what I brought to the job [of tactician] was credibility to this role, which probably wasn't there before. I think today a lot of boats sail—be they America's Cup yachts or ocean racers—with someone acting as tactician..." Asked what a tactician does, Jobson said, "I'm responsible for the game plan. What we do vis-à-vis the competition. I'm the eyes outside the boat."

Asked if match racing (one boat against another, as the America's Cup is sailed) is that complicated, Jobson said, "There are only so many moves and so many countermoves. There's not much to it, actually. The problem is the variables. This whole campaign—this may sound crazy—but in this whole campaign I've learned maybe half a dozen new moves. So it's really a function of how fast you're going, how good the crew's doing. Winning a 12-Meter race is really a function of how many mistakes you make, not how brilliant you are. You don't win on brilliance; you lose on mistakes."

Turner and Jobson went on to defend the America's Cup in 1977, and

Jobson, taking Turner's advice, turned sailing into a business. He lectures on sailing as often as 100 times a year; he writes about sailing; he promotes the sport; he endorses products; and he sails for a living, often with the likes of Herbert von Karajan, conductor of the Vienna Symphony Orchestra, or Walter Cronkite, with whom he sailed to Bermuda. For being a professional in this still-Corinthian world of yacht racing, he is sometimes criticized; hearing himself called "JobCo" was perhaps the unkindest comment of the summer. Asked his reaction to such comments, Jobson said, "I plead guilty. I put my name behind products and allow myself to appear in ads, which is perfectly legal, except if one entertains Olympic aspirations. I lecture and try to get more people into the sport. I write books and work real hard at it. I feel I'm a spokesman for the sport. To the charge of being a 'blatant commercialist'—as Dennis Conner once put it—I don't make that much money. I've got a house, a car, a motorboat, and in fairness I've been able to take a lot of time off in the year to sail, but then again so has Dennis Conner. So I've done okay, but not great. I think if somebody had done the equivalent of what I've done in football, for example, they'd be making $500,000 a year."

Jobson and Blackaller got together in 1980 as the sun was setting on the *Clipper* era. It had already set on *Courageous*, so Jobson had some free time on his hands. He accepted an invitation to sail with Blackaller and Russell Long on *Clipper*. Recalled Jobson, "Blackaller whacks Conner on the starting line, and then Russell took the helm, and Conner just blew by us...I started thinking, Blackaller's pretty good." He also recognized that Blackaller was pretty loud. Said Jobson, "I find that louder guys are really good on the race course. The thing that makes them boisterous is the thing that makes them good on the water." After the *Clipper* campaign, Jobson and Blackaller decided to join forces and try to raise money to start an America's Cup syndicate. This was to prove no easy task.

Around Christmas of 1980, Chandler Hovey III came to Dave Vietor and said that he wanted to back Blackaller and Jobson in an America's Cup syndicate, and how should they go about it? Vietor, who sailed with Russell Long as a senior member of the "kiddy corps," said, "It's simple—buy *Courageous*." Hovey was hesitant about doing that, at least without a bank balance for the project that read several hundred thousand dollars. Rather than taking the bold step and buying *Courageous*, the group printed a slick prospectus that listed an impressive group of potential backers and said they planned to purchase *Courageous*.

In 1981, Leonard Greene, who owns Safe Flight Instruments, which builds stall detectors for airplanes, called Vietor and asked a similar question: "Which boat would you buy for a run at the America's Cup?"

Again Vietor said, "Bar none, buy *Courageous.*" Vietor, an erudite man who has a Ph.D. in German from Stanford, said recently, "I thought *Courageous* was potentially the best boat on the water in 1980; she had the best motion in a seaway. Even though we could hammer her on *Clipper,* I thought it was because we had better sails. I felt *Freedom* was too stiff— she had too much stability for light to moderate air. Although, in heavy air, she might have been better." Greene bought *Courageous.*

This complicated Blackaller's and Jobson's search, which in truth was going nowhere. They called Vietor for another meeting. It was held at the New York Yacht Club. Vietor was asked what they could do. "I said simply build a boat or find a half-million dollars. You've got to have an entry ticket, and you guys don't have one." In April of 1981, Vietor was told by Blackaller that there was no way they could raise the money, so Vietor made plans to sail *Courageous* against a boat to be skippered by Russell Long. However, in the summer of 1981, Jobson met Jane and Nick Heyl. Nick Heyl manages such singing groups as the Kingston Trio, and is fond of backing long shots. His wife Jane is the niece of Tom Watson, of the IBM fortune. They put the money forward—a reported $300,000—to build a new Dave Pedrick–designed 12 Meter to be named *Defender.*

So Vietor had a boat—*Courageous*—and Blackaller and Jobson soon would have one. They both needed money. Then, at the annual St. Francis Yacht Club Stag Cruise to Tinsley Island, Vietor talked about his plans with the eminently wealthy Texans O. L. Pitts and Lee Smith, members of the Fort Worth Boat Club. They played, said Vietor, "what-ifs." Most of those "what-ifs" must have had happy endings because O. L. Pitts and Lee Smith joined the syndicate. Said Vietor, "I went out the next day and made a deal with those guys [Blackaller and Jobson] to join forces."* One of the "what-ifs" must have been "What if we can't get a table in a good restaurant in Newport?"—no small concern of any number of people— because the Texans purchased the White Horse Tavern, the best restaurant in a town well-fixed for better and best restaurants. The elegant White Horse Tavern became known as "Fort Worth Boat Club East."

Defender was launched in June of 1982, having been built by Newport Offshore to the design of Dave Pedrick. Perhaps the prettiest 12 Meter ever, the dark blue *Defender,* with her crew of stars like Blackaller and Jobson, gave every appearance of greatness. That was until she met her stablemate, *Courageous,* sailed by Dave Vietor. The new boat, chockablock full of the best and brightest in sailing, couldn't beat the old and

---

*Russell Long would later sue Vietor for what he termed breach of contract; but the matter went to binding arbitration, and Long's arguments were found unpersuasive. Without a second boat, Long dropped out of the 1983 America's Cup wars.

presumably outdesigned *Courageous*. It is not unheard of in America's Cup trial racing for a new boat to have trouble beating an old one—sometimes these things take time—so there was no panic in the *Defender* camp. *Defender* went back to Newport Offshore for modifications, the major change being the removal of 1,700 pounds of lead ballast.

She seemed marginally better, but still the old boat gave the new one as good as she got. Back went *Defender* for more modifications. Through the magic of chain saws, cutting torches, welding torches, and much money, the leading edge of the keel was changed, the rudder was moved aft, the ballast-displacement ratio was changed, and sail area was cut.

None of this high-tech fiddling surprised the analytical Dave Vietor. "I was a little bit sneaky. When I knew we were going to have two boats competing against each other, I had a guy take the lines of *Courageous;* no one had ever done that before, because she's been modified so much. Then we took the lines of *Defender*. I have a computer study here, called a Velocity Prediction Program [VPP], which is a theoretical assessment, using the lines of the boat, of how the boat should perform. We ran the lines of both boats through the computer. Then we changed things like sail coefficients and hull shapes, and we found that what we were seeing in reality was confirmed by the theoretical computer studies. That is, that *Defender* was basically slow as soon as the wind blew above 12 or 13 knots true. In light air, downwind, she seemed pretty fast, but there was no marked superiority to *Courageous* anywhere. Then we theoretically modified *Courageous*—some of what we evaluated is what the designers actually did . . . We also similarly modified *Defender*. What we discovered was that any change we made seemed to help *Courageous* far more than it affected *Defender*."

Then the boats were shipped by truck to California for a winter of racing at the Balboa Yacht Club in Newport Beach. There *Defender* started beating *Courageous*—at least now and then—and the sighs of relief were loud enough to be heard back in Newport, Rhode Island.

Enter John Kolius into this equation of computer analyses and complicated egos. Kolius, a gunslinger from Houston, Texas, is the future of the America's Cup. Blond and All-American-looking, he is so cool he seems to be powered by a cold-blue flame. Kolius once ran the Ulmer sail loft in Houston, but now does more. On the strength of his performance this summer, and on the strength of his character, he has become president of the company and the name of the company has been changed to Ulmer & Kolius. Even before Kolius became "famous," he owned an Olympic silver medal in the Soling class and had won two J-24 world championships. Kolius was invited into the syndicate to help Blackaller and Vietor tune up their respective yachts.

Describing his supporting role in the *Defender/Courageous* effort, Kolius was typically understated. "I came aboard both boats to make sure they were boat-testing and not sail-testing or crew-testing. Basically, I was there to make sure the crews were trimming sails the same, and tuning the rigs the same. I was just kind of helping out—making sure they were testing boat speed and not testing individuals. I spent a lot of time going on both boats. When either Dave or Tom headed out of town, I would slip in and drive."

Although Vietor's record with *Courageous* was very creditable in Newport in 1982, he relinquished the helm in California. Jobson describes Vietor as "a good ocean-racing sailor, a good straight-line sailor, but weak in the clinches, such as at mark-roundings." When Vietor left the boat, although not the syndicate, *Courageous* was given to Kolius. Asked why he was given this command, Kolius had a sensible answer. "Basically, the idea was to find someone that he [Tom] could get along with. You see, I'm pretty low-key, and Tom is pretty up. It would have been difficult, for example, to get someone like [Ted] Turner and Tom together, although it would have been a riot to watch."

The dynamics of this group were indeed a "riot to watch" even without such an addition as Turner, who is no beginner at stirring up interpersonal trouble. The battle for control of the *Defender/Courageous* syndicate, if it flared now and then, truly began in California in January of 1983.

Heading the *Defender/Courageous* syndicate was Chuck Kirsch, a true gentleman from Michigan whose fortune was made in curtain rods. Then there was Martin "Max" O'Meara, an insurance magnate from Hartford and race-track owner, who ably filled the role of operations manager. Finally, there was the cigar-smoking Jim Mattingly, who worked as the syndicate's co-manager. Both O'Meara and Mattingly have sailed with Turner and have worked for him in similar capacities during his highly visible and highly audible America's Cup campaigns.

The first of the syndicate's crises became known as the "flow chart" incident, and it was nearly Blackaller's last stand. A syndicate member put it this way: "We were getting too big. So it was decided in January to reorganize the syndicate and to define duties with a flow chart—you know, those little boxes with arrows and things that show who does what to whom. In the top box was Kirsch, as chairman. Beneath Kirsch were two boxes—one had O'Meara's name in it as operations manager and the other Mattingly's name as co-manager. Then there were two other boxes under those—one that said *Defender* 12 U.S. 33, and the other *Courageous* 12 U.S. 26. And in those boxes it said skipper U.S. 33, tactician U.S. 33, and it had the same for *Courageous*. Only the names weren't filled in.

"Well, Blackaller saw that—the box conspicuous by the absence of his and Jobson's names—on the way out to a race one day. He stood on the stern of *Defender* and shouted, 'Hey, Jobson, they can fire us!' There was no racing that day as the matter was mediated. And, although practice racing commenced the next day, this battle for control of the syndicate raged for three and a half weeks. Blackaller came close to being fired several times, because he was so close to being out of control. Finally, the names were printed in, and we were able to continue with the boat racing.''

John Kolius is the sort of man for whom everything seems to come easy. Whether this is mere appearance or reality, Kolius managed to avoid the clash of egos all during the summer of '83 and to concentrate on sailing. Perhaps he knew what he was getting into, or perhaps he is one of those rare people who have the ability not to take themselves too seriously. Not an easy thing to manage, for, on the surface at least, the America's Cup has to be one of the world's most serious sporting endeavors. Much of the time it is hard to remember that a Cup summer is just sport.

Kolius has raced against Blackaller for years. Recalling a Half-Ton Championship from years ago, he commented, "I think Tom threw me out of one race there. I don't really remember what it was about, but I probably deserved it. Sailing is a good sport. You don't have to beat up the other guy, like you do in boxing or football; you just try to outsmart him, and outsail him, and then you go out and have a beer with him."

Sailing has been a good sport for John Kolius since he was five. He discovered sailing at that tender age after his sisters took up the sport. "I sailed with my sisters a lot. The rule in my family was that I had to crew for them until I could beat them. It took me until I was 15 to do that." At 17, he won the Sears Cup—the North American Junior Sailing Championship—after five years of trying. Kolius attended the University of Houston, "virtually because of sailing," he said. He had a Soling then, and the local fleet was quite competitive, so there was no compelling reason to stray far from home. At college, he majored in computer science, not because he had any great love for bytes or basic programming, but "because there was this girl there, who was a computer major, who I was trying to hustle." He left college with eight hours remaining before he would take his degree; but an Olympic campaign seemed more important to him then.

Important, perhaps, but Kolius keeps things in perspective. As he said, "For three and a half years I practiced for the Olympics with Buddy Melges [one of America's greatest sailors, who lives in Zenda, Wisconsin]. After we won the Olympic trials, and beat Melges in the process, he mooned us on the way in. That was the extent of the hatred out there;

there just wasn't any. I think you can sail against someone and still be friends—you don't have to be a jerk about it.''

Kolius won the Olympic silver medal in the Soling class in 1976, losing the gold medal by two-tenths of a point. Suddenly sailmakers began to pay attention to him. ''I interviewed with North and Hood Sails,'' said Kolius, ''and a bunch of other lofts, but I decided I liked Butch Ulmer [head of Ulmer Sails] the best. I put a lot more stock in people than I do in companies.''

What was his reaction to being awarded the helm of *Courageous*? Said the 32-year-old Kolius, ''I'm still excited, every time we leave the dock. My entire crew is.''

Who could resist this aw-shucks style, especially when played against the egos expressing themselves in other camps? Kolius and his tactician, John Bertrand of Laser and Finn fame (not to be confused with the Australian John Bertrand), were the stuff of myths, and the charisma that surrounded this boat—in fact, that has always surrounded this boat—and this crew was perhaps the brightest bit of sunlight in an oft cloudy summer.

When Kolius was given the helm of *Courageous* in the winter of 1982–83, the S&S-designed boat had fallen on hard times. She was being beaten regularly by *Defender* and its talented crew. There was talk of building a new boat, and there was talk of redesigning this veteran of a decade of America's Cup competition. It was natural that the *Defender/Courageous* group should talk to Sparkman & Stephens, the designers of *Courageous* in 1974, who had just left Dennis Conner's *Freedom* syndicate under unhappy circumstances. Commented Jobson, ''We went to S&S because they had been pushed out of the Conner camp. We knew they had a lot of good information, and politically I think it's good to have Olin Stephens on your side.''

Said Bill Langan of Sparkman & Stephens, ''Kolius came here, and we met with him a couple of times. They had come to the decision to make *Courageous* work; she had to be modified. That was a good opportunity for us, in view of what happened [the difficulties with the *Freedom* syndicate]. The feeling around here was to totally forget what had gone on in the past, and to work as hard as we could on the redesign . . . I busted my tail to make *Courageous* go fast.''

And *Courageous* went fast. The S&S changes, Kolius believes, accounted for 20 percent of the boat's improvement. ''The other 80 percent came from us getting better. S&S turned a boat that was barely off the pace to one right in there, and we turned a crew that was way off the pace to one right on.'' Asked to characterize his crew, Kolius said, ''I wanted guys that are fun. I was looking for guys who could make a real effort out there. I mean, we went into this not knowing if we were going to be competitive. We thought we could be; but that is where you begin. I wanted guys who could stick it out. That month in California, when we were so slow, we just really hung in there. The crew had faith in the boat, faith in me, and faith in my tactician, John Bertrand. No one gave up.''

The boats were trucked back to Newport in the spring of 1983, and *Defender* failed her measurement test by a nautical mile. The boat wasn't close to being a 12 Meter, and despite the fact that she measured more than 12 meters and should have been faster, she was slower than the rebuilt *Courageous*. Said Jobson, ''That was pretty devastating. You know, we'd been feeling pretty good about our speed in California; we were clearly faster than them there, and then we get back here where it counts, and nothing we could do could touch them.''

Adding injury to insult, the boat had to be reconfigured to become a legal 12 Meter. It was decided to move the rudder forward two inches to shorten the sailing length and thus conform to the measurement. However, because of structural members, the rudder could only be moved forward $1^9/_{16}$ inches. Because of that $^7/_{16}$ inch, the only alternative was to shorten the boom. That took eight inches out of the foot of the mainsail, and by the time they were done making the cut fair, they had lost 20 to 30 square feet of sail, a not inconsiderable amount. A seemingly slow boat was getting slower.

On June 18, the Preliminary Trials began with the brand-new *Liberty* sailing against the veteran *Courageous*. In light air—supposedly *Liberty*'s strong suit—*Courageous* beat Conner and *Liberty* by 34 seconds, and the old boat was ahead at every mark. On the first leg, Conner chose a ratty old headsail that dated back at least to the *Freedom* campaign of 1980, if not before. On the second weather leg, his jib was only slightly newer. Thus began the charge of ''sandbagging.'' On the next day, again in light wind and fog, *Courageous* murdered her stablemate *Defender* by one minute and 56 seconds. When the series ended on June 25, the unofficial* score sheet read: *Courageous* 6–5, *Defender* 5–6, and *Liberty* 5–5. That muddle aside, *Courageous* seemed the best boat; with *Liberty*, the verdict was not in; and *Defender* seemed slow. That verdict—this early in the game—was sure.

Blackaller discounted his troubles beating *Courageous* and Kolius as interpersonal. As he said, ''I think I sail better against Dennis than against Kolius because Kolius is a good friend of mine. I think that's really true.'' He had, in fact, been better against Conner; but in June *Defender* seemed stalled in the designer's office.

---

*The results in the defense trials are unofficial, because this is a selection process, says the NYYC's America's Cup Committee, not a race-off.

Jobson was more troubled by the boat's lack of speed. "I spent three days not sleeping . . . My expertise is not in boat speed; it's tactical sailing. I'm not someone who can look at a mast and say it should be racked two inches; but what I am good at—thanks to Turner—is getting the right people talking to the right people." After conversations such as that, it was decided to template the boat: to see if what they had was what the designer wanted. "We found," said Jobson with some relief, "that the boat had sagged down in the ends, perhaps because of the two cross-country truck rides. It wasn't anything like a 12 Meter; it was completely out of whack. It wasn't even faired on one side, compared to the other side . . . We spent 10 days getting the boat together—interestingly enough, at the end of those 10 days, we were able to add six inches to the J-measurement [the distance from the headstay to the mast], and we were able to add 10 inches to the main boom. The waterline length remained the same; the volume changed because we had to bring the ends up during the changes. We were allowed to put 760 pounds of lead in the keel, and to add sail area. We ended up with more sail area than we lost when we failed the measurement.

"Dave [Pedrick] was under extremely heavy pressure to get the boat right. We were coming down on him like a ton of bricks," said Jobson.

Blackaller had a slightly different view of where blame lay. "I wasn't angry at Pedrick. The problems we had with Pedrick were self-induced. We didn't treat him very well in the beginning. We got cheap with him; our program has suffered somewhat from being a little cheap because we haven't had a lot of money, all the way along. It turns out now that everybody loves us—they can't do enough for us. But six months ago I wish they had; it would have made life easier."

Pedrick responded with *Defender*'s so-called "tummy tuck," which despite all the optimism proved to be more cosmetic than real. *Defender* came back looking as beautiful as ever, but proved to be no faster upwind in a breeze, disappointing off the wind, and downright slow in any direction in a moderate breeze. Again, she showed more promise than performance.

If July was cruel to *Defender*, she was getting used to it. It would also prove cruel to her stablemate *Courageous*. In July, *Courageous* fell from grace with a thud. The worst record of the month, 2–13, belonged to *Courageous*. After a sparkling tactical victory against *Liberty* in her first race—the margins at the five turning marks were never more than 12 seconds and as little as three—and a less than convincing win the next day against *Defender*, *Courageous* couldn't buy a victory. She was never far off the pace—indeed, she and *Liberty* waged another epic battle on another day, which *Liberty* won by 15 seconds in a decent breeze over the full Cup course—but she just couldn't hang in consistently with either *Liberty* or

Defender. It was said that her troubles could be traced to a lack of Kevlar/ Mylar for sailcloth—but all 12 Meters suffered from the same problem, to varying degrees, in midsummer. Things went so badly for *Courageous* that the America's Cup Selection Committee was moved to give Kolius and his crew reassurance that they weren't doing as poorly as they thought. And, as it would turn out, they weren't.

Meanwhile *Liberty,* which lacked for nothing—Kevlar/Mylar sails included—sailed to an unofficial tally of 13 wins and five losses. This included nine straight wins between July 23 and 29. *Liberty* was a good boat and she was well-sailed, but something else was happening. July was the month when it became impossible to characterize *Liberty*'s performance. Some days she seemed potent downwind; other days she seemed what they call on the waterfront and other places "a dog." Bill Langan, the S&S designer who worked on the changes in *Courageous,* put it this way: "One day we'd see a boat [*Liberty*] that couldn't get out of its own way downwind, and then there were days Dennis flew by us downwind. Performance downwind is usually weight- and sail-area related. We were kind of saying to ourselves, 'Something is not right here.' Putting two and two together, the guys were able to figure it out; there was weight and possibly sail area being changed, perhaps on a daily basis, and the boat was presumably being remeasured."

This was the "multiple (rating) certificate" controversy, in which lead ballast was being added or subtracted from *Liberty* to conform to weather conditions. Sail area was changed to balance the 12-Meter equation, thus the "multiple certificates." (*Liberty,* it was later divulged, had three weight- and sail-area configurations and three rating certificates.) What troubled Langan was not that this was being done to *Liberty,* but that the other defense camps were not told about it. Said Langan, "The question [about multiple certificates] had been asked in the past. Olin [Stephens] asked it; Ted Hood asked it. They were told not to do it. We were going with the precedent, and then all of a sudden the rules changed. It was a little unnerving."

At a rare press conference, Commodore Bob McCullough, head of the America's Cup Committee, was asked, "Why did the Yacht Club permit *Liberty* to use multiple certificates?" Responded McCullough, "Actually, that was an experiment in the July series, and we think they only were allowed to do that two times." Asked if this was not an unfair advantage, McCullough responded, "I don't think so. Normally if a boat comes to us with something new, we don't tell the other boat or boats..." When we asked McCullough if he or his committee had ever entertained such a request before, he said, "I don't remember any such requests."

At the end of the July series, Tom Blackaller, who managed to go 8-5 that month, announced plans for another application of the torch to *Defender*. The boat was reported to be beastly to steer, particularly in a seaway, and so this time the broad stern would be reshaped. This became known as the "butt tuck." Blackaller, who is not big in the world of secrets, announced to the world his boat's impending surgery and casually pegged its cost at $50,000. The syndicate seemed less than pleased that he mentioned the plan publicly, and seemed even more upset that he disclosed the price. However, the cost was put into perspective by a member of Pedrick's design team. "We can spend $50,000 with one stroke of a pencil—or an eraser."

Only August—and perhaps a little of September—remained to name a defender. And, as Cup watchers know, these are the cruelest months.

> *"As trustees of sponsors' funds, the syndicate management could not see any value in spending good money after bad in attempting to make a silk purse out of a sow's ear."*
>
> —SYD FISCHER, *ADVANCE* SYNDICATE CHAIRMAN,
> REFERRING TO HIS BOAT AND ITS FAILURE TO BE COMPETITIVE

CHAPTER 5
Seven Challengers—A Mighty Armada

The lineup was intimidating from the start. Never before in America's Cup history had so many yacht clubs, representing so many syndicates, from so many foreign nations, decided that they wanted the prize so badly. The America's Cup was up for grabs. Appetites had been whetted by 24 previous challenges, and everyone knew it was just a matter of time.

Powerful men were caught up in it. The Aga Khan, wealthy ruler of 15 million Moslems, backed a challenging yacht. And so did Peter de Savary, a British banker and businessman whose ostentatious moves knew no bounds. And French movie producer Yves Rousset-Rouard, a man with quiet wealth and altruistic leanings. And the unrelenting Alan Bond, an Australian multimillionaire whose obsession with winning the America's Cup had begun 10 years before.

Dennis Conner, skipper of the American defender, saw it as an ominous sign two summers ago. In May of 1981, he said: "It's pretty scary from the standpoint that with four boats last time [1980], the challengers were able to produce a very competitive race series. Common sense would tell you that with seven or eight, the level will go up dramatically. The sheer numbers give them a chance to come up with a fast boat. For the first time, it changes the odds in favor of the challengers. They could have as much as a 2-1 or 3-1 advantage, if the United States doesn't produce a fast boat."

Even then, Conner predicted that the most serious threat could be expected from the Western Australia group. Especially since John Bertrand had been chosen to be skipper of the Aussie boat. Conner was right. "The foreigners are for real this time," he said a year before the

Cup summer of '83. "We've been crying wolf for a long time. Now it's happening."

The new 12 Meters started rolling into Newport in late April, and continued arriving until June—by container ship, by barge, by truck and by tow. When the politics of forming new syndicates had sifted out, there were seven boats representing five foreign nations that had come to challenge for the America's Cup. They didn't want to be called "foreigners." They preferred instead to be known as "international" syndicates. From France, there was *France 3;* from Italy, *Azzurra;* from Canada, *Canada 1;* from Great Britain, *Victory 83;* from Australia, *Advance, Challenge 12,* and *Australia II.*

Trial races were designed to single out one boat—presumably the best—to challenge a U.S. defender for the America's Cup in September. The Challengers' Race Series took the entire summer, from June 18 to September 5. Boats were eliminated from competition in the first three-race series (A–C) based on a complicated system of accumulated point totals rather than win-loss records. The scoring system weighed the later races more heavily than the earlier ones. It meant that at the end of Series C, on August 4, three of the seven boats were no longer in the running.

The 12-Meter *Advance* did poorly from the start. She had a summer total of 0.8 points, having won only two of 36 races sailed. *France 3* wasn't much better with 3.1 points, winning only seven of her 37 races. *Challenge 12* looked promising at the beginning, but fell from grace toward the end of the third set of trial races (Series C), when the scoring counted most. When eliminated from competition on August 4, she had 10.6 points, winning 24 of her 40 races.

Canada 1 and *Azzurra* hung on a bit longer, making it to the Semifinal Series, along with *Victory 83* and *Australia II. Canada 1* slid into the Semifinals ahead of *Challenge 12* by only 1.1 points. *Azzurra* was close, too; she led *Canada 1* by only 0.4 point.

Win-loss records replaced the point system for scoring in the Semifinals. Scores were not carried forward, as they were in the earlier series. The four boats that raced in the Semifinals started off with a clean slate. When the nine-race series ended August 22, *Canada 1* was out, having lost all nine races. Of the 49 races she sailed all summer, she won 19.

Azzurra won four of her nine races in the Semifinals, but it wasn't enough to stay ahead of *Victory 83,* which won six races. *Azzurra* left the summer's competition with a record of 25 victories in 49 races. It had been an unbelievable performance for a first-time effort, and even the Italians admitted surprise.

Victory 83 and *Australia II* were left to fight it out in a best-of-seven Final Series. *Australia II* won the match 4–1, and the men from Down

Under were a bit shaken by the fact that *Victory 83* had managed even one win. *Victory 83* ended the summer with 30 wins in 54 races, but *Australia II* won 48 of her 54 matches. The boat from Down Under was on a roll, and there was no stopping her. Not even a 132-year-old winning streak.

The challengers from Australia were much varied in terms of quality of design and crew readiness. The 12-Meter *Advance,* sponsored by the Royal Sydney Yacht Squadron, seemed to have everything going for it. The boat's designer, Alan Payne, was highly regarded and experienced. He had designed two other Australian challengers—*Gretel I,* which challenged in 1962, and *Gretel II,* a challenger in 1970. Both boats had won one race from the Americans—which, at the time, was considered a very game performance. The Sydney syndicate was connected with the two other Australian Twelves, *Australia II* and *Challenge 12,* only in a scheme that merged their fund-raising efforts. The three had joined with one another a year before the 1983 Cup races in a group called "Advance Australia Challenge," a play on words that was supposed to bring Australian dollars flowing into the coffers of the three syndicates. The idea was to light a flame of national pride and patriotism; but, in fact, the candle never burned.

As a result, *Australia II* relied more heavily on the wealth of syndicate chairman Alan Bond; the *Challenge 12* group found a godfather in Richard Pratt, a Melbourne businessman; and the *Advance* group, by all appearances, never did find enough money. The financing of the *Advance* effort was never clear. Neil Wyld, administrative manager, conceded in mid-July that the syndicate was strapped for funds and was trying to squeak by on a $1.5 million budget, small by America's Cup standards.

Syndicate chairman Syd Fischer, however, maintained that lack of money was never a problem. Midway through the summer, Fischer blasted Newport Offshore Ltd., where *Advance* was docked, for implying in an interview with an Australian journalist that the syndicate was running out of money and not paying its bills. Fischer showed his anger by slapping a $6 million defamation suit on the boatyard. He said he had withheld payment because Newport Offshore hadn't met its leasing obligations. The bill eventually was paid, and Fischer left Newport insisting he would challenge again (now that Australia has won the Cup, his group will go to Perth instead as a potential defender). Fischer cemented his resolve by buying *Australia I* from the *Victory* syndicate for $105,000.

Financial problems took second place to what had become an America's Cup albatross—the boat itself. *Advance* was brought to Newport under a cloud of uncertainty. Plans to race the Twelve in Melbourne during a March, 1983, series with *Australia II* and *Challenge 12* went awry. Word was already out in Sydney that the old 1970 boat *Gretel II* was beating

Advance with disturbing regularity. When *Advance* arrived in Newport, rumors followed not far behind that the folks back home had dubbed the boat "Retard."

After the 1970 America's Cup challenge, designer Alan Payne remarked that the best chance for anyone to win the Cup was with a "different" boat design. With that in mind, Payne created a 12 Meter that would sail well in August and early September, when winds in Newport are generally light. Unfortunately, *Advance* didn't move in anything but extremely light air. The boat looked odd; it was snubbed at both ends with short overhangs; its hull had fuller sections farther forward than most other 12-Meter designs, and it had high topsides and a skinny keel. Bob Tiedemann, a Newporter who owns the graceful 12-Meter *Gleam*, built in 1937 when nearly all yachts were beautiful, commented on *Advance* the day he saw her: "I never saw an ugly sailboat yet that was fast. You can't fool Mother Nature."

Advance's crew work needed improvement, and her sails were mediocre. In addition, *Advance* was plagued with equipment breakdowns and a run of bad luck. On July 3, she won a race against *Canada 1*, but lost it later on a protest. Three days later, she was beating *France 3* when time was called because of light winds. They ran the race again in the afternoon, and *Advance* was winning again until her bowman, who was filling in for another sailor who had chicken pox, fell overboard as he was reaching for a wayward spinnaker pole. The next day, *Advance* was leading *Azzurra*. But then a fitting on the end of the spinnaker pole broke, and *Azzurra* passed her as *Advance* crewmen were making repairs. Finally, after 19 losses, *Advance* won a race, and then another. She beat *Canada 1* by four minutes on July 10, and *Victory 83* by one minute and 15 seconds, two days later. These were the only two races the boat won all summer. Both were on light-air days.

The competition ended as dismally as it started for *Advance*. On July 29, she sailed out to the race course on Rhode Island Sound, expecting to meet *Victory 83* in what was to be one of her last races of the summer. The wind was blowing fairly hard—a blustery 18 knots and gusting under gray skies. The boats weren't far along in the 24.3-mile race before *Advance*'s mast exploded like a gas pipe, ripping open from compression and splintering in half within a frightful few seconds. The crew looked as dejected as it had all summer. Iain Murray, the 25-year-old skipper, spent the next hour with his 10-man crew pulling the shredded pieces that dangled overboard back onto the boat. To his and the crew's credit, they repaired another mast by working nonstop until it was in place two days later. Then they went out and raced against *Azzurra*. It was their worst defeat of the summer; at the finish they trailed the Italian boat by 7 minutes and 27 seconds. The race with *Azzurra* on July 31 was the last time *Advance* competed in the 1983 campaign.

Alan Payne ended the summer dejected and angry. When the racing was over for *Advance,* he came to his own defense as her designer. He said that there was never enough money in the syndicate to pay for adequate tank testing and analysis. He concluded that "The top-performing boats this year are demonstrating that, in addition to the 'capability' ingredients of knowledge, skill, and experience, one must have a great deal of time and money in order to mount a successful campaign. The basic skill of America's Cup racing may well be the raising of money."

Advance's crewmen were sporting to the last. They took continual ribbing from other 12-Meter crews in stride, and they even were able to make fun of themselves. The boat was a dog, and they had no success sailing it. In early July, members of the crew were passing around an appointment card from a local animal medical clinic that read: "The yacht *Advance* . . . has an appointment on Day–14/Month–July/Date–'83/for major surgery." A crewman handed the card to *Australia II* designer Ben Lexcen.

"Tell me, does it roll over?" Lexcen asked.

"Only when you tickle its transom," the crewman replied.

The French were the next to go. They inherited a prepackaged America's Cup campaign from Baron Marcel Bich, who threw in the towel after four unsuccessful challenges between 1970 and 1980. Bich sold his 12-Meter *France 3* to the new syndicate, along with support boats and whatever sails and equipment were usable from the 1980 challenge. The cost was minimal—about $300,000—with the understanding that the new group would take up the French banner. "It was a kind of guarantee that the French spirit would continue, rather than having someone come in who knew nothing about 12-Meter racing," said Bruno Troublé, *France 3*'s skipper.

What the group lacked in financial resources it made up in *l'ambience.* Its chairman was Yves Rousset-Rouard, a 43-year-old movie producer who filmed the well-known *Emmanuelle,* a French soft-core porn film that became popular in U.S. theaters. He also produced *A Little Romance,* directed by George Roy Hill and starring Laurence Olivier. Henri de Maublanc, syndicate manager, was a star in *L'Enfant Secret,* another Rousset-Rouard film. He temporarily left his job with Exxon to help the French try to win the "Coupe de l'Amérique."

Rousset-Rouard had followed the Cup races since 1958, and dreamed of one day becoming involved. More than anything, he wanted to capture the America's Cup as a tribute to France. As it turned out, his dream was mostly a fund-raising nightmare. Frenchmen naturally assumed that a new

French challenge for the America's Cup had plenty of money available; they thought that, once again, it would be Baron Bich's money from the "Bic" disposables empire, which seemed endless. In fact, the syndicate was nearly destitute. It had less than $1.5 million to spend. Most of the other syndicates were working with budgets of $4 to $6 million. The British announced that they were spending $8 million.

"We have only 15 sails for our boat," said de Maublanc in early summer. "The other syndicates have that many mainsails alone. We are working on fund-raising all the time. I spend half my time going back and forth between Newport and Paris in search of more money. It is very difficult to run an America's Cup campaign that way."

The French spent the year before the 1983 challenge trying to spread the word of the new effort being launched under the auspices of the Yacht Club de Paris. They trucked the eye-pleasing red, white and blue *France 3* into the middle of Paris, wheeled her into a department-store parking lot near the Champs-Élysées, and put her on exhibition in hopes of rallying public support.

The syndicate tried to persuade citizens that this was their chance to "participate" in French history. The idea was not a bad one. It wasn't the same as trying to persuade an Australian bushwhacker that he should give money for a yacht race. The French are maritime-oriented, and their outstanding sailors are national heroes. Eric Tabarly, for example, the man who has won numerous solo races across the Atlantic, and, more recently, Philippe Jeantot, the man who won the BOC singlehanded round-the-world yacht race, are sports superstars in France. But this was different. The image of Baron Bich as the last America's Cup tycoon had a firm grip on the French mentality, and it would take more than a pretty boat in a parking lot to erase it.

Rousset-Rouard—wealthy, but not rich by Bich standards—poured more than a quarter-million of his own dollars into the coffers of this fledgling syndicate. The original budget called for more than $4 million. Some French corporations contributed, including Citroën, Mumm Champagne, and Cointreau. Unfortunately, the state of the French economy worked against whatever financial support the syndicate could gather. The installation of a socialist government under François Mitterrand devalued the franc drastically. What had been a $4 million budget slowly deflated to $2 million.

France 3, which had already been campaigned by Baron Bich in the 1980 Cup challenge, was brought back to Newport for another try. The boat was designed by Johan Valentijn, who went on to design *Liberty* for the Americans, and she is not drastically different from others of her genre— *Courageous, Enterprise, Freedom*, and *Australia*. But she lacked a trial horse, a boat to measure herself against. Without a second Twelve, the French had no way of knowing whether new sails made a difference, or whether to continue modifying the hull. They had already enlarged the keel to improve light-air speed, but had trouble gauging how much it helped, or whether it helped at all.

To make matters worse, *France 3* arrived in Newport with an untried crew. Aside from Bruno Troublé, a skipper with considerable experience, and Jean Castenet, a project manager from the Bich days, the team was new to the game. Discipline deteriorated as the summer progressed. A series of gear breakdowns, race losses to almost every competitor except *Advance,* and a penny-pinching budget took their toll. In addition, the French lost their protests time and again, a clear indication that frustrations were mounting. *France 3,* for example, was disqualified from a race on July 3 when she tried barging at the starting line. *France 3* plowed into the stern of the race committee boat, the 70-foot motor yacht *Mirage,* and then bounced off *Canada 1.*

Spirit was low in the French camp at the end of the second trial series; *France 3* had won six races and lost 18. But optimism rose when the syndicate decided to give the boat another facelift by strengthening the rigging, moving the mast forward, and changing ballast in the keel. *France 3* had been steering poorly, mostly due to the heavier Mylar-Kevlar mainsails that were contributing to weather-helm problems on breezy days. It was a dilemma being confronted by most of the Twelves; but for the French it was one more aggravation added to many. The crew started the third and final series with a glimmer of hope, only to have it dashed with another string of losses and gear breakdowns.

In the end, the French went down fighting. Skipper Bruno Troublé gave up the helm to Jacques Fauroux in hopes that the change would give new life to the demoralized crew. Others worked day and night improving the sails, flattening and trimming shapes that had been too full. Then, just as the boat seemed to be going better, the scoring system caught up with it. Even if *France 3* had won every race left in the series, she wouldn't have had enough points to make it to the Semifinals. The French begged the race committee for permission to finish out the series, but were refused.

The early demise of *France 3* and *Advance* came as no surprise. But the elimination of *Challenge 12* from racing was unpredicted and startling. The boat began the summer in the winner's circle, taking 10 out of 12 races in the first series. *Challenge 12* was the first 12 Meter to bring *Australia II* to her knees, beating her by 51 seconds. This victory in late June was a coup for *Challenge 12,* which had been a poor relation to her quick sister since both boats arrived in Newport. It had been only five months since a deal had been made that turned *Challenge 12* over from Alan Bond's syndicate to its new owners, and the Melbourne group was still struggling to establish autonomy.

Ben Lexcen had designed *Australia II,* and then *Challenge 12.* "It doesn't surprise me," said Lexcen after *Challenge 12* beat *Australia II.* "She always used to beat us in real light air back home."

Challenge 12 was built as the "conventional" 12 Meter that would serve as a yardstick for *Australia II*'s "unconventional" lines. In fact, both boats' underbodies were similar. But it was *Australia II* that had the radical winged keel. The boats were built in Western Australia, at Steve Ward's boatyard in Perth. Bond asked Lexcen to design two boats when he saw how different *Australia II* was turning out to be. But when a syndicate from Melbourne offered to buy *Challenge 12,* Bond sold it to them, convinced that two boats would dilute his effort and that if *Australia II* didn't work out he could always take *Challenge 12* back.

Australia II was finished in June of 1982, *Challenge 12* in late October. The two boats were often in the same shed, side by side. The two crews took advantage of the closeness to copy one another. In most cases, it was *Challenge 12* crewmen who copied the crew of *Australia II.* Bond's team was well-seasoned in America's Cup combat, and they had plenty of tricks and shortcuts for improving their boat. "When *Challenge 12* came out of the shed, she was complete," Lexcen says. "She even had all the little pet touches that normally come later. It was like a big vacuum pack. You open it up, and there's an instant 12 Meter. She went in the water in almost perfect racing condition. And she was fast. Straightaway she went fast. They even beat us sometimes. It was a shock, but it was good for us."

The two teams practiced together near Perth in November and December of 1982. *Challenge 12* changed hands back and forth, with the first owners pulling out of the deal and a second group from the Royal Yacht Club of Victoria in Melbourne taking over. Bond, as always, protected himself, allowing the group to charter the boat and crew for a period until they could come up with the necessary funding. He put a clause in the agreement that his group could use the boat one day a week for sail testing if he desired. Another clause guaranteed Bond the use of the boat and equipment should *Challenge 12* be eliminated from competition in Newport sooner than *Australia II.*

Lexcen says that he was happy to see the second Melbourne group take over the boat. Bond had been in control for a time and found that trying to keep two boats on the edge of perfection became a chore. The two Twelves were shipped from Perth to Melbourne in January, with plans that they both would be sailed there until it was time to go to Newport. At the same time, a loan was due that Bond had made to the Melbourne group for control of *Challenge 12*. The syndicate owed him nearly $500,000 and was finding it difficult to come up with the cash by the January 31 deadline. Bond reclaimed rights to the boat when the time limit ran out.

The foundering syndicate was rescued by Richard Pratt, who was a syndicate supporter from the start. He not only brought in the necessary funding, but infused the syndicate with management and public relations expertise as well. Pratt, a Melbourne businessman who manufactures packaging and cardboard box materials, wasn't a sailor. But by the end of the campaign he had turned into a shoreside yachtsman.

The two boats were shipped from Melbourne to Sydney, where, with *Advance*, they were loaded onto a container ship. They left Australia in late April for the journey to the States.

John Savage, the young and relatively inexperienced skipper of *Challenge 12*, got off to a good start. Of all the challenging crews, his seemed the most confident and well-organized. Graeme "Frizzle" Freeman was undoubtedly one of the best tacticians on the Newport waterfront. And sailing coach Mike Fletcher was tough. Their only loss in the first five races was to *Australia II*. "We were jumped at the start and gassed at the first mark," said Fletcher matter-of-factly. "But as soon as we settled down, our performance improved, and our boat speed was good."

The high-flying *Challenge 12* began to go under in the second trial-race series. After 12 races, she had a 7–5 win-loss record. By the third series, she had turned the burner down to a 7–9 record. The only races she was winning were against *France 3* and *Advance*, and occasionally *Canada 1*. She started the series with a new mast, a new mainsail, and new genoas. It turned out to be too much at one time, and it was hard to tell which component was making the boat go slower. By the time the crew had sorted it all out, the series was half over. Then the boat experienced spreader problems on the mast. The timing was bad. They had developed an inconsistent streak just when the races counted most. Either *Challenge 12* was getting worse or the other boats were getting better. It was never really clear.

The syndicate made few changes to the boat—partly the result of the inattention of Ben Lexcen compared to his devotion to *Australia II*. Skipper John Savage had talked about moving the rudder and making other changes before the start of the third and last series, but nothing was done about it. A designer is central to a 12 Meter's ongoing improvement. In the summer of 1983, designers were more crucial than ever. As the *Challenge 12* campaign wore itself thin, Richard Pratt took to reminding Lexcen whenever he saw him: "Remember, Ben, you have two children here."

It was wrenching for the *Challenge 12* crew to be knocked out of the racing so early. It didn't help that the Canadians and Italians were so close in point totals; if it had been race-by-race scoring, *Challenge 12*'s record would have been better than both. The syndicates, however, had agreed to the system before the summer's trial racing started, and they had to live with its realities. If there were bad feelings, they were never apparent. Both the Canadian and Italian teams had worked hard all summer, too. The Canadians, in particular, were expected to do well. Their designer, Bruce Kirby, is one of the most respected in the business. Although he had never designed a 12 Meter before, he had been involved with the America's Cup in one way or another for 20 years. He was primarily a small-boat designer—his 14-foot Laser had taken the sailing-dinghy world by storm nearly 12 years before.

Beyond that, the Canadians had done well in the 12-Meter World Championship in Newport the previous summer. Referred to as the Xerox Challengers' Races, the regatta brought five Twelves together in a five-day match-racing series in late September. The Canadians sailed *Clipper*. They had bought the 1980 U.S. America's Cup contender for use as a trial horse for their yet-to-be-built *Canada 1*. *Clipper* placed second overall, a creditable performance since they were sailing a boat with old sails and the crew had little experience sailing a Twelve. Most, like skipper Terry McLaughlin, who was world Flying Dutchman champion, sailed small boats. Experts within the syndicate expected that, with the winter of practice racing in Florida, as planned, and a new boat, the team would be formidable a year from then. As time went on it didn't work out that way.

As with the *France 3* syndicate, money was a major problem. The syndicate from the Great White North had lived and died 10 times since its inception in the spring of 1981. The Canadians didn't enter the 1983 America's Cup wars easily. Their first problem was finding a yacht club to sponsor them. The challenge was conceived by a group of western oilmen from Alberta. They neither sailed nor belonged to a yacht club. What they did have was the desire to put money into an effort that might unify what they increasingly saw as a fragmented country—the east with its cities and the west with its natural resources. The America's Cup, they reasoned, might be the perfect vehicle to bring Canada full-throttle behind a national sporting quest, a thing that might foster unity on other fronts. They were undaunted by the fact that two previous Canadian challenges for the Cup—in 1876 and 1881—fell to resounding defeats. And it mattered little that they didn't have a yacht club. They would start one.

The rules governing America's Cup contests stipulate that a challenging yacht club must hold annual regattas on the open sea or an arm of the sea. With that in mind, the men from Alberta found a friend who had a place 60 miles north of Vancouver, in British Columbia. He owned an inn where they could hold meetings. It was near a place called Secret Cove, and thus was born the Secret Cove Yacht Club. The New York Yacht Club sat on that one for a while, but finally acquiesced. The challenge was accepted in the spring of 1981, and by the summer of 1982 the Secret Cove Yacht Club was more than an idea; a clubhouse had been built, and a racing schedule set.

The Canadian campaign was designed to be a people's effort. As with *France 3,* the new boat was put on public display at a boat show in Toronto in hopes of attracting donations. The boat should have been sailing instead. It was already running late. The boatyard in Parry Sound, north of Toronto, wouldn't release *Canada 1* until the bills were paid. Construction had been delayed for the same reason. The crew, which was supposed to go from Newport to Florida for winter practice with *Clipper* and *Canada 1,* was sent home instead. For a time, all the cogs in the challenge machine ground to a halt.

Fund-raisers, led by syndicate chairman Marvin McDill, an Alberta lawyer, tried every conceivable way to raise money—selling T-shirts, beer mugs, and baked goods; holding luncheons, dinners, and raffles. It was a grass-roots campaign in search of $5 million—no grass-roots figure. It only came up with a hard-won $100,000 now and then, and to make matters worse the initial syndicate management had made gross errors in its system of priorities. A quarter-million-dollar support boat was bought before the 12 Meter was paid for. Other expensive equipment was being bought before the first bills were paid. In the end, as is the case with so many other America's Cup syndicates, it was a few men and a handful of corporate sponsors who paid the bills. As far as the crew was concerned, it was nothing short of a miracle that they made it to Newport at all for the summer of 1983.

Canada 1 was built to tack easily and maneuver well. She was designed with a longer waterline than most of the other 12 Meters and with a lower freeboard than any except the American-built *Freedom. Canada 1* arrived in Newport with an old mast and a skimpy sail inventory. The crew eagerly awaited new shipments of both. When the mast came, it was put in the boat immediately. The second day out, the mast broke in a mild eight-knot breeze. Two days before, it had stood tall as a tree in a 23-knot guster. The crew found later that the cause was an improperly supported hydraulic ram below decks. The ram controls mast bend. Designer Bruce Kirby described the accident with some wit as ''not too bad. The mast fell over the side, and that does tend to slow the boat down.''

It was weeks before the boat recovered. The old mast, which was considerably heavier than the new one, was put back in the boat. Repairing the new mast was not easy. It had been made of three aluminum extrusions, but there were no more extrusions of that kind available from the manufacturer. A *Canada 1* corporate supporter, Alcan Aluminum, came to the rescue with donations of the required metal, but it still took weeks for repairs. In the meantime, *Canada 1* was off to a less-than-auspicious start. Of the first 12 races, she won only four.

"We took a bunch of very good small-boat sailors and stuck them on 12 Meters," Kirby says. "Then we practiced for a year and a half. After that, we ran out of money completely. As soon as we went up against the other boats here, we realized our sail inventory was completely out of date."

The mast problem was big, and it wasn't until *Canada 1* had the repaired new mast back that she started winning races. The new sails started arriving from the North Sails loft in Toronto, and the Canadian challenge began looking like a class act. By the end of Series B, the Canadians had evened their scorecard at 6–6 and things were looking up.

For the start of Series C, which would determine which three boats would be the first to be eliminated, *Canada 1* was counting on a continued upward swing. The syndicate imported Vancouver sailmaker David Miller as pre-race coach, and Kirby feathered out the leading edge of the keel to improve the boat's light-air tacking ability. Winds had been unusually light in Newport in the summer of 1983, and most designers were reshaping their boats like sculptors working with clay. The lighter mast contributed significantly to *Canada 1*'s stability and upwind performance, and the Canadians were hoping for the best. Then they were plagued by more rigging problems. *Canada 1* pulled out of a race with *Challenge 12* on August 3, and from then on she was on the steep downside of her winning streak.

Canada 1 never was able to pull things together again when she entered the Semifinals. She retired from a race with *Australia II* because of a torn mainsail. She had a gear breakdown and couldn't finish a race two days later with *Victory 83*. And she was beaten by a towering 8 minutes and 53 seconds the following day by *Azzurra*. It was the largest victory margin in all the trial races of the summer. *Canada 1* ended the summer as she had started—with a lackluster performance fostered by marginal funding and lack of experience with these demanding boats.

The Italians were at the opposite end of the campaign spectrum. They had plenty of money, but not much hope. When their *Azzurra* moved successfully into the Semifinals, the team seemed as surprised as anyone. "We will see, we will see," *Azzurra* skipper Cino Ricci kept repeating as it became clear that his boat would edge out *Challenge 12*.

There was no doubt that they had come a long way. Members of the Italian crew first came to Newport in the summer of 1981 to claim their new possession, the former U.S. 12-Meter *Enterprise*. The boat was a serious contender for the defense in 1977, and had been a high-caliber trial horse for *Freedom* during the 1980 Cup-defense campaign. The Italians quietly came to Newport and bought *Enterprise* for $337,000. The acquisition was a brilliant move that gave Italian designer Andrea Valicelli a pattern on which to base his design for *Azzurra*. And it gave the crew an excellent trial horse for two years of practice racing off the coast of Sardinia.

The Italian 12-Meter effort received unwarranted verbal abuse in Newport that summer of 1981. The crew, as green as the Mediterranean is blue, came to take *Enterprise* back to Italy. But first they planned a few weeks of sailing her. "The Italians are out there trying to figure out how to get the mainsail up," was one of the unfortunate waterfront quips. Or, "Look at them. They've got the mast in upside down." By the summer of 1983, the disparaging words had changed dramatically. The Italians rolled into town with a brand-new, azure-blue 12 Meter of their own design. They were well-prepared and organized—perhaps more than any other syndicate except the British—and the crew worked hard and seemed confident, but never boastful. A press reception area and information center on Bowen's Wharf was the envy of the America's Cup waterfront. Italian corporate sponsors were making themselves known—through afternoon sails on the Cinzano charter boat, by a blue Agusta helicopter hovering in the sky, by classy *Azzurra* blue T-shirts and sweatshirts that made other syndicate uniforms look primitive in comparison.

"Our goal is to do as well as we can and try to make an honorable showing," said Ricci soon after arriving. He was quick to point out that his team had no expectations of winning the America's Cup in 1983. Or for that matter, 1986. They figured they would need at least two Cup campaigns before they had sufficient experience. Although Italians have their own strong yachting tradition, they have had no previous experience with 12 Meters. For that reason alone, they felt themselves to be, as the Aga Khan noted, "the last arrived."

The Italians had the backing of 17 Italian corporations and a budget of $5 million. The budget was sizable but not lavish. But there was an aura of wealth—significant European wealth—that permeated their camp. And rightfully so. The mainstay of the *Azzurra* syndicate was His Royal Highness Prince Karim Aga Khan IV, 49th Imam and spiritual leader of 15 million Shia Moslems of the Nizari Ismaili sect. His followers are widely scattered throughout India, Persia, Burma, Afghanistan, the Middle East, and sections of Africa. In Newport, the balding middle-aged prince was referred to respectfully as the Aga Khan. And sometimes, "Your Highness." And occasionally, "Aga," or "H.H." (His Highness), but never to his face.

The Aga Khan is the son of Aly Khan, a flamboyant playboy who was once accused of caring only for "fast horses, fast cars, and fast women." Aly Khan's first marriage produced Prince Karim and Prince Amyn. A second marrige was to the American film star Rita Hayworth. When Aly Khan's father, the elderly Aga Khan III, died, he took the unprecedented step of bypassing his son for his grandson, Prince Karim, to inherit the title Aga Khan IV.

The Aga Khan, 46, seemed at home amid the elegance of Newport. He never stayed there long; jet-set restlessness is a way of life for this man who keeps four homes around the world and has offices in a newly built chateau on a large, wooded estate at Gouvieux, in France. He lives in Gouvieux with his English wife, Salimah (a name she adopted when they married), and their three children. The Aga Khan is reserved and dedicated. He has a wide range of interests, from raising thoroughbred horses (his kidnapped stallion Shergar was in the headlines last winter) to fast yachts. His love for boats was instrumental in his decision to invest in a new yacht club on the northeast coast of Sardinia—the Yacht Club Costa Smeralda—in 1967. Since then, international regattas have been held there, including the Sardinia Cup and the Swan World Cup. The club, which has only 186 members, has berths for 600 yachts. Facilities near the club complex include four hotels, a tennis club, and a golf course. The Aga Khan has now suggested that a World 12-Meter Championship be held at Costa Smeralda in 1984. He has quietly made it known that he might help with the expenses of shipping competing 12 Meters to his Sardinian resort complex and yacht club. It was the Yacht Club Costa Smeralda that sponsored *Azzurra* for the 1983 America's Cup competition.

"It's going to be a breathtaking series of contests that we are approaching," the Aga Khan said in anticipation of the '83 challenge for the America's Cup. "We do so with the humility of the last arrived, but with the conviction to be up to the standards exacted in this peerless event."

By the end of the first race series, *Azzurra* had proved her worth. She won seven races and lost five. The Valicelli design became noted as a hard-to-beat boat in light air, especially downwind. She was built with a higher stern than *Enterprise,* and a shorter and more angular keel. *Azzurra* came close to beating *Australia II* in a race in which she trailed at the finish by only 49 seconds. She finally had her day in the second series, beating the Aussie superboat by 32 seconds on July 13. *Australia II* had an excuse—she broke a backstay runner and genoa halyard, both made of Kevlar—on the first leg. *Azzurra* took advantage of *Australia II*'s breakdown by moving ahead as her crew struggled to make repairs. "I think our boat is fast enough to take the possibilities the other guys give us," said Cino Ricci afterward.

Ricci had been a driving force behind the success of the boat. Unlike other skippers, he rarely took the helm. That responsibility went instead to Mauro Pelaschier, a former Olympic Finn class champion. It was Ricci who maintained crew discipline while at the same time keeping morale high. He was a quick and methodical thinker who learned fastest by being an astute observer of the American organizations on the waterfront.

Azzurra continued to do well in the second series, again winning seven races and losing five. By the third series, she was trampling *France 3* and *Advance,* and sitting on *Canada 1* and *Challenge 12.* Only *Victory 83* showed spurts of superiority, along with *Australia II,* which was leading all the challengers. By the end of the third set of trial races, *Azzurra* was ready for the Semifinals.

The Italians' only success in this fourth stage of trials was in beating the Canadians, who were on their last legs as well. They beat the Brits once, but abandoned a second race because of a broken spreader. When all was said and done, *Azzurra* was eliminated with honor—a first-time challenger that had made her way to the top without scrambling. In the annals of America's Cup history, she will be remembered as having waged one of the more exemplary campaigns—with pizazz.

Of all the campaigns, that of the British *Victory* syndicate was the most relentless. Beyond the staggering dollar figures was a team of more than 50 individuals who had committed nearly three years of their lives to one goal—winning the America's Cup. It was an around-the-clock effort, four seasons a year, and to belong to this dead-earnest group one had to profess complete devotion. There was no room for a personal life. The uniform was yellow-and-blue striped rugby shirts (with shortened sleeves when the weather was hot) and their nickname was "the Killer Bees." There was some truth to the label. Two *Victory* crewmen climbing the mast of a 12 Meter looked like bees on their way up a daisy stem.

Everywhere in Newport was pasted the *Victory* emblem—a cartoon drawing of Winnie, the bulldog mascot, dressed in full British military regalia, pointing a finger and saying: "Your country needs you for *Victory* in '83." In truth, it was British business mogul Peter J. de Savary who needed the support. De Savary, 38, went after the 1983 America's Cup challenge with the determination and good cheer of Attila the Hun. De Savary decided early on that the only way to win the America's Cup was to treat it as a business venture rather than a summer sport. He poured millions into the campaign, and most of the money spent was his own. De Savary was used to wheeling and dealing. For a man who left boarding school at age 16 and began his career by selling encyclopedias and working in a glue factory, he had come far.

De Savary went to Africa to make his first big money; he worked in the shipping business first, hauling cargo. From there, he moved into the oil business—Nigerian oil—then into exporting and importing cement and flour. Then came Arab oil investments. Today he is on the boards of hundreds of companies. With main offices in Nassau, de Savary deals as an investment banker with connections in West Africa, the Middle East, Europe, the United States, and Australia. He is also in real estate development, and one of his projects is the 32-story, $100 million St. James Tower near Sutton Place in New York City.

De Savary knows sailing, but not as a competitor. He grew up in England, close to the Royal Burnham Yacht Club, which sponsored his challenge for the America's Cup. His father, a French aristocrat, moved to England when he was young and was a member of the Royal Burnham for most of his life. His mother was a psychiatrist. The family lived an upper-middle-class life in England, where de Savary learned to sail when he was 10. "I wasn't keen on regattas," he once said. "I liked it better sailing one-to-one with friends."

This attitude belies the aggressive way in which he approached the America's Cup. De Savary, who brought a 50-member support team to Newport in the summers of 1982 and 1983, regrets that he hadn't started sooner. The syndicate's presence in Newport was significant. It included the rental of four large houses, a luxury condominium, a helicopter, a seaplane, the 140-foot motor yacht *Kalizma* (once the plaything of Richard Burton and Elizabeth Taylor), four 12 Meters, and at least 10 smaller support boats. One of the boats, the 53-foot speedboat *Lisanola,* was capable of 44 knots. It was enough to entice de Savary and the Aga Khan, with his otherworldly powerboat *Shahbaz,* into a high-tech speedboat race on Rhode Island Sound one day as the two bored tycoons waited for the wind to come up for the start of a 12-Meter race. (The Aga won.)

De Savary incurred the wrath of the *Freedom* group early on in the campaign. He sent a motorized dinghy with two or three of his crewmen out to follow the American Twelves. They came equipped with video cameras to film every tack and sail change. "It started out that I just wanted members of our team to go out and watch, to see them when they tack, to see them when they jibe, and how their crew works," de Savary says. "No one seemed to mind except Dennis Conner. I have no complaints about Tom Blackaller [skipper of *Defender*]. He's been great."

In fact, the shadowing did bother Conner. And once de Savary knew that, he continued it, half out of curiosity and half to try to psych Conner out. The summer of '82, which the British team spent in Newport practice racing, was enlivened by a series of charges and countercharges. In one incident, Conner sailed two of the *Freedom* syndicate 12 Meters to the other side of Block Island, 20 miles offshore, to try and shake the curious

Brits. It didn't work. In desperation, *Freedom*'s support boat tried to swamp the British inflatable.

Things deteriorated from there. The *Victory* crew charged that *Freedom* crewmen tried to foul the prop of their outboard engine by dragging lines; Conner's team said they caught a *Victory* crewman snooping around their workshed; the *Victory* team said their immigration cards were being suspended, and they charged that the FBI was snooping around.

"The whole thing just got completely out of control," a *Victory* crewman says. The espionage stopped when the summer of 1982 ended. The *Freedom* crew half expected *Victory* spies to show up at their winter training headquarters in San Diego, but as far as they know there were no such visits.

By the time the America's Cup summer of 1983 rolled around, de Savary was too busy trying to get his own act together to worry much about what was happening on the American docks. Beyond that, "Keelgate" loomed like a storm cloud over the Newport waterfront.

Victory 83, the boat that finally competed for the right to challenge, evolved from the first 12 Meter de Savary built—*Victory*. Designed by Edward du Bois, who had no previous experience with 12 Meters, the first *Victory* was a heavier and a more radical design than the second boat. Even after de Savary had *Victory* overhauled (with a redesigned keel and trim tab and a fuller afterbody), he still wasn't happy. He then asked Ian Howlett, who had designed the 1980 British challenger, *Lionheart,* to build another boat—a more conventional Twelve closer to the design of *Australia I.* With almost continual tinkering, the newer boat improved as the summer progressed. The addition of "winglets," which de Savary apparently planned from the beginning, was not as successful as he might have hoped. Still, the boat was decidedly faster in light air than *Victory* had been, and under most conditions she was faster upwind.

De Savary went through personnel the same way he went through boats. He was dynamic to work for, to say the least. Some said overbearing. But in most cases those who worked for him found that self-preservation meant keeping one's lips tightly buttoned. In the end, decisions were made at the top, and no one disputed the fact that this was de Savary's show. One of his more aggressive skippers, Harold Cudmore, left the team midway into the summer. Cudmore, it turned out, is a world-class sailor. But this Irish version of Ted Turner couldn't keep his mouth shut. Phil Crebbin, helmsman for most of the 1983 trial races, was sent "on vacation" in late summer. He also said too much.

By August, de Savary had split his crewmen into two teams, "A" and "B." The "A" team took the newer boat, *Victory 83*. Once Cudmore left, Rodney Pattisson, Chris Law, Lawrie Smith, and Phil Crebbin alternated as helmsmen. De Savary was later criticized from within his own camp for refusing to settle on a permanent crew. The merry-go-round in the cockpit created an atmosphere of constant one-upmanship. De Savary insisted that the idea worked. It enabled him to have four qualified skippers on hand, each one ready to take the helm at a moment's notice.

Victory 83 won eight of her 12 races in the first trial series. In the second set, she did nearly as well, winning seven of 12 races. In the third series, she won 10 of 16 races. In view of the numbers, it looked as though de Savary's plan was working. His method was to leave no stone unturned in making the crew and the boat work better together. If it hadn't been for *Australia II,* Peter de Savary might have gotten his wish to win the America's Cup. As it was, he went from being a self-proclaimed "under, underdog" to being "underdog." It was a summer in which money alone couldn't buy everything. But it came close.

> *"If these are the lengths you have to go to win, who needs it? You can argue whether we did a good job for the* Freedom *syndicate or not; but we tried our hardest. Olin Stephens certainly has a good track record—the company has a good track record—so we can't be that far off. But this is crazy. Why were we beating our brains out to satisfy the ego of this one guy [Conner] on debatable speed differences?"*
>
> —BILL LANGAN OF SPARKMAN & STEPHENS

CHAPTER 6
America's Cup Yacht Design

The past and much of the present of America's Cup 12-Meter design was written by a bespectacled and rather shy septuagenarian named Olin J. Stephens II, of the venerable design firm of Sparkman & Stephens (S&S). As a 28-year-old, Stephens helped to shape *Ranger,* the last of the great J-Boats to defend the America's Cup, in 1937. After the curtain fell on these behemoths, Stephens delivered a fleet of winning 12-Meter yachts: *Columbia,* for instance, which defended in 1958, the year of the first modern Cup defense; *Constellation,* which defended in '64; the history-making *Intrepid* in '67; *Courageous* in '74 and again in '77; and *Freedom* in 1980. Only one other yacht designer has ever been behind the design and technology of six America's Cup defenders, and that was Nathanael Herreshoff, whose giant, delicate racing yachts defended between 1893 and 1920.

Olin Stephens was born in 1908 in the Mott Haven section of the Bronx in New York City. When he was five, his father, Rod Stephens, Sr., who was in the coal business, moved the family to Scarsdale, a fashionable suburb of New York City. While growing up, Olin was diminutive and studious-looking, although his grades belied his appearance. His major academic pursuit was doodling boats in the margins of his notebooks.

The family spent several summers vacationing at Sandy Neck on Cape Cod, about 25 miles from Plymouth Rock. And although there was no nautical tradition in the family, his father bought a 16-foot daysailer, which Olin and his younger brother Rod named *Corker*. *Corker* was replaced by a 26-foot yawl, and by this time, remembers Olin Stephens, "sailing was the passion of my life. I can't really remember a time I didn't want to design boats."

Upon graduation from high school in 1926, Stephens enrolled at Massachusetts Institute of Technology, despite serious reservations about this or any other academic pursuit. "Frankly, I was sort of pushed into it," says Stephens of his first and final year in Cambridge. "I wasn't very much interested in school or college. My parents said—I didn't disagree—that for learning naval architecture, it [M.I.T.] was as good as anything ... It was agreed that I would go there for a year to see how it worked." It didn't work well, either socially or academically. Before the year was over, Olin came down with what was diagnosed as jaundice. "I suppose today they would call it psychosomatic, but I really did get sick up there."

While convalescing at home, he had time to indulge himself in his hobby of sketching boats. That fall, Sherman Hoyt, who was once described as "one of the century's most brilliant performers in all types of yachts," helped the young Stephens land a job as a draftsman at the design office of Henry J. Gielow. His salary was $20 a week. Soon he learned that Phil Rhodes was looking for a draftsman. "Rhodes, of course, was doing the type of boats that I was more interested in, so I worked for him; but, again, that was only for a few months before Drake Sparkman came along," says Stephens. His salary at Rhodes was $30 a week.

Drake Sparkman was a successful yacht broker and insurance agent whom the Stephens family knew from Larchmont Yacht Club. In fact, Rod Stephens, Sr., had purchased two boats through Sparkman. The broker let it be known that he was looking to expand his operation by taking a designer into the business. Rod Sr. told Drake Sparkman about his oldest son, who was then 20, and about his dream of becoming a yacht designer. They met, and the shy Olin showed Sparkman the designs he had worked up while convalescing the previous summer. Perhaps Drake Sparkman saw a spark of genius in this quiet and unschooled young man, for he agreed to take him on. Asked what Sparkman saw in him, Olin Stephens responded: "I don't really know if he saw very much in me or not ... He could not have been very positive about the thing when it started because I certainly didn't have much in the way of evidence to show I could draw a boat ... We started the thing in such a way that there were no long-and-hard commitments."

Drake Sparkman convinced a friend, Arthur Hatch, to let Stephens design him a boat. The result was the 30-foot sloop *Kalmia,* which Olin, brother Rod, and their father raced in the 1929 Gibson Island Race, sailing from New London, Connecticut, to that small island in the Chesapeake. *Kalmia* won her class.

Despite that auspicious debut, no second customer stood in line for an Olin Stephens design. Then Rod Sr. stepped in and invested $28,000 in a boat and in his son's future. This, it should be noted, was no minor sum in Depression-era dollars, but history would prove it to be a sound investment. The little yawl was named *Dorade.*

The 52-foot *Dorade,* designed by Olin Stephens, entered the TransAtlantic Race in 1931 as the smallest of 10 boats. Almost immediately *Dorade* split from the fleet, going north when the accepted wisdom was that south was the only way to go in sailing west to east across the Atlantic. The magazines would later describe this tactic as a "long shot," but Stephens described it recently as "a very logical gamble." Since his was the smallest boat in the fleet, he reasoned that the long shot would have been attempting to follow the pack.

Dorade went north, cutting inside Sable Island, across the Grand Banks, then passing within 50 miles of Cape Race, Newfoundland. While the rest of the fleet, well to the south, was beating into headwinds in the lumpy Gulf Stream, *Dorade* was power-reaching across the Atlantic. *Dorade*'s entire passage to England took just 17 days. Not only did she win the TransAtlantic Race, but on her way across she set a land-to-land record (from Nantucket Island to Bishop Rock) of 15 days. This was the fastest crossing a small boat had made since 1869. With brother Rod at the helm, *Dorade* won Britain's prestigious Fastnet Race, which that year drew 17 thoroughbred yachts. When *Dorade,* her young crew, and her 23-year-old designer arrived back in New York, they were treated to a ticker-tape parade up Broadway to City Hall—the track of such notables as Admiral Byrd and Charles Lindbergh. It was the first and only time a yacht designer and a racing crew were afforded such honors.

Typically, the modest Stephens plays down the accolade. It happened, he says, "because we won those two races. An American boat. Also my father . . . was involved in politics. While we lived in Scarsdale, he was in business in the Bronx, and he knew the political figures around town. We were picked up off the ship by a tug. Then we were driven up Broadway to City Hall, where they made some sort of presentation." Asked his reaction to such an honor, Stephens said simply: "It made me feel good."

In 1934 America almost lost the America's Cup. The designer of the Cup defender that year was W. Starling Burgess, who was a second-generation yacht designer and a second-generation America's Cup designer. His father, Edward Burgess, had shaped three successful defenders in the 1880s. In 1934, W. Starling Burgess drew *Rainbow* for Harold "Mike" Vanderbilt. Vanderbilt had grave doubts about the boat, which gave little indication of being capable of beating *Yankee*, an old J-Boat from Boston, sailed by Charles Francis Adams, then Secretary of the Navy. At one point during the Cup summer of 1934 *Yankee* beat *Rainbow* 10 straight times. Vanderbilt and *Rainbow* were chosen to defend at the eleventh hour, and it was a controversial decision. Before the series against T. O. M. Sopwith's *Endeavour*, the British challenger, Vanderbilt was heard to say that he was worried about the future of the America's Cup. After the first two races his worries seemed very real indeed; Sopwith's powerful, sophisticated *Endeavour* led 2–0. Trailing again in the third race, Vanderbilt turned the helm over to the ever-clever Sherman Hoyt, and went below to chew on a sandwich and contemplate the loss of the Cup. He was the first man to have such thoughts in 83 years! However, with tactics that tricked *Endeavour* into tacking four times on the last leg, Hoyt managed to eke out a victory that day. Then with luck, pluck, and one very controversial disallowed protest, Vanderbilt and *Rainbow* went on to win the series 4–2.

England challenged again in 1937, with the same team: T. O. M. Sopwith, skipper, and Charles E. Nicholson, designer. Vanderbilt was forced to go to Burgess again for a design, but decided to shore up the team with the 28-year-old *wunderkind* Olin Stephens, whose ocean racers were now winning everywhere. Stephens was enthusiastic about the collaboration; but he recognized that Burgess must have viewed it as unwarranted. Says Olin Stephens, "He was very nice to me, but I don't doubt he must have seen it, at first, as a necessary evil...He was, however, a very nice person to work with, and I learned a lot from him... I was very happy that we got along as well as we did. We did have some difficult times; but as the younger person I had everything to gain by making it work. And I really liked him personally. He was kind of an oddball in certain ways. I said to myself, 'I'm just going to put up with anything to get this right.' When I say, 'put up with anything,' I don't mean he was in any way unkind to me; but he had his own way of doing things, and I felt that as the younger person, I was the one who should do the adapting."

The Burgess/Stephens collaboration resulted in the J-Boat *Ranger*, which soundly defeated the British and *Endeavour II*. The final tally was 4–0, and in one race *Ranger* won by a margin of 18 minutes. Olin and his brother Rod, known on the boat as "Tarzan" for his aerial feats, were in the afterguard. Vanderbilt gave Olin the helm during the fourth race as the unbeatable boat charged for the finish line and a successful defense of the America's Cup. For the entire summer, in different types of racing,

Ranger won 32 of 34 contests, and was never defeated in 12 match races. She was perhaps the most successful racing yacht ever designed.

World War II ended America's Cup racing for almost two decades. But in April, 1955, Commodore Henry Sears of the NYYC went to England to see if there would be any interest in challenging for the Cup if the Deed of Gift were changed so that smaller yachts might be used and the requirement waived that a foreign yacht arrive at the competition on her own bottom. Sears discovered some interest. Upon his return, the America's Cup Committee was revived. On December 17, 1956, the New York State Supreme Court agreed to two amendments: minimum waterline length would now be 44 feet (down from 75 feet), and the phrase "proceed under sail on their own bottoms..." would be deleted. The result of these changes was the 12-Meter era in America's Cup racing, and here Olin Stephens would enjoy some extraordinary design triumphs, despite the strictures of the 12-Meter design rules.

The 12-Meter rule is what is called a developmental rule, as Alan Bond would point out very frequently. It is a yacht-design formula that encourages creativity on the part of yacht designers. The opposite of a developmental rule is a one-design rule, whose goal is to produce boats that are as identical as possible to provide a maximum test for sailors rather than designers. A fleet of Sunfish is a good example of boats racing under a one-design rule. A fleet of ocean racers competing under the International Offshore Rule (IOR)—which, incidentally, Olin Stephens helped to write— is a good example of different-shaped boats racing with relative parity under a developmental rule.

Although the 12-Meter rule is a developmental rule, it is—compared to some other exercises in yacht-design mathematics—a strict one and its formulas do not encourage excessive creativity. That said, there have been only two revolutionary 12 Meters in the 77 years that the 12-Meter rule has been around. They are *Intrepid*, designed by Olin Stephens in 1967, and, of course, *Australia II*, designed by Ben Lexcen for 1983.

Olin Stephens' 12-Meter *Intrepid* is worth some attention, for all 12 Meters, up to 1983, paid homage to her and her sisters *Courageous* and *Freedom*. Says Olin Stephens, "*Intrepid* was a breakthrough...probably the most forward step in the 12-Meter class." (It is interesting to note that Ben Lexcen agrees with that assessment, calling *Intrepid* "the biggest step in 12 Meter design.") In designing *Intrepid* for 1967, Olin Stephens turned to the world of offshore-racing yachts for inspiration. He took a long, hard look at the Cal 40, a Bill Lapworth design that in 1964 crashed the racing circuit with extraordinary success. The Cal 40 was distinguished by a *separate* fin keel and spade rudder, the latter hanging well aft. Prior to that, at least since the 1920s, the keel and rudder of a racing yacht had been contiguous. The Cal 40 was comfortable, easy to sail, and easy to control, even downwind where doomsayers expected the separate rudder to cavitate (lose solid contact with the water) and cause the boat to spin out of control. And the Cal 40 was fast—so fast she seemed to have a lien on racing silverware.

A contiguous rudder and keel (such as on all 12 Meters prior to *Intrepid,* and on most offshore yachts) was an arrangement that tended to make both rudder and keel larger than they probably needed to be for directional stability alone. Their excessive area typically made the hull's wetted surface greater than it needed to be. Because there is friction between the hull, its appendages, and the water, designers who shape hulls for racing yachts are intensely concerned about the amount of wetted surface. The more boat in contact with the water, the more friction generated, the more inertia a boat displays, and, of course, the more the speed potential is affected. Excessive wetted surface is particularly a problem in light winds.

Wetted surface, however, is not the only factor that influences a boat's performance. By juggling the 12-Meter equation, a designer can add sail area, which is also a boon to light-air sailing. A third important factor in yacht design is waterline length, as speed is a function of the square root of the length of the waterline: thus, the longer, the better. And, finally, there is displacement, which can be thought of as the weight of the boat. Obviously, the lighter, the better. If a designer could maximize sail area and waterline length and minimize wetted surface and displacement, the yacht would likely be fairly fast. But the rule is not that generous. The 12-Meter rule both giveth and taketh away, which to the designer of America's Cup machines means a complex of tough choices.

On *Intrepid,* Stephens separated the keel and rudder, following the Cal 40, decreased their size and realized a wetted-surface saving of about 40 square feet over previous 12 Meters.

In the design process of *Intrepid,* Stephens also considered decreasing the depth of the keel to save further on wetted surface. He worried, however, about a corresponding increase in leeway—the undesirable sideward slip of a hull with the wind. It is when sailing upwind that leeway is most apparent and least acceptable. And it is upwind sailing that is most important to an America's Cup yacht, as more than half the 24.3-mile course is into the wind. Before building *Intrepid,* Stephens tank-tested the model with the short keel as well as six other models with different configurations. As he suspected, the model with the shorter keel showed a marked increase in leeway.

The test tank shows a yacht's upwind characteristics in a measurement called "velocity made good" (VMG). Except for a disturbing VMG,

Stephens liked what he saw in this short-keeled model, and he looked for ways to increase her VMG without significantly increasing wetted surface. He found, once again, that the answer to this design conundrum lay in the offshore-racing world.

There, a few yachts had been using a second rudder on the trailing edge of the keel to minimize leeway with some success. Called a "trim tab," the second rudder worked something like an elevator in the tail section of an airplane. When sailing upwind, the trim tab was set a few degrees off center, which in essence deflected the yacht to weather. Drag was increased somewhat by having a rudder set this way, but evidence suggested that it was not enough to offset the benefits. With *Intrepid,* Stephens proved the concept correct. Today all 12 Meters show trim tabs; in fact, *France 3* in 1980, designed by Johan Valentijn (who incidentally studied under Olin Stephens, and who drew *Liberty* for Dennis Conner in 1983) had two trim tabs for a time until the difficulty of controlling them canceled the experiment.

Stephens also looked long and hard at quarter waves when designing *Intrepid.* As a hull moves through the water this is what occurs: At the bow, the water is parted neatly as if by a knife. As the hull thickens, the water pushes against the sides with more force. Where the hull narrows again, there is a sudden decrease in pressure. Here the water separates from the hull and the quarter wave forms, and tends to be sucked along by the yacht. The bigger the quarter wave, the slower the yacht.

By experimenting in the tank, Olin Stephens discovered that by keeping the afterbody full underwater (i.e., with a slower curve aft) the quarter wave could be brought aft and its size diminished. This, he felt, would likely contribute to boat speed. In *Intrepid,* he kept the hull full with an underwater appendage called a "kicker." As the tank had predicted, *Intrepid*'s quarter wave under actual sailing conditions was farther aft and smaller than such waves generated by more typical Twelves. And, as was proved on the race course, *Intrepid* virtually flew.

There were other great 12 Meters designed by Sparkman & Stephens after 1967, such as *Courageous,* which defended in '74, '77, and almost again in '83. And, of course, *Freedom,* which defended in 1980 in the capable hands of Dennis Conner. But, that said, these latter boats were more evolutionary than revolutionary, and it was thought that 12-Meter design had reached the point of diminishing returns.

In his 70th year, Olin Stephens went into semiretirement, passing his mantle to Bill Langan, a young and talented Webb Institute graduate, who reminds one of the young Olin Stephens. Stephens was around for the big projects, such as the 12-Meter designs, but left the day-to-day running of the firm to Langan and to his brother, the indefatigable Rod Stephens, a man who, though in his seventies, still runs up 12 flights of stairs each morning to stay in shape for snow skiing.

Everyone thought that Sparkman & Stephens would design Dennis Conner's newest 12 Meter for the 1983 America's Cup. After all, the firm's *Freedom* had been brilliant. *Freedom* won 32 of 35 trial races and beat Alan Bond's *Australia I* by a score of 4–1. However, after the Florida ocean-racing season of 1981, which Dennis Conner won on a boat called *Williwaw* (until her rating certificate was revoked due to irregularities, which was declared no reflection on Conner), Conner told S&S's head designer, Bill Langan, that in addition to S&S a second designer would be working with the *Freedom* syndicate. The competition, Langan was told, was former Dutch citizen and now naturalized American Johan Valentijn, who studied for years under Olin Stephens at S&S. After leaving S&S, Valentijn worked with Ben Lexcen on the design of *Australia I* for '77 and designed the innovative *France 3* for Baron Marcel Bich for 1980.

For the 1983 America's Cup, Conner ordered two new 12 Meters, one from Valentijn and one from the designers at S&S. His design parameters were simple: the new boat had to be faster than *Freedom*. For S&S, the design competition was complicated a bit by the fact that Valentijn, whose innovative practice is more that of a one-man band, would also wear the hat of "project manager."

To the question was Conner happy with S&S's participation in 1980? Langan said, "No. I think what was very difficult for Dennis to realize is that I have to run a business. [Some 25 people work at Sparkman & Stephens: about 12 in the design office and a similar number in the brokerage side of the business.] He expected a two-year commitment from me, which, basically, I couldn't give him. I've got other things I'm trying to accomplish. What Dennis likes is a group of guys to hang around him and give him their time. And the guys who don't do that, he tries to push aside. In some ways, I can understand and agree with that, but in other ways, it is awfully hard for a company like this to give him all the support he needs." The competition between designers in the same syndicate—though seemingly a first—didn't particularly trouble S&S, at least in the beginning. Said Bill Langan, a fair-haired and quietly articulate man, "We had no real qualms about it, although in retrospect it was probably a bad situation to get into because of what happened later. At that point we felt that we would be fairly treated. You go in and you design a boat and you compete. Whether you compete against a guy in the same camp or another on the race course doesn't really make much difference."

Conner already had a good boat in *Freedom*, which was designed by S&S, and which everyone considered to be the state-of-the-art 12 Meter, so the Madison Avenue design firm decided to go fairly far afield. The result was *Spirit of America*. "*Spirit* was an attempt to do a boat with a lot of stability," says Langan. The stability was induced primarily through the use of a fatter keel. "We got so much stability," he adds, "that the rigging began to stretch."

Valentijn responded with *Magic,* a similarly unconventional boat, but representing goals other than those of *Spirit*. According to Valentijn, "I was trying to create the first light-displacement 12 Meter, about 45- or 46,000 pounds." To build a lightweight boat, he traded waterline length (*Magic* was 44 feet on the water—the minimum length under the America's Cup Deed of Gift, though interestingly enough not under the 12-Meter rule), and he also traded off ballast—the only place you take weight out of these boats. "I took a couple of thousand pounds displacement penalty," said Valentijn. Asked the boat's weakness, Valentijn said simply, "She wasn't fast enough to win." He continued, "Downwind, she was fast; upwind, except in very light air, she was slow. When the breeze came in, you'd get 17 or 18 knots across the deck—the boat wouldn't stand upright."

As a result of competition between the two boats, *Magic* was consigned to anchor the Newport America's Cup Exposition Center (where, for a couple of dollars, you can have your picture taken behind one of her wheels), and the better *Spirit* took a cross-country truck ride to San Diego to meet *Freedom* for a winter of racing. The new boat was good downwind, but less so in the all-important other direction.

Dennis Conner was not pleased with *Spirit*. Remembers Langan, "There was a pretty good disagreement at this point. I think Dennis said to himself, 'Screw it. I am going to design the boats from here on out.' He never actually stated this, but that is in essence what happened."

Conner, believes Langan, decided that, since stability didn't pay off in *Spirit,* then added stability wasn't a desirable objective. "Well, we disagreed with that," says Langan. "We said, 'We should try to get about the same stability as *Freedom* has, and then take the advantage of downwind speed on top of that.' So, in the midst of debating this, we learned there was to be a third boat." The newest boat was to be an evolution or refinement of S&S's *Freedom*.

In the summer of 1982, there was a meeting in Newport to discuss the new project. At the meeting were Conner; Fritz Jewett, the lumber baron and longtime backer of 12-Meter efforts; Ed du Moulin, syndicate manager; Halsey Herreshoff, navigator for Conner and grandson of the legendary designer Nathanael Herreshoff; Olin Stephens, the dean of yacht design; and his successor, Bill Langan. At the meeting S&S learned the disquieting news that Valentijn was to be the designer of the third 12-Meter, despite the fact that it would be a development of their *Freedom*.

"We made the argument," says Langan, "that since the boat was going to be a development of *Freedom*—which it was going to be—we should be designing it. After all, we had all the lines, all the information on the boat. It took six hours to work out a compromise." The compromise was that the new boat should be a collaboration between Valentijn and Sparkman & Stephens, which in some ways was reminiscent of Olin Stephens' collaboration with Starling Burgess in 1937. Langan was uncomfortable with the meeting and the result. He remembers taking Olin Stephens into the hall for a private consultation. "I said, 'Olin, I'm new to this. You've been doing this for a long time. I don't mind getting kicked around a little bit, but you're 76 years old. This is likely to be one of the last boats you're ever going to be involved with. I don't want to put you in a compromising situation.' He said, 'No, I really think we should do this boat.' "

One proviso in the compromise was that the designers pool information. In the dusty files of S&S's Madison Avenue offices is a treasure trove of 12-Meter lines, beginning with *Vim*, designed by S&S in 1939 for Mike Vanderbilt, and evolving to *Freedom* and *Spirit*, designed for Dennis Conner. There is also the rich data of decades of tank testing, which the firm pioneered in its application for yachts. Valentijn and Herreshoff came to the offices of S&S to avail themselves of this information over a period of two days. Says Langan, "Johan requested from us the lines of *Spirit*, *Freedom*, *Enterprise*, and *Courageous*. We couldn't really object. In the spirit of collaboration, we had to do it. So I said—although in truth I didn't really want to see his lines—I might as well ask for the lines of *France 3*, *Australia I*, and *Magic*. Big deal! We do our lines in very great detail. They are about six and a half feet long, and they're very carefully done. We got the lines back from Johan, and they were very small-scale. Very little detail. He does a lot of his work on the loft floor, which is fine . . . So reasonably you could say we exchanged information. We also exchanged rating certificates, displacement numbers, and prismatics. Basically, everything we have learned about 12 Meters over five decades was given to him and we got very little back."

While working with Valentijn on the design of the new boat, Langan was also required to redesign *Spirit*, which had to be redrawn and relofted in a terribly compressed three weeks. "I sort of backed off on what we'd agreed to do on *Spirit*," says Langan. "I wanted to get a little more displacement and a little more ballast in there. So, essentially, I had to do the modifications for *Spirit* on the loft floor at Newport Offshore, because of the constraints of time. At one point Johan, as project manager, came up to the loft floor and said, 'What you are drawing is not what we asked for.' I responded that we had the final say . . . That turned into a big mess. I just remember at that point being so tired. I was flying back and forth to Newport at that point three times a week in order to loft the boat and supervise it. Things happened so fast; it got out of control, what with all the people involved—all these people trying to come up with two boats that were sufficiently compromised enough that everyone could feel happy. It was a pretty nasty situation.

"So we finished the stuff on *Spirit*—made her lighter, the way Dennis wanted. We got her out of the loft floor on time, or maybe it was two days late . . . We finished our work on the new lines. It was Labor Day. We'd worked overtime on everything. Basically the office stopped for these two 12-Meter projects. Then I got a call from Fritz [Jewett] saying, 'Thank you very much, we appreciate all the effort you've put in; but we've decided not to build your design, and we're proceeding with the design of Johan.' "

The response in the office, says Langan, was one of "stunned silence." As he recalls it, "I've never seen Olin so mad—the entire time I've known him, I don't think I've seen him mad more than a couple of times. I think Rod has only seen him mad about four times in his whole life. Olin was so angry that someone could do this. I mean, I was more upset for Olin than I was for me. That someone could do that to Olin Stephens, after all the years he has put into the sport. Everyone was acting in good faith, and Olin had gone a long way to make the compromise work, and then they essentially kicked him in the teeth . . ."

The *Freedom* syndicate had an agreement of exclusivity with S&S; that is, that the firm not be allowed to design any new 12-Meters for other syndicates. "So at that point we asked if we could be released from our agreement of exclusivity. We just knew that, more than anything else, Dennis feared us doing another boat. And we asked to be released from that because of the way they'd handled the thing. As gentlemen, we said that they should release us from the agreement. Basically, they said no," comments Langan. "At this point we were advised by our lawyers that we should stop this thing at all costs. We also considered going to the America's Cup Committee and saying, 'This isn't cricket; this is not the way the game should be played. It is supposed to be a sport . . .' "

Continues Langan, "I felt so bad last fall that I strongly considered quitting. If these are the lengths you have to go to win, who needs it? You can argue whether we did a good job for the *Freedom* syndicate or not; but we tried our hardest. Olin Stephens certainly has a good track record—the company has a good track record—so we can't be that far off. But this is crazy. Why were we beating our brains out to satisfy the ego of this one guy [Conner] on debatable speed differences? Dennis is good. That's the one thing you can't argue about; but I don't think you have to attain greatness the way he goes about it. I sure hope he's an oddity, not the rule, because I'd like to stay in this business.''

So Johan Valentijn went on to design *Liberty* for Dennis Conner. Valentijn is very much his own man, and the boat seemed not at all influenced by the brief cross-pollination between designers. Sparkman & Stephens, at the same time, put their heart and soul into a redesign of the veteran *Courageous*. (Their agreement of exclusivity with the *Freedom* syndicate did not deny them the right to work on existing Twelves of their design.) Both boats were good 12 Meters—refinements on the theme first written by Sparkman & Stephens. But on the other side of the world, something very different in yacht design was being created. It was a boat with wings, and it flew.

"If the closely guarded peculiar keel design of Australia II *is allowed to remain in competition, or is allowed to continue to be rated without penalty, the yacht will likely win the foreign trials and will likely win the America's Cup in September."*

—HALSEY HERRESHOFF,
YACHT DESIGNER AND *LIBERTY'S* NAVIGATOR

CHAPTER 7
Keelgate

From the dock at Newport Offshore, it was possible to see eight 12 Meters this summer: *Freedom, Liberty, Courageous, Defender, France 3, Azzurra, Challenge 12,* and *Australia II.* You could see only the topsides of *Australia II,* however, due to her now famous "modesty skirt." Save for the last two, designed by Ben Lexcen, the Twelves were similar in appearance, shaped in the tradition of *Intrepid-Courageous-Freedom,* the Sparkman & Stephens lineage. The similarity of these yachts was not surprising, since for the past 10 years we were told—and told others—that 12-Meter design had reached the point of diminishing returns; each generation of boats represented—it was hoped—only minor refinements on a basic theme perfected by S&S.

The 12-Meter design world was also fairly inbred. Johan Valentijn, the designer of *Liberty* and *France 3,* and Ben Lexcen's collaborator on *Australia I,* learned his trade at Sparkman & Stephens, as did Dave Pedrick, the designer of *Defender* and *Clipper.* And if the Italians didn't have an S&S graduate (although for a while they tried to hire the firm's Mario Tarabocchia, who has worked as a draftsman at S&S for 25 years and in that time drew the lines for *Constellation, Intrepid, Valiant, Courageous, Enterprise,* and *Freedom*), they did have as a trial horse the S&S-designed *Enterprise,* built for Lowell North in 1977. It is fair to say that the brilliant *Azzurra,* designed by Andrea Valicelli, was an S&S-style boat.

At the end of the dock, however, something very different was seen: *Challenge 12* and *Australia II,* both Ben Lexcen designs—similar in hull shapes, masts, and sailplans, one with the magic keel and one without— and both either very right or very wrong. Here there was no allegiance paid to *Intrepid/Courageous/Freedom*. The one with the magic keel, *Australia II*, turned out to be very right indeed, as the world now knows. She was the most forward step in the 12-Meter class, and perhaps in modern racing-yacht design.

It was *Australia II*'s winged keel that caught the world's attention this summer. Its reasons for being were twofold, explained Alan Bond. "We looked at where we got beat last time, and it was at the starting line. So the theme of the new keel isn't breakaway speed, although we seem to have that; it's maneuverability." The other part, said Bond, quite candidly, was a "psych." He continued with obvious pleasure, "We've kept the keel shrouded because we think Dennis Conner is susceptible to psyching. He looked like he fell apart in 1980, when we beat him in that one race, so a little mystery wasn't going to do us any harm."

A "little mystery" indeed. The phantom keel, more than anything else, dominated the America's Cup summer of 1983. At times it seemed that the racing was but a footnote to the shoot-out that surrounded the keel.

News and views of the keel had been circulating through the small world of yachting for nearly a year. Several designers, in fact, claimed to have drawings or even photographs of it. If one wasn't privy to this select information, *Sail* magazine published in late June of 1983 a rough drawing of the hull and keel. Its concept was provided by the magazine's well-connected correspondent Jay Broze. In July it was thought that the keel had a bulbous bow, two trim tabs, and two downward-sloping, delta-shaped wings. (When all was revealed after the Australians won the Cup, the keel showed neither a bulbous bow nor the two trim tabs; it had a more conventional single tab.)

Lexcen would finally describe the keel this way on the night it was revealed to the world and on the night the America's Cup belonged to his homeland. "The keel?" said Lexcen. "Well, there are about 500 Americans hanging on it at the moment. When we lifted the boat out tonight there were just heaps of them hanging on, like leeches when you walk out of a swamp. But I'll try to describe the keel. The keel is somewhat shorter than a regular keel; it's what you could call upside down. It's narrower where it leaves the hull, and long at the bottom. So if you had a regular keel on an ordinary yacht and sawed it off and put it back on upside down, that's something similar to our keel. It doesn't have a bulb like everyone thinks; it just gets a little thicker at the bottom in accordance with its chord. For about half of its length on the bottom it has protrusions [wings] that stick out on each side; they poke down at about 20 degrees, and they are about a meter wide and about two or three meters long. They are made of lead and are very thick and heavy. On the back of the very sloping trailing edge is a somewhat narrow trim tab that is faired in with a plastic flexible membrane, which gives the lie to it having a double trim tab. It only has a single trim tab, but this plastic fairing bends and fairs the trim tab into a nice, smooth curve.''

That is what the keel looked like. Bruce Kirby, the designer of the estimable Laser and the 12-Meter *Canada 1,* tells us what it does. ''When a designer looks at the 12-Meter rule, he thinks these boats are awfully heavy; in fact, they're lead mines. They have a displacement-length ratio of something like 263. So typically a designer investigates making the boat lighter. The rules are pretty tough on that. If you take the lead ballast out of these 12-Meter hulls, you find the hulls all weigh the same; they are built to Lloyd's specification and thus weigh 8,500 pounds. The rest of the weight is all lead ballast; in a 55,000-pound boat you've got 46,500 pounds of lead.

''The only way you can reduce the weight of a 12-Meter is to shorten the waterline length, which permits you to reduce weight; but the only place from which you can take the weight—since you have the Lloyd's hull requirements—is out of the keel. That means you are throwing away stability; you've got to be careful about that. That is why these boats rarely get below 45 feet on the waterline. What Ben [Lexcen] did—and this is just speculation—is to go down to a 44-foot waterline, which meant, I suspect, that he could reduce the displacement to 52,000—a saving of about 3,000 or even 4,000 pounds over a typical 12-Meter. But instead of just throwing it away, he came up with a keel that allowed him to pack a lot of weight at the bottom—the best place. The wings supposedly weigh 1,000 pounds apiece . . . You then have 2,000 pounds at the bottom of the keel—8½ feet below the water—and as the center of gravity on a 12-Meter is very close to the waterline you can multiply those 2,000 pounds by eight. That means you have 16,000 pounds of righting moment that wouldn't ordinarily be there.

''I don't know if Ben had an idea for the keel and made it work, and then said, 'I can make the boat lighter,' or whether he thought, I've got to make the boat lighter, and set out to design a keel to help him do that; but he must have done one or the other.''

In July, however, when all of this was presumably very much a secret, Johan Valentijn, designer of *Liberty* and the stillborn *Magic,* explained the keel's advantages to supplement a weighty letter of protest sent by the NYYC to George Andreadis, chairman of the Keel Boat Technical Committee of the International Yacht Racing Union (IYRU). Valentijn's arguments, although some of them—such as the bulbous-bow discussion—are incorrect, provide additional insight into the Lexcen keel. His arguments can be summarized in four points: (1) The wings are endplates as used in aerodynamics; properly designed endplates for the right conditions can increase the lift coefficient, and thus lift, by as much as 50%. (2) With the increase in lift, the keel can be smaller, and thus present less wetted surface; the end result could be a keel that has 33% less lateral area; to be specific, the keel on *Australia II* has an average chord length of 10 feet versus 14 feet for a standard Twelve, and this results in 20% less lateral area. (3) Turning and maneuverability are controlled by lateral surface; a short-keeled boat can turn more easily than a boat with a longer keel; the disadvantage of a normal short-keeled boat is that it lacks stability, and *Australia II* solved this with her bulb on the keel bottom.* (4) Added draft was obtained by situating the wings in such a downward manner that, when heeling, the wings extend beyond the normal draft.

The subject of all this technical analysis was a yacht that sailed circles around her foreign sisters, winning 48 races and losing only six all summer before being named the foreign challenger. Along the way, more than a few people had something to say about the winged wonder.

The questions about *Australia II* revolved around three points: Were the wings legal? If they were legal, was the yacht rated fairly with the wings? And did Ben Lexcen actually design the keel and hull, or were they a product of the Netherlands Aerospace Laboratory and the Netherlands Ship Model Basin, where Lexcen worked on the keel for four months?

Perhaps the best way to sort out "Keelgate" is to provide a chronology of the high and low points; of the latter there were more than a few. The protagonists of Keelgate were the New York Yacht Club, primarily in the towering form of Commodore Robert W. McCullough, also of the America's Cup Committee, versus *Australia II,* primarily in the diminutive but just as combative form of Alan Bond and his right-hand man, Warren Jones. Bond had been in training for this battle for a decade.

Although it seemed that at times the New York Yacht Club wasn't playing fair in this technical controversy, and aspersions were broadly cast that they would do anything to keep the Cup, this simply wasn't the entire story. The Australians gave as good as they got, and were perhaps just as aggressive as the New York Yacht Club. They were just quieter about it and, publicly at least, were responding—defending themselves—rather than taking the offensive. Privately, they apparently did plenty of attacking. Unfortunately, when all was said and done, the New York Yacht Club handled the matter with all the finesse of a sledgehammer. And the sledgehammer was wielded by Bob McCullough.

The recorded facts about the controversial keel date from March 4,

---

Author's note: Actually, she solved this with the weighted wings.

1983, when *Australia II* was first measured in Australia by Ken McAlpine, an IYRU-appointed measurer from Australia. The rating certificate was signed by the Australian Yachting Federation (AYF) as a matter of course. (Later, the NYYC would allege that McAlpine doubted that *Australia II* was a legal 12 Meter and that he asked the AYF to refer it to the IYRU; but this, like many of the NYYC's charges, could never be substantiated.) *Australia II* arrived in Rhode Island in June, late compared to the other foreign yachts. Even while being offloaded from the freighter, she sported her so-called "modesty skirt," a shroud around the keel made of ugly green-and-blue spinnaker cloth. She was measured at Cove Haven Marina in Barrington, Rhode Island, on June 16, by the three men of the measurement committee for the America's Cup competition. On the committee were an Australian, John Savage, an Englishman, Tony Watts, and an American, Mark Vinbury. This usually straightforward procedure was accompanied by typical Bond intrigue.

In a letter of August 1, 1983, Paul Doppke, of Cove Haven, where the measurement took place, described the secrecy surrounding the measurement to Bob McCullough. Doppke wrote, "Please be advised that at the time of the measuring of *Australia II,* I was asked to provide a complete shed with no other boats or work to be done in it for the purpose of complete secrecy.

"After hauling *Australia II,* it was decided that I would be the only person allowed to see the keel since I had to block the hull. They asked me to keep all of my employees out of the shed, and then they supplied two armed guards to make sure that no one would get a look at their keel. The boat was hauled and launched with the shroud in place. When the boat was measured, the shroud was rolled up onto the deck."

A footnote to this summer of secrecy and wild speculation is that, by the rules, the NYYC and in fact any official persons representing the foreign challengers had the right to see the measurement take place, armed guards notwithstanding. All of the secrecy could have been dispensed with in June. On the day the New York Yacht Club capitulated in the matter of the keel, Commodore McCullough said, when asked about this, "As you remember, the boat was late arriving, and she was the last one measured. Frankly, it was a slip-up on our part. We were supposed to have Bill Luders [technical adviser to the America's Cup Committee] there to see it, and we missed the measurement date."

After passing muster in Australia, *Australia II* was again deemed a legal 12 Meter by a unanimous vote of the three-man committee. Mark Vinbury, the American on the measurement committee, was quoted as saying there "was no question that our committee measured *Australia II*'s keel according to the rule." But apparently Vinbury privately wondered whether the keel might be a "peculiarity" of design, as spelled out in 12-Meter Rating Rule 27 or Rating Rule Measurement Instruction 7.

On July 20, after *Australia II* had started her nearly unopposed march through the foreign competition, Ed du Moulin, head of the *Freedom/Liberty* syndicate, sent a telex to the Netherlands Ship Model Basin (NSMB) in Wageningen, Holland, where Ben Lexcen had worked for four months on keel design. It read, "I understand you and your team are responsible for development and design of the special keel for *Australia II*. We are finally convinced of her potential and would therefore like to build same design under one of our boats. We will keep this confidential as not to jeopardize your agreement with Alan Bond. However, due to the complexity of problems, need your maximum input. We can start next week and be ready by August 25."

Du Moulin received this no doubt uncheery response from the NSMB: "We have received your telex addressed to our Dr. van Oossanen and would ask you to note firstly that we were associated with the *Australia II* campaign by way of a tank-testing contract. Their designer Mr. Ben Lexcen resided at Wageningen for four months whilst he completed the design for both *Australia II* and *Challenge 12*.

"As we are contracted to them not to test 12-Meter models for any other 12-Meter syndicate until the completion of the 1983 campaign, we have today advised them [the Australians] of your query and requested their permission to undertake work for you. But unfortunately they have advised us that they are not prepared to allow such dispensation. We thank you for your enquiry and would be only too delighted to discuss work for you related to any campaign in 1986."

When the telex became public in August—released by the Australians when the war of words had escalated—the *Freedom* syndicate announced that it was du Moulin's intention merely to modify *Magic* with wings to provide a suitable trial horse for *Liberty*. "It was never our intention to enter an American boat with a winged keel in competition," says the press release, dated August 14.

In October, in the wake of the New York Yacht Club's loss to the Australians, Fritz Jewett, Dennis Conner's primary backer and a longtime supporter of America's Cup defense efforts, would characterize this stratagem in slightly different terms. He said that the telex was partly an effort "to smoke out" Dr. van Oossanen about who owned the rights to the keel. (It turned out that Ben Lexcen, rather than van Oossanen, was awarded a patent on the idea in the Netherlands in February, 1982.)* Jewett continued, "But it was also an effort to see if we could learn something about what this [keel] would do... because if we were to be selected, it would be worthwhile to have something to practice against."

There was, however, a more serious attempt to enter an American boat with a winged keel, and that boat was none other than *Magic*. In July, Russell Long, the young skipper of *Clipper* in the 1980 America's Cup defense wars, returned from a Boston Red Sox game to find a message from Bob McCullough marked "urgent." Said Long, "When I called McCullough back, he said that the *Freedom* syndicate was willing to provide 'at no cost' the use of *Magic* and a few of her sails to a skipper who would be willing to put wings on the keel. He said that the idea was Dennis Conner's, and that he [Conner] had spoken to McCullough and most of the others on the America's Cup Committee about the plan . . . He said Dennis was concerned about *Australia II* and wanted to see an American syndicate come up with another boat that had wings on the keel. McCullough said that Dennis had personally gone out and timed *Australia II* one day, when he had a lay day. He found that the boat was able to tack on this day in five seconds—much faster than *Liberty* or *Freedom*."

Long called *Magic*'s designer, Johan Valentijn, to discuss the idea. Valentijn felt *Magic* would be perfect for the new-style keel, as the boat was light to begin with (45,000 pounds), and light weight was one secret of *Australia II*'s success. Valentijn said, according to Long, that "there was a very good chance that we could make her a fast boat."

Russell Long also needed crew. The underutilized crew of *Freedom*—*Liberty*'s trial horse—seemed perfect. Long decided that, since it was McCullough's idea, the commodore should work out the details. At that point Fritz Jewett, who didn't seem to be aware of Dennis's original offer, wouldn't agree to the conditions. McCullough explained to Long that Jewett was concerned about Valentijn having to divide his time between the two boats. He also felt that they couldn't do without the *Freedom* crew. "Dennis and I talked at length about it," said Long. "I said, 'Okay, I can put a crew together and I can work out arrangements where Johan would only work with us for an hour or an hour and a half each day. We agreed that Jerry Milgram [professor of ocean engineering at M.I.T.] would be a good person to help out, and Milgram was in favor of the idea."

Long again called Jewett, who acted surprised that anyone would want to change *Magic*. Jewett claimed to have talked with Valentijn, who told

---

*In the middle of the summer, a gentleman named Riejos Salminen arrived in Newport from the Pacific Northwest to claim that he, in fact, had a patent on the Australian keel. Such occurrences, it should be noted, are not uncommon in the history of patented inventions. Ben Lexcen had this to say about Salminen: "He wasn't a bad guy—just emotional. We said, 'Look, we'll sign an agreement that says straight after the America's Cup we'll have a meeting with you about it, if you'll just leave us alone now.' We were afraid he'd come down with lawyers and force us to lock the boat up. We thought at first he was a New York Yacht Club stooge, but he wasn't. He was for real. If he wants to take us to court, he can; but he'll lose. But I don't think it will go that far. He has a patent on what amounts to an upside-down hydrofoil that just adds displacement to the boat."

him he couldn't make the boat any faster. He also told Long he couldn't give the boat away; it belonged to the Fort Schuyler Foundation, which for tax reasons owned all four of the syndicate's boats. But he said he could sell it for $100,000. Said Long, "I couldn't believe it when I heard that. I went back to McCullough. I'd been busting my chops for three days trying to put this deal together. I got the backers I needed . . . I told McCullough, 'I'm out! If you want me to continue, the NYYC is going to have to buy the boat.' He called back in 24 hours and said the NYYC would buy the boat. He wouldn't say where the money came from, but he said that it was available."

Long recognized that he needed to get a look at the keel of *Australia II* if they were to duplicate it. "We had the idea of taking pictures of *Australia II* from an airplane, when she was under sail." They reasoned that, with a decent breeze, the boat might heel sufficiently to reveal the secrets of the keel. "We knew it might be difficult. The day we decided to charter a plane, the wind died, so that didn't work. The other idea was to put a diver down 10 feet at the leeward mark—to get someone down there with scuba tanks. I thought it was perfectly ethical. The water's free; no one can claim it as their privileged domain. We contacted professional divers about the plan, but they felt it was too risky.

"The [other] plan to take pictures at Newport Offshore while the boat was hoisted probably would have worked. We just had to put a diver in the water, have him swim over to the boat, pop up, take a picture and leave. Unfortunately, I didn't think it was ethical to do that, so we decided against it.

"As a result, we couldn't come up with the exact design of the keel. I sat down with Johan and Jerry, but suddenly Johan had changed his tune, too. He said that he felt the chances of designing a keel faster than *Australia II* were slim." There and then the project died, and *Magic* remained at the Newport America's Cup Exposition Center.

If Long had qualms about diving under *Australia II* at Newport Offshore, a Canadian didn't. On July 23, Jim Johnston, a boat driver for the Canadian challenge, was apprehended at 5:45 A.M. by security guards for swimming under the shrouded keel of *Australia II* with an underwater camera. The guards, who leaped into the murky morning water, believed that Johnston was accompanied by another scuba diver, but were unable to catch his accomplice. Johnston, still in his wetsuit, was turned over to the Newport police. He was arrested, and the camera and film were held for evidence. When he appeared that afternoon before Justice of the Peace Charles Levesque, he was still wearing his wetsuit, was barefoot, and sported an Atlanta Braves baseball cap. The Australians dropped the case when they were given the film and assurances that there had been only one diver. Shortly after this bizarre incident, rather crude drawings of the Australian keel began to be offered for sale in Newport shops. They were signed by "Frogman II." (This matter seemed trifling until the morning of the seventh America's Cup race, September 26, when the Toronto *Globe & Mail,* and then newspapers around the world, published photos of the keel, obviously taken by that unapprehended multimedia artist "Frogman II.") The Australians informed the world that they were strengthening their security net with the addition of a 12-volt electric screen in the water around the yacht. Such security, it was said, was costing them $1,000 a week.

On July 24, the day after the diving incident, a letter was sent by Bob McCullough to Mark Vinbury, the American on the international measurement committee, questioning the rating of *Australia II.* Eventually the other foreign syndicates were given copies of McCullough's letter, presumably in the hope that they would join the battle to outlaw the maverick design. When this letter broke, McCullough was conveniently off on the New York Yacht Club's annual summer cruise, and thus was unavailable for comment. At a meeting of the foreign crews, held on August 1 to discuss the letter, the other challengers offered their support to the Australians. Warren Jones, of *Australia II,* claimed to be "comforted and delighted" by this support, but he doubted that he'd seen the end of such harassment.

On July 25, Mark Vinbury acted on his private doubts and sent a letter to Tony Watts in England. Watts was the IYRU measurer who, like Vinbury, was involved in the June measurement of the troubling Australian Twelve. Wrote Vinbury, "I have no question that our committee measured *Australia II*'s keel according to the rule. I am concerned, however, that the rule as it is currently written is not able to assess the unusual shape of this keel and thereby fairly rate the yacht." He asked that the Keel Boat Technical Committee of the IYRU rule on this matter.

On August 3, war was openly declared by the New York Yacht Club. In its heaviest missive of the summer, the yacht club posted 34 pages to George Andreadis, chairman of the KBTC. It described the winged appendages on *Australia II* as "a peculiarity," and asked for redress under Rule 27 and Instruction 7, which deal with such matters. Naval architects such as Bill Luders, Johan Valentijn, and Halsey Herreshoff described the Australian boat as a 12.45-Meter yacht at 20 degrees of heel, charging that the downward-sloping wings gave the yacht added—but unrated—draft. (Extra draft makes a yacht faster upwind.) One of many fascinating things about this document is the precision of the numbers used to support this charge; one had to wonder, as the Australians shortly would, whence they came. The NYYC asked for an immediate ruling about the keel, despite the fact that the KBTC was not scheduled to meet until the following November.

In the yacht club's 34 pages was a statement of Herreshoff's that put forth what had never been stated before: "If the closely guarded peculiar keel design of *Australia II* is allowed to remain in competition, or is allowed to continue to be rated without penalty, the yacht will likely win the foreign trials and will likely win the America's Cup in September."

Win the America's Cup in September! No foreign yacht had ever won the America's Cup; no foreign yacht had ever even come close in 132 years.

After the New York Yacht Club delivered its declaration of war, which must have taken weeks of work to assemble, it was pointed out that the club, no matter how far-ranging its power, was not an entity recognized by the IYRU. Thus noted, the United States Yacht Racing Union (USYRU) entered the matter through the offices of Thomas F. Ehman, Jr., its executive director, who happens to be a member of the New York Yacht Club. It was the USYRU's turn to call for an immediate ruling by the KBTC.

The New York Yacht Club made an attempt at rapprochement on August 7. Commodores McCullough, Stone, and Emil "Bus" Mosbacher, a defending America's Cup skipper himself, went to Alan Bond's mansion, Midcliffe. They met with Bond and Warren Jones. The meeting disintegrated rapidly. It was reported, and has been confirmed by two reliable sources, that Bond threatened that the NYYC could expect big trouble over this matter if it continued on this course, and that he intended to smear the club, to drag it through the gutter, and to embarrass the club in every way he could. Bob McCullough, it was said, left the meeting quite shaken.

Within a week, Warren Jones, executive director of the *Australia II* syndicate, issued a manifesto. Jones, no stranger to bluster either, argued that "no entity, and certainly not the NYYC or the USYRU, has any right to request that the IYRU re-rate or comment on the rating of our boat." Next Jones invoked the good name of Olin Stephens, that institution of naval architecture, who knew a thing or two about designing world- and rule-beating 12-Meters. Jones said that Olin Stephens had recently indicated to the International 12-Meter Association that, "in his opinion, *Australia II* was correctly rated and that her designer, Ben Lexcen, should be congratulated for the innovative concept he has employed."

Jones's charge that neither the NYYC nor the national authority "has any right to request that the IYRU re-rate or comment on the rating" bears explanation. There were two agreements governing the running of the 1983 America's Cup competition. The first, dealing with the organization of the actual America's Cup races in September, was signed by the New York Yacht Club and the Royal Sydney Yacht Squadron, which was the challenger of record. The second agreement was signed by the seven foreign challengers to govern the running of their matches: in June, July, August, and September, if necessary. Signing the second agreement were the Royal Sydney Yacht Squadron, which entered *Advance,* the Royal Perth Yacht Club *(Australia II),* the Royal Yacht Club of Victoria *(Challenge 12),* the Yacht Club Costa Smeralda *(Azzurra),* the Yacht Club de France *(France 3),* the Secret Cove Yacht Club *(Canada 1),* and the Royal Burnham Yacht Club *(Victory 83).* Rather conspicuous by its absence in that second agreement is the New York Yacht Club. Thus, in truth, they had no standing in this matter at this point, and they wouldn't have any standing until the remeasurement of *Australia II*—if she was named the challenger—just before the first race of the America's Cup, when the other agreement took effect. Thus all of the NYYC's sound and fury may have been based on legitimate claims, but was premature at best. At that point, the New York Yacht Club had no credentials.

Jones's second charge, that similarly the USYRU had no right to request that the IYRU investigate or re-rate the boat, is interesting. The USYRU does not have authority over foreign yachts. In the case of Rule 27 and Rating Rule Measurement Instruction 7 ("If from any peculiarity in the build of the yacht or other cause the measurer shall be of the opinion that the rule will not rate the yacht fairly . . . he shall report the circumstances to the National Authority"), the national authority, Jones argued, is the Australian Yachting Federation, not the USYRU. Jones would put it this way: "Even though the USYRU is *a* national authority, they are not *the* national authority to which Measurement Instruction 7 refers in this case." (You may recall that in Australia—or so alleged the NYYC—when Ken McAlpine measured *Australia II* he had grave doubts about it, and asked the AYF to rule on the matter or query the IYRU; but the allegation couldn't be proved.)

Even more intriguing is the fact that the IYRU did not seem to have any authority in this matter, either. Cup Condition 22 and Selection Condition 20 read: "The decision of the Committee on questions of the measurement rule of the International 12 Meter Class shall be final." This committee of Vinbury, Savage, and Watts had unanimously ruled that *Australia* was a legitimate 12 Meter.

Jones scored two other major points. He made public for the first time Ed du Moulin's attempt to secure a similar keel from the Netherlands Ship Model Basin. Charged Jones, "We now feel compelled, however, to make sure that people are aware of the extent to which some Americans have been prepared to go to hold the Cup. We now reveal that only a few weeks ago one of the American syndicates attempted to purchase plans for a keel identical to that of *Australia II,* from the Netherlands Ship Model Basin, which did the tank-testing . . . It appears curious to us that the syndicate backing the leading yacht in the defenders' trials has tried to purchase our keel design while the NYYC and now the USYRU are attempting to have the design re-rated by incurring a penalty.''

Lastly he demanded to know from where the confidential design information, which had fueled these fires for weeks, was coming. ''The NYYC has stated that it had only recently become aware of the details of the *Australia II* keel. We would like to know where these details were obtained, since it is common knowledge that we keep all details of our boat secret, aside from divulging full details in strictest confidence to authorities such as the measurement committee, whom we trust implicitly. If the NYYC is in receipt of specific information, it can only be through improper means, and we have a right to know who passed it to them and under what conditions.''

Not surprisingly, the IYRU did not embrace this nettlesome matter with open arms. Nigel Hacking, secretary general of the IYRU, wanted to be sure his organization was on firm legal ground. He asked why his organization should look into this matter. He also wanted to ensure that the IYRU ''would not be usurping the functions of the measurement committee.'' Finally, after receiving both sides of the story, the IYRU announced on August 18 that it would meet on August 30 to consider the USYRU's request that *Australia II* be re-rated.

Before things went that far, however, it was revealed on August 22 that *Victory 83,* the British 12 Meter, had been built to allow the addition of objects called ''winglets.'' Not only that, but on July 28, 1982—1982!—a ruling was sought from the Keel Boat Technical Committee of the IYRU on their legality. The committee ruled that ''tip wings are permitted so long as the static draft is not exceeded.'' The KBTC also added that winglets may not be retracted, nor can their angle of incidence be adjusted. This interpretation was given in confidence, and would not ordinarily have been made known to the public until November, 1983, after the IYRU annual meeting in London, when it would have been confirmed.

It was supposed to be a secret, as is allowed by the IYRU, but then something strange happened in a summer characterized by strange events. In a meaningless race at the end of the semifinal series, when both *Australia II* and *Victory 83* had won the right to meet in the finals, *Victory 83* decided to try her wings. Mark Vinbury, the NYYC's official measurer, and the only one of the original triumvirate of measurers still in this country, was called to the British yacht ''to decide whether or not the changes [the addition of wings] would require a remeasurement." Upon inspection, Vinbury, acting alone in the neutral role of "measurer of record," said the winglets were neutrally buoyant and "thus they would not affect the yacht's flotation." With neither the flotation nor the yacht's draft changed, Vinbury agreed that her rating certificate should remain unchanged. He was asked to keep this information confidential. Had he objected to the changes, say the British, they would have removed the wings. There were no objections. Immediately upon leaving the measurement, however, Vinbury wrote a letter to the USYRU stating, " . . . I am of the opinion that these foils constitute a peculiarity in the build of the yacht and believe that the rule will not rate the yacht fairly while they are attached." The British, personified in the cigar-wielding form of Peter de Savary, were furious at this breach of confidence.

Long forgotten was the fate of Bob Blumenstock, back in 1980. That year the British had tried out their new bendy mast—supposedly a light-air breakthrough. The French, apparently receiving encouragement and technical information from the New York Yacht Club, protested the British mast, but the international jury determined that it was legal.

Immediately the Australians, under Alan Bond, began building a bendy mast of their own in a warehouse behind the S.S. Newport Restaurant. With the completion of the mast, the Australians called Bob Blumenstock, then the New York Yacht Club's measurer—an officer of the club and the sole member of the three-man measurement committee still in this country—and asked him to measure their new mast. Blumenstock saw his role as that of an "impartial measurer"—despite his NYYC affiliation—and in fact he had assurances from both Bob McCullough and Bruno Bich, representing the challenger of record, that this was to be the case. Remembering that 1980 phone call from the Australians, Blumenstock, a man who has been measuring 12 Meters since 1958, commented that the Australians said, " 'We've got something to show you. We want you to measure it. We want you to keep it quiet because it's rather secret.' I said, 'Okay,' and went over to measure it, to weigh it, and I took sections of it. This was the bendy mast. I didn't say anything; I didn't think it was my place to do that. I was an impartial measurer, which McCullough and Bruno [Bich] said they wanted me to be. So I kept it under my hat.

"Suddenly, about two weeks later, I got a frantic call from Bob McCullough saying that the Australians had a new mast, and they wanted to be present when it was measured. I told him that I'd measured it two or three weeks before that. He was furious. That was my demise [as the NYYC measurer] right there." Blumenstock continued, "I was not about to tell the New York Yacht Club about *Australia*'s mast, just as I wouldn't tell the Australians what the Americans were doing."

Blumenstock is no longer measuring yachts, neither as the New York Yacht Club's official measurer, nor as a USYRU measurer, which he had been since its inception. In fact, Blumenstock, who had been measuring boats since 1948 under the old CCA Rule, trained this country's measurers in the International Offshore Rule (IOR) in the 1970s. Now, at age 62, he is working hard to reestablish his once flourishing surveying business, which he gave up when he became a full-time measurer for both the NYYC and the sport's national authorities, the USYRU and its predecessor, the North American Yacht Racing Union (NAYRU). Asked if he would do things differently today, Blumenstock said with some sadness, "I couldn't do anything differently and live with myself. I tried to do something right, but I got a boot for it."

Blumenstock was asked whether, from what he had seen of the keel on *Australia II,* he would rule the boat a legal 12 Meter. He answered, "I think so. Certainly the way the rule is written she is. You can do anything you want underwater as long as you don't exceed the draft limits or displacement."

(It is interesting to note that the 12-Meter rule doesn't even mention the word "keel." Rating Rule 6 reads, "Draught is the vertical distance below the LWL plane to the lowest point of the hull or moveable appendages in any position." And an IYRU interpretation to the rule, issued in 1972, makes this interesting statement: "The hull may be of *any shape* [authors' italics] 150mm below the LWL. . . . ")

The British on *Victory 83* would remove their wings after one race, claiming to be unable to notice any difference in the speed of the yacht. This failed experiment, however, didn't stop the Americans from trying to bring wings to the conventional keels of *Freedom* and then *Defender* at the end of August. Above *Defender*'s rather crude-looking wings were the neatly taped letters *T.W.A.,* which Chuck Kirsch, the *Defender/ Courageous* syndicate head, would explain as "twin-winged appendages."

Yacht designer Bruce Kirby was skeptical of these attempts at turning two conventional 12 Meters into *Australia II.* As he said, "There is a difference in sticking wings on an ordinary keel and putting them on a special keel, as the Australians did. Ben [Lexcen] made a keel that was much smaller, then put pretty big wings on it, and the total amount of wetted surface probably came out to be the same as a normal 12 Meter. But if you simply take a normal 12 Meter, which already has a lot of wetted surface, and stick wings on it, it's only going to add to the wetted surface. So at best you end up with a boat that is a little bit better in a very narrow range of conditions, but you kill yourself in other conditions."

Three acts remained to be played in the continuing drama of Keelgate. The first occurred when the Australians announced with burning indignation—a pose they had perfected by the end of the summer—that representatives of the NYYC had traveled to the Netherlands to induce officials of the Netherlands Ship Model Basin to sign an affidavit that they, rather than Ben Lexcen, had designed the keel and hull of *Australia II*. (See Chapter 9: "Point/Counterpoint.") The trip was made by Wil Valentijn, the uncle of *Liberty* designer Johan Valentijn, and Tony van Rijn, a boyhood friend of Johan's.

The second involved an odd encounter between *Liberty*'s designer and Alan Bond. Johan Valentijn and Bond had been good friends, dating back to the time when Valentijn collaborated with Ben Lexcen on the design of *Australia I*. Valentijn was putting wings on *Freedom* when Bond drove up on his Moped. Valentijn described in his accented English this strange meeting on the docks: "[Bond] came by and was looking very, very serious. I tried to be jovial. I said, 'Alan, how are you?' We chatted for a minute, and then he took me aside and said, 'I hope you know that the wings are copyrighted [patented]. We can sue you for that.' He also said, 'If you don't stop defaming Ben Lexcen, we will sue you for defamation of character.' I said, 'The wings are patented in Holland, not in the United States. This is a free country, so we can do whatever we like.' I also said that, about Ben Lexcen, I had simply stated the facts, and whatever the America's Cup people ask me, I'll answer.

"Bond was dead serious about this. I never talked to him again," said Valentijn.

Finally, on August 26, 1983, Keelgate ended with a whimper. The NYYC told the world, with great cordiality, that it was "pleased to announce that the question relating to the keels of *Australia II* and *Victory 83* and the design thereof have been resolved.

"We have now received verification from the International Yacht Racing Union that an interpretative ruling respecting the design of the British keel was issued in August of 1982. That ruling under the IYRU regulations is controlling for the 1983 match, and the New York Yacht Club accepts it as such.

"For reasons unknown to us neither the British challengers nor the International Yacht Racing Union saw fit to advise the USYRU or us of this fact and regrettably this omission has resulted in unnecessary controversy." The press release ended on an upbeat note: "With these matters resolved, we now can all focus on the match itself to be settled on the water and may the better yacht win."

Then, in the most fascinating press conference of the summer, Commodores Robert G. Stone, Jr., and Robert W. McCullough faced the world. Asked to characterize their club's conduct, McCullough answered, "I think that our conduct has been absolutely straightforward. We tried not to push our weight around in any way or make a lot of public statements. We tried to keep to the facts. The facts were that we didn't know about *Australia II*'s keel or the ruling on it. Had we known, this whole controversy could have been over before it began. And I think, as far as who designed the boat and so forth—I think unfortunately a lot of rumors get going . . . Maybe it's a lot of fun for some people. It isn't particularly fun for us."

Commodore Stone added: "I think you should realize that this Cup comes under a Deed of Gift. There are conditions for the Cup races that you know. And we feel an obligation to—not only to our own defending syndicates but to other challenging syndicates—when there are some reports that possibly contravene the Deed of Gift, we feel an obligation to check into it. That's all we were trying to do, in a very logical and fair way."

An Australian reporter asked about the New York Yacht Club's specific knowledge of the secret Australian keel. "Would it mean," he inquired, "that the information you have was illegally obtained?" McCullough answered, "I don't think that is true at all. If someone who knows the details of the boat, who is on that boat, or who was at a measurement or whatever tells us of it, I don't think it's illegally obtained. I can assure you that we didn't go after it; it was given to us."

After the press conference, this reporter asked McCullough whether the timing of the yacht club in this matter wasn't unfortunate. "Why did you wait until the Australian boat started winning big?" McCullough said, "I think it was unfortunate, but I think we were forced into it by the secrecy of the Australians. If the Australians had been out front to begin with, and if we hadn't missed the initial measurement, I think the whole thing would have come right to the fore at that time. I've always felt that if the Australians had nothing to hide, why didn't they go to the Keel Boat Technical Committee and get a ruling, just as the Brits did?"

Throughout Keelgate stalked the strong personality of Bob McCullough. Credit must go to McCullough for heavy-handedness and, more to the point, for displaying a disdain for public relations. The litany of misplayed moves and countermoves is shocking: to wit, the fact that the New York Yacht Club missed the measurement date of *Australia II;* the fact that the committee, presumably, like much of the sailing world, knew all about this keel for more than a year, and if they were worried about it might have taken steps much earlier to catch up; the fact that they didn't attack the Australians until the challenger started to look dangerous to them; the club's unsuccessful attempt to secure information from the Netherlands Ship Model Basin, while at the same time proclaiming to the world that they felt the keel on *Australia II* was illegal or unfairly rated;

the aborted attempt to equip *Magic* with wings and a new keel, and the club's apparent condoning—even abetting—efforts to discover *Australia II*'s secrets by any means; the fact that they wasted time, effort, and money putting wings on traditional-keeled boats such as *Freedom* and *Defender*, when the chances for success were less than encouraging; the fact that they threw their weight around—months too early—when they had absolutely no standing in the matter; the fact that they tried to impeach the first Australian measurer (McAlpine) without sufficient evidence; and, lastly, the fact that they tried to damage the reputation of Ben Lexcen, again without sufficient evidence.

Fritz Jewett, of the *Freedom* syndicate, concluded that the New York Yacht Club's major failing was in the area of public relations. Said Jewett, who still strongly believes that the keel was rated unfairly, and that Lexcen was not its sole designer: "The [America's] Cup Committee was dominated largely by one individual—Bob McCullough. He ran the show, sort of in the Henry Morgan tradition, but with very strong leadership, to the point that he really made most of the decisions. I think that he got in trouble because this turned out not to be an ordinary Cup year. He had no plans for dealing with technical issues, legal issues, or public relations issues. In fact, we urged him to please hire a professional public relations service. We were told that Bill Robinson, the former editor of *Yachting*, was going to take over that function. To my knowledge, Bill Robinson was in Newport one day. He's a writer and a publisher. He's not a PR person. As a result, the NYYC had no professional advice from an experienced public relations firm, and as a result their image is just terrible."

*"I had a nightmare about winning the
America's Cup last night. I dreamed
that we won, and no one told me . . ."*
—BEN LEXCEN, DESIGNER OF *AUSTRALIA II*,
IN THE BEGINNING OF THE SUMMER

CHAPTER 8
The Men from the Land Down Under

It was as though the Australians surprised even themselves. When they were named challengers for the America's Cup, finally winning their last trial race of the summer against *Victory 83*, the crew erupted with joy. One would have thought they'd won the America's Cup itself. When they finally won the first race against *Liberty*, they were still expressing their delight. Newporters feared the worst: "If they're like this now, what will it be like if they win the America's Cup?" they asked. Shortly, they'd find out. The second time *Australia II* beat *Liberty* the mood changed. It was more subdued, and one had the impression that the Australians were asking themselves, perhaps for the first time, "By God, is it possible we could win this thing?" By the time they won their third race, evening the score at three, the mood at the *Australia II* dock was one of forced joviality. They were truly coming to grips with the idea that they might succeed.

John Bertrand, who had been the imperturbable skipper all summer, the man who gave the pep talks each morning as his boat and crew were towed out to the race course, assumed a wait-and-see stance early on. "I believe we're going to have a great yacht race," he said just before his first match with *Liberty*. "Who knows what chances we have? You can't predict anything. But this is the chance of a lifetime to create history."

Alan Bond, the head of the syndicate who had invested more than $16 million in the pursuit of the Cup over a decade, was unusually restrained. He ventured that *Australia II* would take the America's Cup in a 4–2 series, but he was reluctant to go beyond that. "It's going to be very tough beating the Americans," he said. And then added, almost as an afterthought, "but we're better prepared now than we've ever been."

Ben Lexcen, the free-spirited yacht designer who came up with the challenger's winged keel, took a devil-may-care attitude. When the Cup series was down to its last race, he said: "It would be great for [us] to win. But I don't really care. We've won three races, and that's never been done before. Now I just want to go home and go windsurfing. Springtime is just beginning at home. The smells are so beautiful. The wisteria is just coming out. The bees are flying around. It'll be so lovely. It will be the best summer of my life."

The Australians had done their best; they had taken advantage of the experience gained in three previous attempts to win the America's Cup and had put it to good use. They knew they had a fast boat. By all appearances, they were confident. But underneath this armored front was a group of quirky individuals who badly wanted the Cup, and who were willing to use anything, including whatever good-luck omens they could find, to get it. No one found that out more readily than Lucas, the 10-year-old son of John Bertrand.

"What happened was, he [Lucas] didn't come the first two times to watch the races, and we lost," says John Longley, port grinder. "The third day, he came out and we won. The next day, he didn't come out. He had to go to school and he'd been seasick the day before, and we lost. The next day, he just happened to come out, and we won. Then someone said, 'That's it. You are going.' And we pulled him out of school and stuck him on the boat. Towards the end, he was getting over his seasickness."

Longley had his own superstitions as well. His had to do with the color of the crew's shirts, which they alternated each day between green and yellow. "We had lost the first two races," he says. "Then we got to the third race, and it was yellow day. But I'd left my shirt at home, and the other one had gotten lost in the laundry. The only yellow shirt I had was the one with the '12 KA 5' on it from the 1980 *Australia I* campaign. So, I put that on, and we won. Next day was green shirt day, and we lost. The next day came along, and it was yellow shirt day again, and I thought, 'Oh bugger, I'll put my other one on, the one I won with last time.' And then I wore it every race. So the shirt won four races and was never beaten. It got so that the guys said, 'Hey, got your shirt on?' I said, 'Yep.' And they said, 'Okay, that's fine. We'll be just fine today.' "

The Australian omens and superstitions were in evidence elsewhere, too. Guests aboard Alan Bond's new 95-foot Australian-built motor yacht, *Southern Cross*, noticed that the day the Australians won their first race there were three Eileens on board. One was Bond's wife. From then on, the three women were instructed to wear the same outfits they had on that day. "It was a bit of a nuisance," said one, "because we had to wash out our clothes at the end of the day so they would be fresh again the next day. We lived for the lay days."

Ben Lexcen says he couldn't even watch during that final race. "When we were 50 seconds behind the Americans, I went below in *Black Swan* with Tom Schnackenberg [sailmaker], and instead of looking at the races we watched the New York Yacht Club's committee boat. We could tell by their faces how we were doing."

Of all the people in Newport that summer, there was no one who was more maligned, and at the same time better liked, than Ben Lexcen. He would go into a rage upon hearing the latest charge by the New York Yacht Club concerning the parentage or legality of his design. But those who knew him also knew that the storm would pass within minutes, and that Lexcen would be nattering on happily about something else.

Lexcen, 47, is a burly bear of a man with dark brown hair, metal-rimmed glasses, and broad shoulders that round off and give him a forward list when he walks. He loves to tell outrageous stories, but his listeners generally can tell when he's crossed the line from truth to fiction to outrageous fiction by the steel-blue eyes that seem to crinkle into a devilish grin. His real name is Bob Miller, but he changed it to Ben Lexcen in 1976 in an attempt to start fresh after a business partnership failed. Lexcen is married, and has two stepchildren through his wife, Yvonne. He treats Yvonne's three grandchildren like his own, claiming that they're the children he never had. "I really like it that way," says Lexcen. "This way, I have grown-up children and grandchildren. I get to play with the little ones now that I'm old enough and have the time to enjoy them. I guess it's like having kids in reverse."

When Lexcen is at home in Sydney, he spends his free time away from yacht design, playing with the children or windsurfing. He lives on a hill overlooking Sydney Harbor, and every evening at 6 P.M. he loads his sailboard on a trailer and wheels it down the hill. Then he's out on the water until dinnertime. "Windsurfing is a wonderful sport," Lexcen says. "It's the best. The only thing bad about it is that I always end up destroying my elbows. When I know I'm going to fall, I always try to land on the board. That's why I smash my elbows. But it's better than falling in the water and having some big, hungry shark come by. There are sharks in Sydney Harbor, you know."

Lexcen is, by most accounts, a genius. He has little formal schooling, but he has designed more than 50 sailboats in his lifetime, including four 12 Meters: *Southern Cross* (1974); *Australia,* which he designed with Johan Valentijn for the 1977 challenge; and both *Australia II* and *Challenge 12* for 1983. His interests are varied. He is always thinking, always tinkering with new ideas. While he was in Newport with the *Australia II* crew, he had a technician working for him in Sydney experimenting with aluminum strips on sails. Lexcen wants to see if he can use radar to control sail shape. And he talks about designing sails with laser beams.

Lexcen is a connoisseur of music, and he can identify most classical pieces by not only name and composer, but often the orchestra playing it. When he has the time, he experiments with whimsical mobiles. He's mad for antique cars, and he keeps three vintage Mercedes at his home in Sydney. He will go into an hour monologue at the mere mention of the name Bugatti, rhapsodizing over Ettore Bugatti and the extraordinary road and racing machines he created in the twenties and thirties. Lexcen says he once drove nearly a day out of his way while in Europe so he could ride by the old Bugatti factory and peer in the windows.

He is a connoisseur of fine, old wooden boats, too, and considers the late L. Francis Herreshoff one of the greatest yacht designers who ever lived. Lexcen visited the Herreshoff boatyard in Bristol, Rhode Island, several years ago, and still talks about how he was allowed to whittle a piece of wood using a knife out of Herreshoff's old toolbox. Lexcen made the trip, oddly enough, with Halsey Herreshoff, nephew of L. Francis and navigator on the 12-Meter *Liberty*. Halsey, it will be recalled, was the man who sounded the alarm that Ben Lexcen's controversial keel could win the America's Cup. Lexcen has read and reread L. Francis Herreshoff's *The Common Sense of Yacht Design*, and considers it to be the best book ever written on the subject.

Lexcen is a world-class sailor himself, and has won the World championship in the Flying Dutchman class, a 19-foot high-performance machine that only the most athletic sailors ever master. He has competed in other Olympic classes, too, such as the Soling and the Star.

In the early 1960s, he designed boats in the Australian 18-Footer Class, and caused an uproar doing it. Lexcen changed the boat's trapeze arrangement and the shape of the hull. Both ideas made the lively planing hull, which was already lightning-fast, go faster. Improvements are generally welcomed among small-boat sailors, but Lexcen's boat made what was already a volatile group of sailors extremely angry. Those who man the Sydney 18s are an unusual group anyway, sailing as if at a race track with professional bettors keeping tabs on wins and losses.

When Lexcen entered this world with a faster boat, they accused him of cheating. It was in his experiments with these boats that Lexcen first came up with the notion of wings on the underbody of a boat. He put wings on the rudder of his 18 Footer for a championship that was being held in a river with mudflats. The fins were designed to keep him from getting stuck in the mud as he sailed through shallow water. He later put fins on the keel of a 5.5-Meter boat, but the owner eventually took them off, convinced they weren't a good idea. History would prove that judgment wrong.

Lexcen's experiments with 18 Footers led him to design a new international class of boats in 1967, the 16-foot Contender, a single-hander with a trapeze. The boat grew quickly in popularity in Australia and was being considered as an Olympic class boat before strong opposition from the Finn class—the Olympic single-hander—nixed the idea.

Lexcen achieved his first widespread acclaim in yacht design with *Mercedes III,* a 40-foot boat he designed for a friend who once sailed with him in Stars. *Mercedes III* was the leading boat in the Admiral's Cup competition in 1967. The series, held in England as perhaps the world's most preeminent ocean-racing event, brought Lexcen to the threshold of international fame. Other designs followed: *Volante,* a 54-foot speedster, and then *Apollo,* a new 58-foot yacht designed for Alan Bond. Bond's *Apollo* was a success in Australia, competing in the famed Sydney-Hobart Race and then in the Bermuda Race from Newport to Bermuda. *Ginkgo,* a 46-footer, was next, another winner. Designs were rolling off Lexcen's drafting table. Some, he will admit, were less than world-beaters. But for the most part, he was successful, and he was making money. He joined forces with Craig Whitworth, a Sydney sailmaker, in the late 1960s, and they put together a flourishing sailmaking and yacht-design business. By the mid-1970s, the business was doing so well that the partners started making plans to merge with a sailmaking firm in England.

"We became fashionable," says Lexcen of that period. "We were doing well and making money, so we started making plans overseas. I was getting a fat head about it. I was driving around in cars like Ferraris when I should have been riding around in boats. We were turning into empire builders; we thought we could rule the world."

Ben Lexcen was born in a small town in the Australian outback called Boggabri. "My father and mother were bushwhackers,"he says. "Sort of country bumpkins. We lived out in the country, and they weren't very sophisticated people. My father was a very restless person; he couldn't keep a job for very long because it was the Depression, and Australia was very hard hit. All I can remember about my childhood is moving about the country and living in tents.

"My father used to cut timber, like a lumberjack. They used to make railroad ties. Australian timber is hard; it's like iron. It's heavier than water. When you throw it in water, it sinks. The wood smelled so good when it was being cut. I've often craved to go back to that spot, but I don't think I could find it. I roughly know the area. There were deep gorges with running water and huge trees. It was so beautiful. I can remember my father taking the pith out of the center of the trees—it was like mud—and carving little cars and trucks for me.

"I remember once that I got lost. I was seven miles into the woods with my father, and I just disappeared. My mother was frantic. But I just walked to where they were cutting the trees down through the bush and undergrowth—I followed the sound of the axes.''

Lexcen eventually moved to Newcastle, a seacoast coal-mining town about 80 miles north of Sydney, when he was about six. His father had left home to go into the Australian Air Force, and he never returned. Lexcen says he found another woman. His mother then sent Lexcen to live with his maternal grandmother, who was married to a man named Mick Green. Green had a strong influence on the young Ben Lexcen. He was an old, silent codger, Lexcen says, who rarely spoke to him when he was a child. But Lexcen's grandmother died when he was nine, and it was Mick Green who made sure he was washed and fed.

Lexcen didn't enter school until he was 10, and he left when he was 14. ''I was embarrassed because I couldn't do anything,'' he says. ''The biggest cross I have to bear today is that I can't spell. I'm embarrassed to write. I write badly. It's scribbling. So I print. I print as fast as a normal person can write.''

Still, the experience of going to school relatively late, after living in the woods, had a great impact on Lexcen, who believes that most children start school too young. ''Look at how many people send their children to school when they're three years old,'' he says. ''They send them because they want to get rid of them. Little three-year-old kids are beautiful and lovely. That's the best age. But their mothers are distracted. To be a mother is a bloody hard thing. I don't think you should send children to school until they're 10. I think kids should live like Huckleberry Finn until they're 10. Think of the life they lose. They get regimented when they're three years old. The world might be full of bloody geniuses if they weren't allowed to go to school until they're 10. Once they're in school, they should stay in longer, go to university and all. But I think they learn quicker when their brain is empty. I think an empty brain learns fast. So if you keep the brain empty until it's more developed, it must learn quicker and do better things.''

Lexcen learned about boats by sailing toy models at the beach with friends, a Huckleberry Finn experience that guided him into the design work that is his passion today. ''I used to go down to the beach every day,'' he says. ''The beach was surrounded by huge sandstone cliffs 300 feet high. At one end of this cove, there was this huge pond that was sort of man-made; it was about 150 yards in diameter, with a retaining wall around it. Inside of it, there was another pool about 50 yards in diameter, and it was a map of the world, with all the continents, and the canals—the Suez Canal and the Panama Canal—and the oceans about four feet deep. The continents stuck up about an inch and a half from the water, and the water used to lap against the sides. It was a geography lesson. That thing is so beautiful, and now it's all covered with sand, and nobody knows it's even there.

"We used to sail boats in there. One of the kids' fathers was real handy. He used to make him boats out of sheet metal. They were very buoyant and used to sail nicely. So, I begged my grandmother to buy me a boat, and she bought me a boat for a dollar. But it only sailed when the sail wasn't wet. I decided I had to make one like this kid's, so I went and bought some balsa wood at a model airplane shop. I made a boat similar to his as best I could guess. It was faster than his, so I gave mine to my friend, and I made another one so we could race."

Lexcen was hooked after that. He started ordering yacht-model plans from a company in England and made little boats that were more and more intricate. "There was a lake about 20 miles from us, so we used to get on the train with the models under our arms and take them to this huge bay that was only about a foot deep. You could walk in the water next to the boats. We used to reef the boats when they had weather helm and sail them with a piece of cotton on the tiller. My friend would sail on one tack and I'd sail on the other.

"That's all pretty much what makes me go," says Lexcen in a classic understatement. "I have a belief that everybody in the world is like a computer card. Everyone has one of those things inside when they're born. Walking around the streets of Newport, there is probably an Albert Einstein. He might be a short-order chef down at the local diner, only he's gone through life and his card has never matched up with the situation. My card made me what I am by my being exposed to that pool and those little toy boats for a minute. The slots fit, and my life was set. Like Mozart. If somebody never put a violin in front of him, he'd probably have been a bloody bus driver. His absolute use might not have been there because he wasn't put into the position of being Mozart."

Lexcen says there's nothing he'd rather do in life than design boats. Now that he's become well-known, it's more difficult, because people are always approaching him with a new idea. But he thrives on it. "I'd pay Bondy to let me design these 12 Meters if I could afford it," he says, grinning.

Lexcen worked in an iron foundry right after he quit school, but lasted in the job for only three months. He knew he wanted to build boats. He went from one boatyard to the next, looking for work. But with so little education it wasn't easy. He settled finally for an apprenticeship as a machinist with a shipyard. But his love affair with sailboats went on despite the work. He built a 20-foot boat in his backyard just to gain experience. The self-education paid dividends when he was finally hired to learn sailmaking with a small group in Sydney. From there he moved to Brisbane and opened his own sailmaking loft. Within a few years, he had joined forces with Whitworth in a Sydney loft, and the path to fame and fortune was set. At least for a time. Lexcen's involvement with 12 Meters was then a few years in the future.

In 1970, Bob Derecktor was building what proved to be the unsuccessful America's Cup yacht *Valiant* in his woebegone yard in Mamaroneck, on Long Island Sound. Lexcen and Alan Bond happened to be there, preparing for the Bermuda Race. Bond, a man of boundless curiosity, and Lexcen, a boundless man, went over to look at the new Twelve.

Recently Alan Bond recalled their visit to *Valiant*. "We had *Apollo I* there for the Bermuda Race. She was right next to the 12 Meter. Vic Romagna, who has sailed on many American 12 Meters, was there, and he didn't seem to want us around. He felt that the 12 Meter was a big thing, and we should keep our boat and ourselves away—far away. He said—if I recall it—'This is a 12 Meter; it's something really important in yachting.' He asked Bob Miller [Lexcen] and me to leave, immediately, in fairly strong terms." Miller, not a man easily pushed, responded in kind. He said that he wasn't interested "in your bloody Cup or boat. If we were, we'd come back and win it."

When Alan Bond did decide to come back and win it, he turned to Lexcen for a design. Bond, when asked why he selected Lexcen to design his Cup challenger in 1974, rather than the far more established Australian designer Alan Payne of *Gretel I* and *Gretel II* fame, said, "He [Lexcen] had done very well with the design of *Apollo I*. I'd gone sailing with him, and he taught me all about sailing. He also became a friend at the same time."

Constancy, Bond added, has been one key to his success. "Having the same people involved in the boats is no different than having the same people involved in your business. You'll find there's been no change in the top executives of the Bond Corporation for 14 years . . . I like the team to grow with us . . . So I've really built the team as a yachting team, the same way as I've built a business team."

Lexcen's 12-Meter *Southern Cross* was a great disappointment. Built as a light-air boat for winds of 12 to 15 knots, she was too sharply focused for racing off Newport. In addition, she was slow upwind compared to *Courageous,* the American defender that year. The Australians hadn't acquired enough experience yet, and wouldn't for another decade. The Americans were the experts, and they won the series easily, 4-0. Still, Alan Bond, first and foremost a businessman, got what he wanted out of this challenge in terms of publicity. His entry into the America's Cup arena put one of his ventures, a 20,000-acre land development called Yanchep Sun City, on the map and in the black. Bond would eventually realize millions of dollars from this resort town that some called "Yanchep Fly City."

When Ben Lexcen designed the 12-Meter *Southern Cross,* he was still Bob Miller. But after the boat was finished, and the Bond campaign of 1974 went up in smoke, Lexcen and Whitworth had a falling out. They had decided to try to buy into a sailmaking firm in England owned by John Oakeley, a sailmaker who subsequently entered the America's Cup arena in 1980 with the British yacht *Lionheart.* Negotiations took a long time, and by the time they were completed Lexcen wanted out. He packed his bags and moved from England, where he had temporarily relocated, to the Continent. For the next two years, he wandered aimlessly, spending more than all of the fortune he had amassed, and designing boats only now and then.

The name Miller & Whitworth caused confusion, because the Miller end of the business was gone. Lexcen says his mail was going to the wrong place, among other things, and he decided he needed a new identity to set things straight. To open a business of his own, as he thought about doing, would best be done with a new name. Lexcen had a friend with access to the *Reader's Digest* computer bank. He asked his friend to go through the computer list and find him a name that no one else had. The friend agreed and came up with six names, all of which were the same number of letters as "Miller." Miller chose Lexcen—Ben Lexcen. He was now a man with a name no one else claimed—or so he thought. "It didn't work," Lexcen says. "I got a call last year from a guy in Washington, D.C., who said his name was John Lexcen. I didn't know there were any other Lexcens around. But there are eight more: two in California and eight in Minnesota. All his relatives."

That's Lexcen's version of the name-change story, a tale that varies slightly every time he tells it. Johan Valentijn, who was working with Lexcen on the design of *Australia I,* has a different version. Valentijn says that Lexcen's wife Yvonne helped him find a new name. They were living in Sydney—it was after Lexcen's time in Europe, when Alan Bond brought him home to prepare for the 1977 Australian challenge. Valentijn and Lexcen had just finished designing the boat's hatch covers. The two talked about having their names engraved on the covers as they were being molded. The covers were made of a clear plastic called Lexan. Yvonne was in on the discussion and suggested that if her husband planned to change his name, this was a good time. She convinced him that if the Australians won the Cup, the new name would become a household word.

Yvonne's first suggestion was Ben Lincoln: "Ben" after their favorite dog Benjie, who had recently died, and "Lincoln" after Abraham Lincoln—a fitting name for an Australian on his way to America. The idea seemed good. Valentijn says Lexcen didn't seem to care one way or the other; it was his wife who was carried away with the idea. They went ahead with the plans to engrave BL in the hatch cover, but afterwards Lexcen decided he didn't like the name Lincoln. The problem then was to substitute a name beginning with L. The hatch covers were made of Lexan, so why not "Lexcen"? If Valentijn is right, this may be the reason Lexcen's story involves *Reader's Digest* computers and one-of-a-kind names—it certainly has a lot more appeal than references to dead dogs and plastic hatch covers.

By the time Bond asked Lexcen to design *Australia I*, Lexcen was ready. He had run out of money and was eager for a new challenge. Lexcen says Bond spotted him in a supermarket in Europe one day, striding down one of the aisles with that typical forward-listing Lexcen gait. Bond, a man who goes after what he wants, had tracked Lexcen down and come to him from the other end of the world. "All of a sudden Bondy popped out of nowhere," says Lexcen. "He said he heard I was out of work and that I had run out of money and that I must come to work for him." Lexcen agreed.

Alan Bond is English, but he moved to Australia at age 13 because his father's ill health necessitated a drier climate. The steamer *Himalaya* brought Bond and his family from Ealing, a suburb of London, to Fremantle's Swan River in Western Australia. Like Lexcen, Bond quit school at 14. But Bond's dreams grew as he went along. He started out as a $50-a-month sign painter and bought a firm called Nu-Signs two years later. He turned the sign-making venture into a home-remodeling business, taking derelict houses and making them livable. From old houses, Bond graduated to new subdivisions, then to oil and minerals at Robe River, 800 miles north of Perth. Then came Yanchep Sun City, which Bond has since had the good sense to sell to the Japanese.

Today, Bond has interests in oil and gas. He also owns the Swan Brewing Company, which was responsible for mountains of empty beer cans in Newport. When Bond's *Australia II* returned to the harbor on September 5 after thrashing the British for the Louis Vuitton trophy—and for the right to challenge against *Liberty* for the America's Cup—she was flying her enormous Black Swan spinnaker. Ahead of her was her tender—named *Black Swan,* of course—accompanied by a tape of Australia's hard-rocking band Men At Work, working up a sweat with a song entitled "Down Under." It was a commercial and patriotic moment made all the more riveting by a decibel level that could collapse a spinnaker.

Before the summer of 1983, Bond was well-known for his personal decibel level; he was a man with a bark and a bite, and Newport didn't like him. But commercial success apparently has permitted polish to appear on the surface of Alan Bond, the wild colonial boy. "I've built up a large collection of French Impressionists—from Renoir, Gauguin, Picasso, Monet, to Manet—as well as a big collection of early Australian works," Bond says. He is particularly proud of a recent purchase, an oil painting by Thomas Webber, the botanist who sailed with Captain Cook. Bond funds the game of cricket in Australia, and actively supports his country's equestrian teams because of his daughter Susan's interest in riding.

Bond has four children, most of whom spent last summer in Newport living in a rented oceanfront mansion named Midcliffe. Bond and his wife Eileen, whom he married when she was 17 and he was still painting signs, mingled nicely with members of Newport's social élite. "She is so totally open and lovable," says one Bellevue Avenue socialite about the red-headed Mrs. Bond. "The only trouble with the summer was that I didn't see more of the Bonds . . . As the summer continued, my feelings for the Bond family rose and rose. Stalwart Alan. Gay Eileen."

Bond's first significant plunge into the nautical world came when he acquired the 49-foot sloop *Panamuna,* which he took in trade for some real estate. Within two months, Bond had destroyed two masts and learned much of the lore of seasickness. But he persevered, becoming an adept and experienced ocean sailor. His next boat was *Apollo,* the Bob Miller/Ben Lexcen design that catapulted a bushwhacker's son into the international yacht-racing arena.

Throughout the summer of 1983, Alan Bond was constantly protective of his crew. When he wanted to, he would lash out at anyone he thought was trying to take advantage of him. But to his team, which he started forming in that first campaign back in 1974, he was a gentleman. When the crew was invited to attend a Rolex watch presentation on September 11, Bond refused. He maintained that they wouldn't accept Rolex watches as gifts unless the entire crew and support team of some 22 individuals received watches. When Rolex wouldn't go along with the request—as it hadn't in 1977 and 1980—Bond ordered his crew to boycott the presentation at Beechwood mansion on Bellevue Avenue. The *Liberty* crew appeared and went home with new $1,000 watches on their wrists.

Bond insisted that his entire team had worked hard, not just the *Australia II* crew, and that they all deserved recognition. As a way of making up to the team for the watches they never got, Bond bought them all 1983 America's Cup gold coins that were minted especially for the *Victory* syndicate in England. Each coin was worth $2,000.

There was no doubt that Bond had picked a good crew. "*Australia II* was very much a crew of 11 people who were all of equal standing," says John Longley, project manager and the boat's port winch grinder. In the past, in the campaigns since 1974, it had been an "us and them" situation, says Longley, with the "black coats," the men steering and navigating the boat, being the "them" and the rest of the crew the "us."

"With our boat, the shoreside management looks after the boat and crew and plays the game," he says. "The helmsman is allowed simply to get on with the job of being the helmsman. John [Bertrand] doesn't have to worry about any of the fund-raising, any of the ordering, anything. All he has to worry about is driving the boat, training the crew and seeing that the boat goes fast."

Beyond that, John Bertrand was superb in what he was doing. Bertrand, 37, was named by Bond to be his 1983 skipper. Bond made the public announcement before the sails were even dry in that last fateful race of 1980 after the America's Cup had slipped through his fingers for the third time. Even Bertrand didn't know about the decision until it was announced.

Bertrand was a natural for the job. He had sailed on 12 Meters in four campaigns. He had experience on ocean racers, including time as crew with Dennis Conner. He started sailing at age seven, having lived near a beach in Chelsea, a suburb of Melbourne. Although neither of his parents sailed, he developed a love for it. Bertrand started winning titles at an early age. He won Australia's national junior sailing title in 1964 and was recognized as the best all-round sailor in Australia in 1968.

Bertrand had his first experience on a 12 Meter in 1970 when he sailed as crew on *Gretel II*, the Australian challenger that year from Sydney. He and his wife, Rasa, stayed on in America when the unsuccessful challenge was over in September. Bertrand worked on his master's degree in naval architecture at the Massachusetts Institute of Technology. Rasa worked as a nurse in Boston to help pay the bills.

From there, Bertrand's sailing career escalated. He was a member of the 1972 Australian Olympic sailing team. After the 1974 America's Cup fiasco with *Southern Cross*, Bertrand chose to stay in the United States for yet another stretch—this time to learn sailmaking at the North Sails loft in Pewaukee, Wisconsin. It was then that he became interested in sailing in the Finn class. He competed in the 1976 Olympics in Montreal, where he won a bronze medal. Bertrand returned to Melbourne after the Games to manage the North Sails loft there. He had planned to compete in the 1980 Olympics, but joined Bond's team instead when Australia decided to boycott the 1980 Games in Russia.

Jim Hardy was skipper of *Australia I* in the 1980 challenge, but Bertrand made himself invaluable as sailtrimmer. When the Australian crew lost to the American defenders, Hardy announced that he preferred to let someone else take over for the next challenge in 1983. For Bond, the obvious choice was Bertrand.

Bertrand came to Newport in June of 1983, bringing his wife and three children, ages 4 to 10, with him the 12,000 miles from Melbourne. At the end of the day, he would disappear from the docks to join Rasa and their two sons and daughter at their rented home downtown. When he was sailing, he gave the boat and crew his undivided attention. Bertrand, who is tall and slim, sports a kung-fu mustache that belies his gentle nature. He has a sense of humor that comes in spurts. "We're going to change the rules," he said amid the turmoil of the summer-long keel controversy. "All future sails will have to be made with kangaroo cloth, and we'll run a bulldozer over the Cup and turn it into the America's plate." While pressure from the New York Yacht Club came down heavy, Bertrand seemed not to notice. Although management, such as Warren Jones, allowed him to avoid much of this theater of the absurd, Bertrand would have been cool and collected anyway. His unruffled presence seemed to calm the rest of the crew.

"The crew respected his ability enormously," Longley says. "He worked very, very hard at binding the crew together as a unit. There was absolutely no hierarchical strain on the boat. The bowman had just as much right to put his oar in as the tactician.

"There was only one thing he asked the whole time, and that was that the crew keep their eyes on the wind. The whole thing here is to sail where the wind is. One of our mottoes during the summer was the dear old sailing thing: 'Don't sail where the wind ain't, because that's slow.' And we didn't want to sail where the wind ain't—anytime.

"We were very conscious of not only looking for the wind, but looking for the other boat and being able to anticipate what was going on. It was up to the grinders and everybody. The whole crew fed information back. There is always this thing about how the crew should sail quietly. We didn't sail quietly. There was no idle chatter; but the whole time there were comments like, 'The wind is coming...' Continual conversation, continual input the whole time."

In an interview with Robert Hopkins, a sail expert with North sailmakers, who at the end of the summer would work as a coach for the British on *Victory 83*, Bertrand said he never dwelled on whether he was good enough to be leading the *Australia II* team. "Sure, I can get fired if I don't deliver the goods, but that doesn't particularly worry me," he said. "It's not an important issue, I must say. I think that in a sporting contest, if you are really worried about failure, you should never start participating."

"As a group of 11 people, we were incredibly close," says Longley. "Basically, that came from John's leadership; there's no doubt about that. His talks at breakfast. His talks going out to the starting line. Things he came up with..." Longley recounted the time that *Australia II* lost its first race in the final trial series to the British boat, *Victory 83*. It had been a light-air day, the kind in which *Victory 83* excelled, and the boat beat *Australia II* by 13 seconds over a 24.3-mile course. It was the only race she was able to claim in that final four-out-of-seven series. When *Australia II* finally won the series, she won the right to challenge *Liberty* for the America's Cup.

Bertrand knew just what to say the next day after the loss to *Victory 83*, says Longley. "Now look, fellas, I don't want you to think about what today means mathematically in relation to yesterday, or what it will be like tomorrow," said Bertrand. "I don't want you to think about what it means in the overall series in winning or losing this race. What I want you to do today is take today's race as a separate entity and just race today's race."

"That became our attitude for every race from then on," says Longley. "Each race has its own pressures. We agreed that we would treat each day as it came, and we would not think what it meant. We wouldn't think that if we were 3-1 down, and if we lost today, we were gone. We didn't even think that if we were 3-all and we won today, we were going to win the America's Cup."

Australia II steamrolled her way through a summer of trial racing in which she lost only six of the 54 races she sailed. It had been a team effort all the way, made easier by the fact that Lexcen had designed a boat faster than all the others. Still, the competition to be chosen challenger was not without its drama, not the least of which was that loss to *Victory 83* in the final elimination trials. The Australians had done their homework. They had taken the experience of the previous three campaigns and put it to good use.

Going into the America's Cup Races, they had everything their way, including a skipper who badly wanted to win. Bertrand put it this way in talking to Robert Hopkins: "It's interesting why people want to win. Dennis, as I read him . . . wants to prove himself to the rest of the world. Tommy Blackaller has a large ego. I think you have to have a combination of those things.

"You've got to be egotistical, to have an incredible desire, a perseverance, to win. I suspect I've got that. Having to prove oneself to other people possibly is an ingredient. All those things mount up. Anyone who gets involved obviously has a definite desire to win. I think the proof is— well, I hate losing."

*"The hard part of the 12-Meter chal-
lenge is gone. I feel like I could
design a 12 Meter in my sleep . . ."*
—BEN LEXCEN

CHAPTER 9
Point/Counterpoint

The question of how much Ben Lexcen had to do with designing the keel of *Australia II* and how much Dutch testing laboratories contributed was never fully resolved. The New York Yacht Club opted out of the controversy in late August, bruised and battered from the adverse publicity it had aroused over the issue. But even after its public retreat, members of the club and officials within the American syndicates continued to stew about who actually designed the keel. Many remained convinced that it was not Lexcen's brainchild. But no one could prove it.

Among others, Johan Valentijn was sure Lexcen couldn't have designed the keel alone. He had worked closely with Lexcen on the design of *Australia I* in preparation for the 1977 Australian challenge, and he felt he knew Lexcen's strengths and weaknesses. Beyond that, Valentijn had done his own investigating.

The question was crucial. Rules governing the America's Cup Races require that challengers compete in a boat designed by nationals of their country. To have had an Australian boat designed by Dutch lab technicians would have been illegal. If proved, it would have been enough to disqualify *Australia II* from the 1983 challenge.

Hearing Lexcen's version of how he designed the keel, and then superimposing Valentijn's version of what he was told happened, is a classic exercise in point/counterpoint. Both designers were willing to discuss the keel controversy a short time after the America's Cup summer had ended—after the America's Cup was in Australian hands and members of the New York Yacht Club had gone home.

Ben Lexcen was already planning another 12 Meter within days of winning the America's Cup. It was intended for the 1987 defense, and he wanted to get the idea down on paper as soon as he returned to Australia. "It's so easy to do a 12 Meter now," he says. "I'll just jot one off—just so that I won't forget what the next one should look like." He claims to have a boat in mind that will be even faster than *Australia II*. And it will have wings, assuming such things are still legal in 1987. He laments the fact that he didn't have more time with *Australia II* to work on the hull. "I really only worked on keels," he says. "I should have been working on the hull, but there wasn't enough time. If we hadn't had to drag that bloody hull around, we'd have gone twice as fast."

The *Australia II* syndicate had received special permission during the design stages to work up the lines of their 12 Meter at a Dutch tank-testing center, the Netherlands Ship Model Basin at Wageningen. Australia has no comparable testing laboratory. Lexcen takes umbrage at the fact that the New York Yacht Club approved the center, but then became upset with the results of the experimentation. "They were just doing what I told them," Lexcen says of the Dutch technicians. "Sometimes they'd tell me things back. How the hell can you stop them from telling you things? It's like in a jury—'Well, disregard that remark . . .' You can't disregard that remark. If someone says, 'I think this could be a good idea,' you can't say, 'Well, I didn't hear that.'

"The situation at the tank puts you almost under conditions that would contravene the spirit of the bloody ruling of the New York Yacht Club. But as far as I'm concerned, if you can use the tank, then you can talk to the people at the tank. The only time they [the NYYC] brought it up was after the boat was good. But they never would have brought it up if the boat had been a turkey.

"That's the attitude . . . that before this America's Cup, the American yacht designers were the only ones who were any damn good. Like Sparkman & Stephens. And that was pretty well true in those days . . . "

Lexcen says he was aware that Dutch technicians spread rumors that they were responsible for the keel design. Their version of the story, Lexcen says, was largely an outgrowth of the way he works. He used the example of an elderly Dutch draftsman who was able to take Lexcen's line drawings of the boat and reinterpret them on a smaller design scale for use in a computer. He says he believes in complimenting those around him when they do well or are innovative. But he occasionally ends up boosting their egos to the detriment of his own.

Lexcen concedes that he cannot use a computer, and that he is not a draftsman. "Even now, I can't program a computer," he says. "I spent a couple of days reading through the basic CPM method of programming, and I sort of stumbled into doing some real crude, ham-fisted attempts at making a program . . . But why should I do that? Down the street from me is the most brilliant computer programmer in the world probably. So if I walk his dogs, he'll write me a computer program that talks to me.

"To stimulate these people [at the Dutch center], I would sometimes say things like . . . 'You're doing a great job' to make them think they're doing it. And give them heaps of credit all the time. I don't mind doing that, but unfortunately, you occasionally get a guy who you give heaps of credit to, and he goes and says he designed the boat . . . I don't mind sharing credit with those people as long as they take second billing."

This 12-Meter workup required the testing of one-third-size models to get a realistic picture of the design. The 20-foot models, in every way miniature 12 Meters, are expensive. Made of wood with a lead keel, they weigh more than two tons and cost about $10,000 each.

Lexcen used the tanks at the Ship Model Basin for towing the mini Twelves through the water. The tank is about 750 feet long and 30 feet wide. Lexcen describes how he initiated the project: "I sent first the line plans from our boat [*Australia I*] to make a base model to work from and to try to beat. When I got there, that was made. It hadn't been run. We had a first run, and we had a disaster with the equipment because it wasn't strong enough. They had to rebuild the equipment overnight. The way we tested had never been done before in the world—we towed the boat by the mast. It had been done first in a small way by a man in Canada, and he wrote a paper on it. That's why I decided to go there [Holland]. Peter van Oossanen, who was in charge, told me there was this new way of testing, and he convinced me of it."

Lexcen toyed first with the idea of changing the counter of the boat where the stern rises above the waterline. The idea didn't make any difference in the boat's performance, but the rating went down. That meant that more sail area could be added. Lexcen decided to hold off on that. He wanted to be open-minded at this stage. Sail area was something he could add later if all else failed.

Lexcen says he had it in the back of his mind to add wings to the boat, but he first wanted to learn more about ordinary keels. Then he modified the tank model with a more upright leading edge to the keel. And he made a model keel with thicker sections. Lexcen says the "more upright" keel was a disaster, but the thicker keel was promising. "Then we had a big confab, and we said, 'Let's go two-pronged, with a conventional and an unconventional attack on this thing.' That's when we got involved with the aerospace people. Peter [van Oossanen] said, 'Let's get their program, and then we'll be able to get on the inside of both tracks.' We had to decide, do we want to do a conventional . . . [or unconventional boat]?"

Lexcen refers to Joop Slooff, who worked at the Dutch NLR Aerospace Laboratory. Slooff apparently took credit for design of the keel in May of 1983, but later in the summer—when the heat was on—minimized his role in the project. "He was a very knowledgeable guy, and he had a program we wanted to use," says Lexcen. The program belonged to the Aerospace Laboratory. Technicians modified the program to fit yacht design and then fed in the new information. Lexcen says he and the Dutch analysts were able to come out with a set of computer numbers that measured performance almost as accurately as tank testing. And it cost about 10 percent of the price of tank testing. The program worked so well that the Ship Model Basin bought the computer program from the Aerospace Laboratory for $100,000 when the Australian project was completed.

"It gave us a lot of insight into what was going to happen when we tank-tested," Lexcen says. "At least you could sort out the real duds. Sometimes when it showed [a design] was as good as it was, I'd say, 'Well, maybe the computer's wacky.' " The only way to test it then was to build a model and watch it perform in a tank of water.

Lexcen says he and van Oossanen plugged his design ideas (12 Lexcen sketches) into the computer program. The results looked promising: "It came out that these wings and things were going to be okay, so then we decided to go ahead and test them. The test program went very gradually. I think we did six or seven variations of that. You can see the progression as the thing grew. Like evolution, from this to that. Each test. Cut off a bit here. Cut off a bit there. Add over here. And so on."

Lexcen says he had no preconceived ideas before he went to Holland about what he wanted to do. In the past, he was unable to prove that the fins he designed on smaller boats were good or bad. He is the first to point out that other designers have also experimented with wings. When he put them on a 5.5 Meter, the boat was fast downwind, but it wouldn't go in a breeze. On *Australia II* there was no doubt that they worked—in any direction, at any time.

"When I went to the tank [the Ship Model Basin], I tried to empty my head before I left home," Lexcen says. "That's why I didn't take a lot of stuff. I didn't take any drawings or anything. They gave me an office when I got there. I took all my pictures. But I borrowed stuff off the people there, like splines [strips of wood used to lay down a curved line when lofting a boat] and battens and paper and stuff. And then I moved a huge drawing board into a little office near a sea-keeping tank. So I went in there, and they just left me alone. Then I would just sketch stuff, and draw stuff, and take it to van Oossanen, and he would draw it up to feed it into the machine to make the models."

Lexcen says he didn't have much contact with Alan Bond until he knew he had something that might work. "I said that I had a real bloody wild boat. I said, 'This really works,' because I had to convince him that it worked." Bond was going to London on business, so he told Lexcen that he and John Bertrand would stop in Holland to see the design.

"John Bertrand was a bit skeptical," says Lexcen. "He's always very careful about what he does. Bondy just looked at me with his big, blue eyes and said, 'You sure?' I had Peter talk to him, too. I had to convince him. Then he was convinced and he said, 'All right, we'll do it.' "

When the tank testing was over, the Ship Model Basin issued a thick report compiled by the scientists who had worked on the testing program. Lexcen concedes that it was full of things "that even I can't understand." He wanted to use the report to further convince Bond that the design was credible. But he also knew that he couldn't expect Bond to wade through the report.

"Bondy has an attention span of about a minute," Lexcen says. "If you want to sell Alan Bond something, if you haven't sold it in a minute you aren't going to sell it. So I condensed the report down to about 20 pages of real straightforward [material]—what every person in the street can understand. With sketches and photographs." Bond looked through the report quickly—it described a boat that was an improvement on *Australia I*. That design became *Challenge 12*. The report also discussed the design of what Lexcen called "the funny boat." That was *Australia II*.

After they all returned to Australia, Lexcen suggested to Bond that they build two identical boats. But Bond refused. He wanted one "ordinary" boat and one "funny one," Lexcen says. "He wasn't absolutely convinced in his mind. And I can't blame him . . . I'm surprised he built it at all, actually."

Johan Valentijn also had a Dutch connection, but his was, first of all, by birth. Valentijn was born in Holland. He was back and forth to Newport during the 1977 and 1980 challenges—first for Alan Bond, and then for Baron Bich. Eventually, he settled in Newport, buying a home with a huge backyard and plenty of room inside for his design office. Like Lexcen, Valentijn made use of tank-testing laboratories in Holland in preparation for the 1983 challenge. He was a naturalized American citizen by then, and therefore qualified as a designer for the *Freedom* syndicate.

Valentijn's approach to tank testing differed from Lexcen's. He designed his version of *Magic* while in the United States and then sent the lines to a tank-testing center at Delft University in Holland. (*Liberty* never was tank-tested.) As soon as the drawings arrived, the center went ahead and made a model of Valentijn's design. When it was finished, Valentijn flew to Holland and tested his model 12 Meter in the tanks. The center also had a sophisticated computer program with which to analyze results. Valentijn, who is a trained naval architect and has his own computer in Newport, took the data back home with him. Soon afterward, he proceeded to build *Magic* at Custom Marine in Old Saybrook, Connecticut.

Valentijn says he had heard about the *Australia II* keel, but he didn't know that much about it. Then, in May, 1983, just before the start of the America's Cup summer, he was approached in Newport by Joop Slooff. "I was on the dock next to *Liberty,* so he introduced himself," says Valentijn.

"Are you Mr. Valentijn?" Slooff reportedly asked.

"Yes," answered Valentijn.

"Well, I designed the keel on *Australia II,*" Slooff said.

"You what?" asked Valentijn.

"I designed the keel on *Australia II,*" Slooff repeated.

Valentijn says that Slooff explained he was in the United States to attend a seminar in Massachusetts and had decided to stop in Newport. He had heard about Valentijn and had looked him up. Valentijn says he asked Slooff for more details of *Australia II* and about his participation in the project.

"He felt very strongly and was very proud that he had designed this keel," says Valentijn, who also was experimenting with winged appendages on keels at the time. Valentijn, however, was working with aeronautical engineers at Boeing Aircraft in Seattle. When he told the Slooff story to a friend at Boeing, he was told in turn that Dutch engineers were repeating almost the same tale to Boeing employees—that is, that the Dutch designed *Australia II*'s keel. (In midsummer, Slooff was interviewed by telephone at his office in Holland. He conceded that he had met Valentijn that day in May, but he denied that he said anything to Valentijn about *Australia II*'s keel.)

Valentijn approached Dennis Conner with news of Slooff's disclosure. "At that time, we didn't even know how good *Australia II* was," Valentijn says. "She hadn't even sailed against anyone yet." In fact, the boat still had not arrived in Newport. Conner seemed surprised. "Well, if you want to start a third world war, this is a great time to start it—bringing this up now," he said to Valentijn about prospects of pressing the issue. Valentijn backed down, and little more was said for more than a month—until *Australia II* started winning races.

"Suddenly, I was asked to come on board *Fox Hunter* [the New York Yacht Club committee boat]," says Valentijn. "They started talking about this keel and the concept and whether it would be legal under the rating. So I casually mentioned that 'I hope you guys remember it was designed in Holland.' " Cup Committee members didn't seem to know, so Valentijn says he described his conversation in May with Joop Slooff.

"Whether it's true or not, I don't know," Valentijn told them. "I assume he told me the truth. The way he told me—he seemed so proud of himself—I tended to believe him. Maybe he was on an ego trip. Who knows?"

Club members asked Valentijn to find out what he could. Valentijn says that was when they devised a telex to van Oossanen at the Netherlands

Ship Model Basin and to Slooff. In the telex, the *Freedom* syndicate asked for plans of the keel. The syndicate said publicly that it wanted the design plans so it could attach wings to the 12-Meter *Magic,* which by then had been replaced by *Liberty* as a Cup contender. By putting wings on *Magic,* the syndicate said, it would have a better idea of how *Liberty* was performing in comparison.

Valentijn says the telex was no more than a ploy to find out who designed *Australia II*'s keel. "We wanted to see if they would give a little feel as to who owns what and whose idea it basically was," Valentijn says. "At the same time, we felt that it would look as if we wanted to change *Magic.* But *Magic* was just a story that was put in there to make it look legitimate for what we were trying to do...It was really a smoke screen."

The telex ploy didn't work because van Oossanen sent a message back saying that he was working for the Australians and couldn't disclose anything about the design until after the 1983 challenge.

Next the America's Cup Committee of the NYYC—specifically Bob McCullough and Jim Michael—asked Valentijn to go to Holland and investigate. Conner agreed and suggested that Valentijn go with Ed du Moulin, the *Freedom* syndicate's manager. In the meantime, Michael, the Cup Committee counsel, drew up a three-page list of questions to ask the Dutch. Du Moulin backed away, asking that he be kept out of it.

Then it was up to Valentijn. "I didn't mind going, but I thought that everyone would think it was pretty much sour grapes if I went," he says. "Well, it's not sour grapes. I don't care who designed the boat, but rules are rules. That's about all. But if the selection committee wants to find out, they should send their own people. So I decided I was not going to go either."

Instead, Valentijn telephoned Tony van Rijn in North Carolina. Van Rijn had been a friend of Valentijn's for more than 20 years. They grew up together in Holland in the same village, and then as adults both moved to the United States. Van Rijn was in the fiberglass manufacturing business and understood yacht design.

Van Rijn agreed to go to Holland and speak to Slooff. He went first to the Dutch patent office and found out that a Bond company—Norport Pty. Ltd.—had filed a Dutch patent application on the secret keel. Van Rijn then went to see Slooff. "He tried to get Slooff to say something," Valentijn reports. "But Slooff didn't want to say anything because he suddenly feels, 'Oh, my God, what's going to happen next?'"

Valentijn says Slooff was upset when informed about Bond's patent. He apparently didn't know anything about it. Beyond that, he refused to talk. Van Rijn left frustrated and went to visit Valentijn's uncle, Wil Valentijn, a

Dutch boatbuilder whom he also knew from his youth. The two decided to visit various Dutch government agencies to see what they could do, and then to talk with the scientists at the Aerospace Laboratory.

Valentijn says they later visited van Oossanen at the Netherlands Ship Model Basin in Wageningen, and that van Oossanen conceded that his laboratory designed the keel. "He talked to my uncle and Tony for an hour, and he told them everything," Valentijn says. "He told them that Slooff most likely did the wings. He told them all the work they had done on this whole bloody boat. And he said, 'Well, Ben Lexcen is a nice guy. He's a great team leader. But Ben doesn't understand what's going on.' "

Van Oossanen at the time apparently agreed to repeat the same story to the New York Yacht Club. He had wanted to become involved with a 12-Meter syndicate for years, and this was his chance. He talked at length about the design process. "At first they did very standard 12-Meter models and 12-Meter keels," Valentijn says. "All with medium success. Then it was van Oossanen who came up with the idea to use Slooff's special computer program to make 12-Meter keels that nobody ever dreamed of . . . He painted it in black and white."

After the meeting in Wageningen, Wil Valentijn and Tony van Rijn drafted an affidavit reflecting statements made by van Oossanen. The affidavit reads, in part:

☐ I [Dr. van Oossanen] put together a team of highly trained technical experts (varying in number from 6–8) from NSMB plus Mr. J. W. Slooff, the head of the Theoretical Aerodynamics Department of the Netherlands Aerospace Laboratory. Ben Lexcen was the team leader and maintained an office at NSMB for four months. However, the project, from beginning to end, was a team effort, and the results represent the combined talents and contributions of all members of the team.

☐ As is customary with research and development projects of this type at NSMB, we then proposed, and it was agreed, to develop a special set of computer programs that would permit complete testing by computer of wholly new ideas and even radical types of keels. . . .

☐ After trying various concepts, a basic keel shape began slowly to evolve from the computer program. However, it also had a serious problem of excessive tip vortexes, that is, a swirling of the water starting ahead of and becoming concentrated at the trailing lower tip of the keel, all of which retards the flow of water and would reduce the speed of the yacht. To cure this problem, Mr. J. W. Slooff, of NLR, came forward with a proposal to add end plates [wings] to the bottom of the keel, as was customary in the aircraft industry. This addition to the program, even in its early stages, showed promise, so an all-out effort was then undertaken by the team to refine this type of keel with a form of end plate or wing-like appendage that would maximize its beneficial effect.

☐ Consistent with the advances in keel design . . . there was a corresponding computer development of a compatible hull form, which exploited the advantages offered by the keel. . . .

☐ To complete the effort, there was produced by the computer at NSMB a set of full-scale lines of the yacht plus full-scale templates from the computer of all frames and the plating. This was done, and the entire package was then shipped to Australia.

Van Oossanen later denied the remarks he allegedly made to van Rijn and Wil Valentijn. Johan Valentijn is convinced that van Oossanen wasn't aware at the time of the America's Cup rule that a challenging boat should be designed by nationals of the country she represents.

On August 24 the New York Yacht Club sent Cup Committee member Richard Latham, and Wil Valentijn, to Wageningen. In a letter to Dr. M. W. C. Oosterveld (Oossanen's superior), Latham outlined his version of what happened at the meeting. Wrote Latham: "I had with me at the August 24th meeting a draft of an affidavit, per copy enclosed [quoted above], which, it was believed, accurately reflected the statements made by Dr. van Oossanen at the earlier meeting on August 10, 1983. The accuracy of those reported statements already had been confirmed by Mr. Wil Valentijn and Mr. Antoon J. van Rijn, both of whom were present at such earlier meeting. After again emphasizing that my mission was not to 'put words in Dr. van Oossanen's mouth,' but rather to assure that there were no inaccuracies in his reported statements, I asked him to read carefully the draft.

"He did so, after which he said that the contents of the draft were basically correct and that he could only offer minor corrections. I then asked him to point out each correction, indicating I would make *any* changes he requested."

When it came time to sign the document, Latham reviewed the NYYC rule about who should design the boat. Valentijn says he wanted to make sure van Oossanen and his boss, Dr. M. Oosterveld, understood the consequences of signing—that it would be evidence that the Australians had violated the rule that the boat be designed by an Australian.

At that point, van Oossanen wouldn't sign, Valentijn says. He refused on the grounds that Lexcen was his friend. And he said that even though the information in the affidavit was true, he didn't want to see *Australia II* lose its chance to win the America's Cup.

Immediately after this visit, Dr. van Oossanen sent an angry telex to Warren Jones, manager of the *Australia II* syndicate. He said, in part, that the "affidavit contained many incorrect statements which attempted to suggest that Ben Lexcen was not solely responsible for the design of *Australia II*.

"I refused to sign the document as the contents was [*sic*] incorrect. What is more disturbing to me is that the New York Yacht Club representatives asked me to sign this affidavit knowing that the contents is [*sic*] incorrect, because they were told so by me once before.

" . . . Mr. Latham further informed me that the New York Yacht Club was considering challenging the design of *Australia II* based on work done with the NSMB and NLR Aerospace Laboratory here. There would be absolutely no truth to a claim that *Australia II* was designed to any extent by anyone other than Mr. Lexcen. I told him that we acted solely pursuant to Mr. Lexcen's directions at all times. I further informed Mr. Latham that the computer support work provided by NLR Aerospace Laboratory and tank testing by NSMD for Mr. Lexcen is similar to the computer support work and tank testing provided by the Delft University of Technology here to the designer of *Magic* and *Liberty* [Johan Valentijn] in 1981."

In retrospect, Johan Valentijn insists that the country-of-origin rule was violated by the Australians, but there wasn't much anyone could do about it. "Ben Lexcen is a nice guy," says Valentijn. "And I have no doubt that he's a genius. But this stuff is high-tech. It's not something you just dream up."

Even though they had given up on the Dutch connection, the NYYC's America's Cup Committee didn't give up on the important issue of Keelgate. Committee attorney James Michael prepared a three-page "certification of compliance" affidavit that the committee wanted the Australians to sign just prior to the start of the America's Cup series on September 13. The Australians refused.

Cup Committee chairman Bob McCullough presented the document to Australian syndicate chairman Alan Bond on September 11, the day before the official America's Cup Captain's Meeting. The meeting was scheduled for Rosecliff, a Newport Preservation Society mansion, in the early evening. The affidavit, full of "whereases" and "therefores," spelled out in detail certain assumptions* concerning the design process of *Australia II*. By agreeing to the 10 points delineated in the document, the Australians would have stated publicly—under penalty of perjury—that they had complied with the "Conditions" governing the races. Bond didn't sign.

When McCullough hit a dead end with the Australians, he went to William Fesq, former commodore of the Royal Sydney Yacht Squadron and liaison chairman for all the challengers. McCullough showed Fesq the affidavit and told him the story of how the *Australia II* syndicate wouldn't sign it. At that point, McCullough reportedly said to Fesq: "Find another challenger." That was two days before the America's Cup Races were to begin, and Fesq had little sympathy. He refused to consider a challenger other than *Australia II*. McCullough, frustrated and demoralized, went back to the committee with news of yet another Australian bushwhacking.

The Cup Committee met the next day aboard *Summertime*, the luxury

---

*See Appendix A for full text of affidavit.

motor yacht owned by committee member Bus Mosbacher. The meeting was held two hours before the America's Cup Captain's Meeting, to which both defenders and challengers were invited. Victor Romagna, secretary of the America's Cup Committee, says that members were convinced of allegations that the Australians cheated in designing *Australia II*. But they had run out of time, and the question before them that day on *Summertime* was whether to let the whole thing drop or keep pressing. In fact, the decision to be made was whether to proceed with a match between *Liberty* and *Australia II* or cancel the America's Cup Races. Cancel the America's Cup Races! "We were in a tight spot," Romagna says. "We didn't want to appear to be spoiling it for the sake of spoiling it, but we were convinced the Australians had overlooked nearly every rule."

A few members of the nine-man committee were absent, but those who were there had a good idea of where each man stood. "We went around the room, and everyone said their piece," Romagna recalls. "Then, all of a sudden, the discussion came to a shuddering halt. At that point, if we did vote, it was clear that four members agreed to continue, and five wanted to pull out."

Romagna declined to say how the members aligned themselves, but he made clear that he wanted to force a confrontation. "We didn't have the guts to stand up and say we won't race," Romagna says of that meeting. "...And so we just folded up our tents and went off into oblivion."

He says that members who backed down seemed concerned about the public outcry that would develop if the New York Yacht Club stopped the racing at that point. He concedes that the committee's biggest problem all summer was its inability to convey to the press and public the reservations it had over how the Australians went about designing *Australia II*. Just when the committee thought they had concrete evidence—getting three Dutch engineers, for example, to agree to sign documents confirming that they helped Lexcen design the keel—the rug was pulled out from under them. Romagna alleges that higher-ups within the Dutch organization quashed the attempt to get signatures.

On the day of the Captain's Meeting, the Cup Committee showed up powerless by its own decree. Bond agreed to sign a statement, but it was a whitewashed version of the Michael affidavit. It said, in effect, that he agreed to the "Conditions" for the America's Cup as stated in the "blue book" that governs the races. The language in the book is loosely written in regard to rules for designing a boat. It states in Section 12 that: "Yachts shall comply in every respect with the requirements regarding construction, sails and equipment contained in the Deed of Gift and the Interpretive Resolutions applying to national origin of design and construction."

The Deed of Gift itself is vague. The document, drawn up between

George L. Schuyler and the NYYC, is filed with the Supreme Court of the State of New York. Changes to the deed must go through the court. Since Schuyler first signed the deed over to the club in 1857, it has been amended twice (1882 and 1887), and has gone through three sets of interpretations (1958, 1980, and 1982). A resolution adopted in 1962 was later rescinded.

The key clause in the deed relating to the 1983 skirmish relates to the design of the challenging boat. The deed says that it must be "constructed" in the challenging country. The 1958 change to the deed interprets this to mean "designed and built. . . ." Designed in a country means that "the designers of the yacht's hull, rig and sails shall be nationals of that country. . . ."

The affidavit the Cup Committee wanted the Australians to sign was far more detailed than that. Whether the *Australia II* syndicate was guilty of deception or not, there was no doubt it was an intimidating document. The content was almost constructionist in style; it was like rewriting the Constitution to fit the circumstances. For example, the fourth statement guaranteed that the computer programs the Australians used at the Netherlands Ship Model Basin were standard programs used at that facility for model testing. It implied what could not be used: "No proprietary or confidential computer programs were developed for or made available to Ben Lexcen or the *Australia II* syndicate for use in developing by computer the design of the keel, hull and/or rig of *Australia II*."

It was clear from reading the affidavit that the NYYC wanted to pin down its distrust of the design. It states: "Whereas: information available to the New York Yacht Club has raised certain questions regarding *Australia II*'s compliance with said Section 12 [of the race Conditions], as to which the Royal Perth Yacht Club, the *Australia II* syndicate, and the designer of *Australia II* desire to provide such clairifications and assurances as will insure that the New York Yacht Club has fulfilled its obligation, as trustee under the Deed of Gift, to it, 'that it will faithfully and fully see that the foregoing conditions are fully observed and complied with by any contestant for the said Cup.' "

The Cup Committee had asked the *Freedom* syndicate to sign a similar document, which it reportedly did. It was normal procedure to ask challengers to sign statements agreeing to the "Conditions" of the Cup. But it was unusual to have a syndicate's compliance with the "Conditions" spelled out in such detail. For whatever reason, the Australians wouldn't bite. Lexcen says that by the end of the summer the Australian syndicate already had spent $75,000 "on New York lawyers" to confront allegations from the NYYC.

The Cup Committee was persistent in its effort to unearth the origin of the keel. But American critics claim it was "too little, too late." The Michael affidavit, surfacing as it did only hours before the races were to begin, lends a certain amount of credence to the criticism that it was too late. But it may have been too much rather than too little: the Australians were asked to swear that Ben Lexcen was sole designer of *Australia II* without "foreign consultants"; that Lexcen supervised the tank testing; that neither the Netherlands Ship Model Basin nor the Aerospace Laboratory added any design concepts that affected the outcome of *Australia II*; that the Dutch patent application listing Ben Lexcen as the inventor of the keel was correct; and that the hull was built and lofted (full-size design plan) in Australia.

Other guarantees related to equipment on board the boat. For example, the NYYC wanted to affirm that the design details on an American-made mast extrusion were Ben Lexcen's and that the computers and electronics on *Australia II* either were standard "shelf items" or, if custom-built, were made by Australians. Finally, the affidavit wanted the syndicate and the Royal Perth Yacht Club, as represented by Commodore Peter Dalziell, to swear that each of them had complied, and would continue to comply, with the race "Conditions." Spaces were left for Dalziell to sign, along with Alan Bond, Ben Lexcen, and Warren Jones.

Romagna says that 40 minutes after the Captain's Meeting, written proof was available to the committee that *Australia II* received an American-made mast that was designed in detail by a U.S. company. It was legal under the rules to use American extrusions (12-Meter masts are made in three parts), but it was up to each challenger to design how the metal fit together and was rigged. The club may or may not have had a case. Lexcen was seen tinkering with an American-made set of spar extrusions on the waterfront one day in midsummer. He had ripped off all the fittings, complaining that they weren't strong enough for his tastes, and that he would design a better mast himself. He was further angered by the fact that he could only order a fully rigged mast, rather than just the extrusions. He felt it was the company's way of making extra money. As it lay on its side at Newport Offshore Ltd., all that was left were the three lengths of mast that Lexcen apparently had sealed together himself. Lexcen, who served an apprenticeship as a machinist in his youth, was hand-tooling new fittings for the spar.

How many of the other NYYC allegations are true remains to be seen. Fritz Jewett, chairman of the *Freedom* syndicate, says he was bitterly disappointed when the NYYC halted its investigation of the Australian design process. "They put expediency ahead of principle," Jewett says.

"We were counting on the New York Yacht Club to represent us in these issues, and as far as we were concerned, the New York Yacht Club let us down."

Romagna is convinced that it is only a matter of time before what he perceives to be the true story is told. In the meantime, he has no aspirations about trying to get the America's Cup back. He says that Cup Committee members who resisted his pleadings to pull out of the America's Cup match with *Australia II* have had second thoughts. Some have indicated they wished they'd persisted, despite the certainty of a public scandal. "I want to get out of it and stay out of it," Romagna says about further involvement with the America's Cup. "I don't want to have anything to do with a situation where you have to cheat to win . . .

"We don't want it back," he says of the America's Cup. "It's just so degraded now. It's . . . it's busted!"

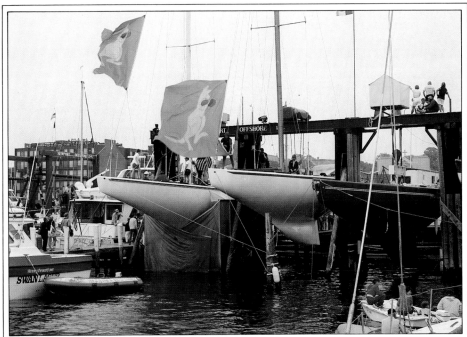

Above are three foreign challengers. From left to right: *Australia II, Challenge 12,* and *Azzurra.* At left is Ben Lexcen posing on a wing of his famous keel; and at right is John Bertrand, skipper of *Australia II.* Below left is the high-tech keel again, and below is Alan Bond being jubilant with the Cup.

Australia II is seen moments before the start of the first America's Cup Race. The Australian boat won the start this day and led *Liberty,* seen on the same day in the next spread,
by eight seconds at the first mark. On the second reach, *Liberty,* showing the only speed

advantage she seemed to have, passed the challenger to lead at the third mark by a slim 16 seconds. Then *Australia* showed a side she wasn't supposed to have: she romped downwind until a steering-gear failure—seemingly—gave the race to the Americans.

At left, *Liberty* wins the second race. Above is a rare look at the NYYC's America's Cup Committee. Below left is Dennis Conner, and below are ranking members of the *Freedom* Syndicate: Tom Whidden, Conner, Ed du Moulin, Halsey Herreshoff, and John Marshall.

Above, the beautiful *Defender*, Tom Blackaller's charge, surges upwind during a trials race. Nothing they did to *Defender*, however—and she was under the torch more than any other Twelve in Newport—could make her go fast. The result of sailing a slow boat is seen below as Blackaller is consoled by friends after his *Defender* was excused from the action. At right is Blackaller's tactician, Gary Jobson. Below right is John Kolius, who was named skipper of the aged *Courageous*. Age notwithstanding, *Courageous,* on the next page, gave Dennis Conner and *Liberty* a summer full of trouble in the defense trials.

Above, crew members on *Defender* are seen in the midst of a spinnaker change. In front of them is stablemate *Courageous* in an orientation *Defender* saw much too much of— ahead and doing better in the defense trials. Below, *Liberty* leads *Courageous* in their last meeting of the summer. At the end of this day, *Liberty* would be named the defender.

Above, journalists from around the world view the action from the *New Englander II*. Left, the *Liberty* crew celebrate being named the defender from the deck—and off the deck—of their stablemate *Freedom*. Below, the Australians win something called the Louis Vuitton trophy in a contest sailed against *Victory 83* just before they were chosen to meet the Americans in September.

On the preceding spread, *Liberty* and *Australia II* spar before the start of the seventh and final race. Owen Torrey, of Ulmer Sails, has described this moment as the "mating dance of the lead-bottomed money-gobblers." Conner won this particular "mating

dance'' by a commanding eight seconds. On this page is the moment that changed history. *Australia II,* by sailing lower and faster than *Liberty* on the fifth leg, takes the lead. A leg later she took the America's Cup in the seventh Cup race on September 26, 1983.

On the third leg of the first race, *Liberty* makes her move on *Australia II.* At the moment *Australia* took *Liberty* up, to protect her lead, the white boat lost steering and broached. *Liberty* sailed around the crippled challenger to win the race by 1 minute and 10 seconds.

"In all my years of designing, I've learned that if you have a bad boat, you are stuck with a bad boat. You can work on it and work on it, but it will never become a superboat..."

—JOHAN VALENTIJN,
DESIGNER OF FOUR 12 METERS, INCLUDING *LIBERTY*

CHAPTER 10
The Cream Rises to the Top

In an America's Cup summer, August is the cruelest month. With millions of dollars on the line, as well as so many highly prized egos, it was not surprising that high pressure characterized the start of August's Final Trials. The skippers and crews of the three American yachts were aware that the last boat standing would defend the America's Cup in September, and each did what had to be done to be chosen. They hadn't come this far and given up two years of their lives to be good losers. Even *Courageous'* skipper, John Kolius, who in June seemed so perfectly poised, was accused in July of being overconfident. So he regrouped, and once again assumed his well-practiced cool. "We're taking it one day at a time," he said after winning the first three of four races in August. "Every race is so close, you just can't get overthrilled."

Tom Blackaller and Gary Jobson were defensive, covering for what was obvious—that *Defender* was within days of being eliminated as a contender. Dennis Conner kept moving forward—his characteristic direction—but he was haunted by a deepening realization that *Australia II* was turning out to be even better than she was rumored to be. Before he could face that colossal problem, though, he had to prove that his *Liberty* was better than the other two American Twelves. He had more or less dismissed *Defender* as a viable competitor; but *Courageous* was another matter. She seemed unwilling to go without a fight, and time was running out. There was so much to do.

What could not be ignored was that the fate of the three American boats was in the hands of the New York Yacht Club's America's Cup Committee, whose job it was to choose a boat to defend the America's Cup by September 8. The *Liberty* team felt sure that it was the favorite. The

NYYC felt threatened by what appeared to be its most potent challenger ever, and much of the *Liberty* team, which had been there in 1980 with *Freedom,* had been bloodied in battle. They had not been found wanting. They were also well-known to the committee. "I think [this familiarity] was an advantage as far as communication was concerned," Fritz Jewett, *Freedom*'s syndicate chairman, offered in retrospect. "You know the people [Cup Committee members], and you feel you can pick up the phone and call. When I first came here in '74, I thought they were next to God. They were up there on a pedestal, and you came at their request. Otherwise, you didn't talk to them. Subsequently, I learned that they're very human, and there are very appropriate areas in which you can talk to them.

"As a matter of fact, I think it's only prudent to do so—to make darn sure they know what your crew is all about, what you've got going for your sail program; and they ought to understand why you think your hardware is better than the other guy's ... My point is, we initiated the communication much of the time."

Jewett says that his syndicate approached the committee in the same way in 1980, when it defended with *Freedom.* "The consensus of the whole group was that we should stick with our program," he says. "The same thing this year. We took the initiative to talk to those people on the committee and tell them what we were doing. And I see nothing wrong with that. I think, in the final analysis, they're going to pick the boat and the skipper they think are most likely to cope with whatever's going to happen in those conditions that year. I think the fact that they picked Ted Turner, who was not exactly popular in 1977, was a pretty good confirmation of that."

Bitter feelings between the syndicates often deflected attention from the racing in August, which on occasion was inspired. The crewmen on *Defender,* in particular, were rankled by what they perceived to be an increasingly cozy relationship between the *Liberty* team and the Cup Committee. In part, they were right. Men like Jewett, who is a member of the NYYC board of trustees, Dennis Conner, Halsey Herreshoff, and Johan Valentijn were seen more than once sitting on the upper deck of *Fox Hunter II* having comfortable chats with committee members before the start of a race. No one could tell if it was racing they were discussing, or whether it was new information on the continuing keel controversy. Whatever it was, it became apparent in August that *Liberty* was first among equals.

The public battle over *Liberty*'s multiple-rating certificates and the Cup Committee's admitted complicity in this matter widened the gap even further. Increasingly, the *Defender* team was pushed onto the periphery of

August's events, both on the water and ashore. (The leadership on *Courageous*, wisely enough, kept its distance from this particular storm.) Both Dennis Conner and Gary Jobson had their combative moments, drawn from the same source: frustration. Conner took a wild poke at the Australians in mid-August, accusing them of "sandbagging" when they lost a race to the British. He surmised that the loss was an effort to obscure the threat of their secret keel. That one turned into an inside joke at the *Liberty* dock later in the week. "We were sandbagging," Conner's tactician, Tom Whidden, quipped as he strolled down the dock the day *Courageous* led *Liberty* in two races.

Jobson, meanwhile, seemed the most frustrated, both personally and professionally. It was becoming clearer every day that, regardless of major surgery, *Defender* was going nowhere fast, except perhaps to oblivion. She only showed speed in very light winds. In any breeze above nine knots, *Liberty* and *Courageous* were gone. Being aboard the slowest boat was not easy for Jobson, who had careened his way into sailing stardom as tactician with Ted Turner in 1977, watched a preoccupied Turner falter in 1980, and pinned his hopes on *Defender* in 1983.

Finally, it was as if Jobson couldn't contain himself any longer. He lashed out at Conner with undisguised ferocity. He accused him of lying about his boat's multiple certificates. Then he attacked Conner over an August 25 race in which *Defender* lost to *Liberty* by one second. The *Defender* crew blamed that loss on an errant shrimp boat that got in the way just before the finish. Conner's comment was succinct: "What shrimp boat?" Finally Jobson suggested that Conner "subconsciously" wanted to lose in the trial races so he wouldn't be responsible for losing the America's Cup to *Australia II*.

These intramural tempests disturbed the America's Cup Committee, which was not without its own problem: the looming threat of *Australia II*. McCullough summoned Conner and Jobson to *Fox Hunter II* one day in late August and "scolded" them for their public outbursts. "Dennis and I were alone on the bridge for a few minutes afterwards," Jobson says. "He just looked at me and said: 'I'm going to get you for this.' " To this day, the two are bitter enemies, each scarred in his own way by a summer in which the heat of competition had burst into flame.

Competition on the water was nearly as intense. Despite her preferred status, *Liberty* still had to keep winning to be selected, and that wasn't always easy. *Courageous* and *Liberty* went at it in heated matches that had *Courageous* improving with each race she sailed during the waning days of August. Besides, *Courageous* had other things going for her as well: she had history on her side—two successful Cup defenses—and a certain amount of nostalgia for the "old boat." In addition, John Kolius, as the golden boy of the summer of '83 and a newcomer to the scene, exhibited the qualities the committee demanded in a defender: an uncanny sense of match-racing tactics, a killer instinct on the course, and the good sense to avoid extracurricular warfare ashore.

Courageous' only black mark in the eyes of the selection committee was a loss at the protest table after a collision with *Liberty* on August 23. Race officials were unimpressed with Kolius' explanation that Conner had tacked too close, forcing Kolius to steer *Courageous* into *Liberty*'s stern. It had been a close duel—one that exhibited the best in match-racing techniques—an aggressive interplay between two good men and two good boats. *Liberty* was working her way into the lead on the first weather leg. In her third attempt to clear *Courageous'* bow, *Liberty* headed over on starboard tack. She crossed, and then tacked back. Just as she was completing this maneuver, *Courageous*—on port—hesitated and then tried to tack under *Liberty*'s stern. Not only did she fail to clear, she left a six-inch hole in *Liberty*'s side and knocked out the backstay and antenna. To Conner's credit, *Liberty* continued racing.

Conner didn't appear overly concerned by the day's carnage. Repairs were made overnight, and *Liberty* was out to meet *Courageous* again the next day. The Cup Committee wanted to see the two boats together again, officially because thick fog had cut short the racing the day before. But also, as many insiders concluded, to allow *Liberty* and *Courageous* more time on the water together.

By this time hope had departed the *Defender* camp. Good sportsmanship and oft professed claims of good will and admiration for the *Courageous* crew ended in bitterness over what had happened—that the new blue boat, with all that talent, had turned out to be slower than the old white boat. Despite the fact that *Courageous* was a mere shadow of her former self—she had been reworked and overhauled too many times to count—she was still the "old boat." There may have been something in the fact that John Kolius never thought of her that way.

Then *Defender* performed something of a miracle on August 25 by winning three straight races against her stablemate, *Courageous*. Unfortunately, her fate was already written. Those races were sailed in light winds—mostly eight to nine knots—her forte. Two days later she was beaten by *Liberty* in winds of 17–22 knots. The committee had seen enough of the blue boat. "The men in the straw hats," as the waterfront called the Cup Committee members, arrived at the *Defender/Courageous* dock the afternoon of August 27 and politely excused *Defender* from further racing.

The next night, under cover of darkness, *Defender* left Newport—to be decommissioned, or so it was said. In the light of day, *Liberty* and

Courageous continued to battle one another with all the match-racing machismo they could muster. And that was plenty. The Cup Committee, it was obvious, wanted one or the other to show some clear indication of superiority. Meanwhile, it let them race; this could only improve whichever was selected. By this time *Courageous* had found some friends on the committee boat, too. She had proved herself competitive in every range of wind and her crew was well-behaved and well-liked.

Both syndicates, by this time, increased their efforts to win Cup Committee approval. Some of this went in strange directions. The first indication that something was up had come the morning of August 29. Questions arose as to why *Defender* was missing from her slip at Newport Offshore Ltd. They were met with unsatisfactory and evasive answers. "*Defender* has been taken to Cove Haven Marina [in Barrington, Rhode Island] to be disassembled..." Or, "No comment." Chuck Kirsch, *Defender/Courageous* syndicate chairman, hedged. "We're not going to try to play games with the press...," he said. "Now is not an appropriate time to talk."

Telling an America's Cup press corps that had sharpened its teeth on Keelgate to wait for a more "appropriate time" was like tossing a sirloin steak into a lion's den and telling the animals to leave it until morning. It didn't play. If the *Defender/Courageous* syndicate would not talk, others would. Jeremy McGeary, a designer with Pedrick Yacht Designs, was the first to discuss the matter. McGeary and his boss, *Defender* designer David Pedrick, had learned that morning that "their" boat had been taken to Cove Haven to have wings installed on the keel. The news came as a complete surprise to both. McGeary, who figured he had little more to lose than a reprimand from his boss, leaked the story to the press. Pedrick, meanwhile, rushed to Cove Haven to find out what was going on.

The plot unfolded through a bizarre twist of circumstances. Johan Valentijn had called Pedrick that morning to ask if he might use one of the group's $2,000 epoxy models of *Defender* for tank testing at M.I.T. Valentijn was working on a last-minute plan to add wings to the keel of *Freedom*. If the idea worked, he planned to add them to *Liberty*'s keel should she be selected to defend the America's Cup. Pedrick suggested that Valentijn check with the *Defender* syndicate—with either Kirsch or syndicate manager Max O'Meara. He did, and was told that the three-foot models belonged to the syndicate and as such were not available, even on loan.

Shortly after, Pedrick received a phone call from O'Meara, who inadvertently mentioned that wings were to be put on *Defender*. He learned that the syndicate had hired Sparkman & Stephens to develop wings, since they had already done some work on the idea. The plan apparently came from conversations between John Kolius, *Courageous* tactician John Bertrand, and Kirsch. The two crewmen reportedly stated that if their boat was chosen to defend the Cup, they wanted wings. They concluded that a winged boat might prove invaluable as a trial horse, and that perhaps those wings could be used as prototypes for wings on *Courageous,* should the idea prove successful. There wasn't much time to take such a radical step, but the American syndicates were scared of the winged marvel from Perth, were scared of each other, and were looking to curry favor with the America's Cup Committee, which likewise feared the potential of the Australian boat.

When Pedrick arrived at Cove Haven, he found *Defender* hauled out of the water and moved inside a large shed. A spinnaker cloth was draped around her underbody. No one seemed to be around. Pedrick, a soft-spoken man who looks more like a choirboy than a prominent naval architect, approached the Twelve he designed. He slipped his arm into the spot where the cloth separated, and pulled it apart. There was the keel, but there were no wings. Yet two holes were drilled where wings might be installed. At that point, Pedrick heard a voice behind him. It was Chuck Wilson, project manager while *Defender* was being built. He was a friend of Pedrick's, a man who had worked side by side with him as the boat was being built at Newport Offshore.

"I have been instructed not to let anybody in here, including you," Wilson said. There was a pause, then Wilson touched Pedrick on the arm and said; "I know how you feel, because we only learned about this yesterday."

When Pedrick returned to Newport, he went immediately to see Kirsch and O'Meara. They discussed what had happened and assured Pedrick that it was a last-minute decision done with great secrecy. Not even the *Defender* crew knew. Pedrick calmed down, but he was still angry that he had not been consulted. "Despite disagreements, I respect the efforts of the *Defender* group to do what they want in private," he said that night. "But one thing I will say—I am out of the 12-Meter business for 1983." *Defender* showed up in Newport two days later—with wings on her keel. The incident only crystallized feelings that Pedrick was harboring at that point—that the syndicate's habit of resisting his attempts to stay involved had happened once too often.

Pedrick had developed a solid working relationship with Blackaller and Jobson and the rest of the *Defender* crew. But he had found himself in the untenable position of having to convince the syndicate executive committee—of which Kirsch was chairman—that he was still needed once the design was complete and the boat had been built. The syndicate agreed to send Pedrick out to California only once during winter practice sessions in Newport Beach. He would have preferred to go more often; he felt he needed more time to evaluate *Defender*'s weak points. Instead, he learned about budget constraints. Pedrick was working on a fee-for-services basis.

When the boat was brought back to Newport in April, 1983, Pedrick had to convince Kirsch that his help was needed. The committee finally agreed, but its reluctance caused friction in the camp. "We were all in this together," Pedrick says. "If you can't do something as a 100 percent team effort, then you shouldn't try to develop an America's Cup campaign at all. That was one of the reasons why I decided not to go with Conner. I don't think Sparkman & Stephens and Valentijn had a whole lot of fun."

The day after Dave Pedrick visited *Defender* at Cove Haven, *Freedom* appeared at Newport Offshore with wings on her keel. Valentijn says in retrospect that he put them on partly to see what would happen and partly to appease the winged-keel mania within the syndicate. Valentijn says he was almost certain that attaching wings to an existing keel—rather than designing a keel to fit wings—would only slow the boat down. "But...I didn't want to be the spoiler of the party," says Valentijn. "So when Dennis said, 'Hey, can't we make some fins for *Freedom*?' I said, 'Sure. You can have them in a few days if you'd like.' So, we fiddled around with a bunch of stuff, and three days later we had fins on the boat." Valentijn says he had discussed the idea of wings with Conner many times before, and more or less convinced him that it wouldn't work to put wings on an existing boat. "I think he just wanted to have proof of it," Valentijn says.

While designers fiddled with wings, the two remaining American boats continued racing. The finale of the Final Trials was marked by a series of races in which the lead changed several times within each match. The Cup Committee frequently ran two races each day, abandoning them at will by raising the familiar checkered code flag. In the end, *Liberty* established herself as the superior boat, able to beat *Courageous* in the critical range of wind speed: 7–17 knots. In anything above that, *Courageous* appeared to have a slight edge. In the last eight matches after *Defender* was dismissed, *Liberty* won six and lost only two. On September 2, the cream had risen to the top. *Liberty* was chosen to defend the America's Cup.

It had been an epic battle, rife with uncertainty. There was no such thing as an easy win; only a tough—and sometimes bitter—defeat. Depending on whether abandoned races were included in total scores, race results from June to September looked dramatically different. The Cup Committee insisted that they weren't counting; they only wanted to know who was winning in the end. Abandoned races were frequent, since the committee was presumably interested in which boat rounded the weather mark first. The summer's unofficial win-loss record, including abandonments, was: *Liberty,* 39–19; *Courageous,* 20–35; *Defender,* 19–24.

The *Liberty* team fought tenaciously. It hadn't been an easy Cup summer for Dennis Conner, certainly not as easy as the summer of 1980. This time he suffered many more setbacks, but each time forged ahead again. Race by race. Crisis by crisis. It had been disheartening for him to find out in midsummer of 1982 that both of his new boats, *Magic* and *Spirit of America,* were slow. He had been blinded by the fact that he had only sailed those two boats against each other. *Freedom* was out of commission. It wasn't until he brought *Freedom* out of the shed that he realized that both boats were slower than his 1980 defender of the America's Cup. Valentijn says that they weren't just slower—they were "disastrously" slower. Valentijn knew that *Magic* was somewhat sluggish sailing against *Spirit* in the early part of the summer of '82. With that in mind, Conner decided to test *Spirit* with *Freedom* first.

"It was a most beautiful day," Valentijn remembers. "There was about 18, maybe 20 knots of apparent breeze. We put a beautiful mainsail on *Freedom* and the best mainsail on *Spirit.* Then they started to tack. We were counting. It was *Freedom* gaining . . . *Freedom* gaining . . . *Freedom* gaining. In 10 minutes, *Freedom* had gained seven boat lengths!

"I said, 'Dennis, look!'

"He said, 'This can't be right! We must do it again . . . '

"We did it again, counting exactly the same way.

" 'My God!' I said to Dennis. 'We don't have one problem, we have two problems.' "

Valentijn says that the disparity in speed was very discouraging. Both he and Conner knew that if *Spirit* was that much slower than *Freedom,* then *Magic* must be worse. When it's one or two boat lengths, you can make relatively minor adjustments to make up the difference, Valentijn says, but when it's six or seven it's a catastrophe. "It was just horrible! It was a rude awakening." That was when Valentijn decided to cut the entire after end out of *Magic* in an effort to make the boat faster. Even with major surgery the boat wasn't good enough.

"In all my years of designing, I've learned that if you have a bad boat, you are stuck with a bad boat," he says. "You can work on it and work on it, but it will never become a superboat."

Sparkman & Stephens, which had designed *Spirit,* drew plans to rectify the problems by changing the design of the keel and shifting the lead ballast higher up. The result, says Valentijn, was that the boat lost a great deal of its stability. She was faster in light air, but in anything above 18 knots of apparent wind she heeled too much and slowed down. S&S has maintained that the fault lay with Dennis Conner, who overruled their original recommendations for the boat.

Late in the summer of '82, Conner decided that he had only one other choice: to build another boat. At the same time, he would ask S&S to redesign *Spirit* in time for winter practice sailing against *Freedom* in San Diego. If the changes were good enough, there was still a chance *Spirit* might sail as the America's Cup contender. Conner told Valentijn from the beginning of the campaign that there was always the possibility of building three new boats. But first he wanted to take a chance and build two extreme Twelves—boats at both ends of the design spectrum. Hence, *Magic* and *Spirit of America*. When it came time to build the third boat, the decision created factions within the syndicate and a virtual standoff between Valentijn and Bill Langan, the chief designer at S&S. (See Chapter 6: "America's Cup Yacht Design.")

Valentijn's version of these events is different from that of Langan. Valentijn talked about the negotiated decision to work together on a new boat, but with Valentijn acting as project manager. S&S was to be responsible for the changes to *Spirit*, Valentijn says, and both parties agreed, but both were highly reluctant. Valentijn went into the meeting thinking that he was to design the new boat using S&S as consultants. He came out of the meeting upset over the compromise. "I was very strongly against combining design offices together to design one single boat," he says. "I felt that if that was going to be the deal, I didn't want any part of it. I knew that S&S would be looking after themselves, and I would probably want to be looking out for myself, so it wouldn't work."

By the end of the meeting, the *Freedom* syndicate had persuaded Valentijn to go along with the combined effort. Halsey Herreshoff agreed to work with Valentijn—largely as a liaison between him and S&S. "Halsey would be the neutral ground to help sort out any problems," Valentijn says, adding that it seemed like a good solution. Valentijn says that there were subsequent meetings in Newport, at which time the group examined the performance of other 12 Meters, such as *Courageous* and *Freedom*—successful 12 Meters—and compared them to *Magic* and *Spirit*. Finally, they came to a few general conclusions as to how *Liberty* should be shaped.

Valentijn is adamant that he never received the line drawings for S&S 12-Meter designs. "The only thing they gave us was some material on *Freedom*," he says. "But *Freedom* was a syndicate boat anyway, so that didn't matter. They claim they gave us *Enterprise* and *Courageous* and *Spirit*. But they never gave us any of that stuff." Valentijn confirms what Langan said about exchanging drawings—about Valentijn's wanting to look at the lines of S&S 12 Meters in exchange for line drawings of *Australia I*, *France 3*, and *Magic*.

The S&S team went back to its offices in New York to consider what had been discussed. It was agreed that Mario Tarabocchia, a highly respected and experienced draftsman at S&S, would start on the lines, but only after Tarabocchia visited Newport and consulted with Valentijn. He never came. Nearly three weeks had passed. Conner encouraged Valentijn and Herreshoff to visit S&S in New York, and to check on the progress of *Spirit* while they were at it.

Valentijn says he met several times with S&S after that to discuss the work on *Spirit*. Eventually, the *Spirit* modifications cost the syndicate about $100,000. Valentijn insists that they were never done right, largely because S&S lost interest in the project. S&S felt the opposite—that they had done their best under extremely difficult circumstances.

The *Liberty* project was another story. When Valentijn and Herreshoff arrived in New York in early September, they found that Tarabocchia had completed the drawings, but they didn't look much like what had been discussed in Newport. "He rolled out a drawing, and it was a completely new 12 Meter," Valentijn says. "It was a very nice boat. But here the whole boat was designed. It was, in general, along the parameters of what the syndicate had discussed. But that wasn't the point. They had gone ahead and not given me a chance to provide any input."

Valentijn says he was impressed with Tarabocchia's work. He had drawn a beautiful Twelve. It incorporated ideas Valentijn both liked and disliked. He went back to Newport and thought about it for three days. Then, when he pulled his nerve together, he went to Dennis Conner and quit. "I don't feel part of the boat," he told Conner. "I don't feel I've been consulted. It's a Sparkman & Stephens boat. It's fine. So I've decided—I quit. I'll finish my commitment to you over the next month or two. After that, you can have Sparkman & Stephens take care of it. I can't be part of it, and I don't want to be part of it. I don't want to work for Sparkman & Stephens because I worked for them 10 years ago."

Valentijn felt rejected at this point, as Langan had felt only a few months before in the meeting with the *Freedom* syndicate and Valentijn. "I felt I had to stand up for my own principles, and one of my principles is that I'm not working for Sparkman & Stephens," says Valentijn. "I was supposed to be co-designer on the job, but here I was just given a little bone in the end—'Well, your name is on the bottom, and here, just be quiet.' But I didn't feel like that."

Valentijn's resignation apparently shook the syndicate. The next morning, syndicate manager Ed du Moulin reportedly spent three hours trying to bring him back. Valentijn remained firm. The next day, Valentijn ran into Conner, along with Fritz Jewett and his wife Lucy on the *Freedom* dock. They asked him if he'd changed his mind. He said no. Then Conner said to him: "If we give you the boat by yourself, would that change your mind?"

"I'll have to think about that," Valentijn replied.

"How long do you have to think about it?" Conner asked.

"I'll think about it for a minute or two," said Valentijn.

"So okay. Start thinking," replied Conner.

"All right. I have two minutes. If you'll give me the boat by myself, yes, I'll do the boat. I'll be part of the team. I'll design the boat and just be here until we win or lose the America's Cup."

Conner agreed and said that he'd tell S&S somehow that the deal was off. It was soon afterwards that Langan received the phone call from Fritz Jewett—the bad news which Langan remembers brought "stunned silence" to the S&S offices in New York.

Valentijn went ahead and designed *Liberty*, which he says was nothing like the S&S drawing. "Even though I finally designed *Liberty*, I felt pretty bad about the way the whole thing went," Valentijn says. "It's really sad as far as I'm concerned... I think he [Bill Langan] has some right to be bitter, but I think he should go back and try to understand what happened. If he can understand what happened, maybe he'll be able to understand why it happened that way. It was not because of me—I was really pushing the job to Sparkman & Stephens because I felt there were so many in the syndicate who wanted them to have an S&S boat instead of somebody else's boat... I said, 'If that helps you raise money, please go ahead. Your campaign is more important than me.'"

Valentijn says that the final *Liberty* design was an amalgamation of ideas between Dennis Conner and himself. He says that the boat began to take shape, oddly enough, in a discussion the two had in early 1982 as they were driving back to Newport from Old Saybrook, Connecticut, where *Magic* was being built. Conner pointed out that, since the design plans for *Magic* and *Spirit* were so different, chances of having a good boat and a bad boat, or two bad boats, certainly existed. "Say both boats are bad," Conner reportedly said to Valentijn. "How should we put this new boat together?"

The two decided on the boat's design characteristics: the amount of freeboard (the height of the hull above the water), length, sail area—all the basic parameters. "You know, the basic *Liberty* is exactly those parameters that we talked about nearly a year before," says Valentijn. He concedes that part of the reason Conner appeared to side with him rather than S&S is because Valentijn was willing to devote his full time to a 12-Meter project. Valentijn says he would also like to believe that it was because Conner thought him more innovative.

"If you create a new toy," Valentijn says, "no matter how busy you are, you're going to find time to go out the first couple of days on that new toy. A new toy, and a very expensive campaign to come... I felt I still had to prove myself, and I still feel I always have to prove myself, so I work so much harder, I think, at trying to be successful...I think that's why Dennis picked me over S&S. If I was in his shoes, I would think the chances of having a good boat from S&S or myself are pretty even.''

There was little doubt that Conner demanded a lot from his designers. A perfectionist himself, he required the same exhaustive dedication from the people who worked with him. Langan says S&S had a business to run and didn't have the time Conner seemed to need. "All he wanted was somebody holding his hand," Valentijn says. "If you really look at it, the people who are successful—or the boats that are successful—have their designers with them. Not that designers are the greatest assets in the world. Some are a pain. But, at the same time, they can be extremely useful, at least more than half the time.

"These things have become so high-tech and so demanding that, to be successful, you have to be involved all the way or not at all.''

The friction between S&S and Johan Valentijn was just one of the onshore battles Conner found himself fighting in his rise to the top. Once the design dilemma was resolved, the next crisis was which boat to choose, *Liberty* or *Freedom*. *Freedom* still was faster upwind in a breeze, but *Liberty* had a slight edge in light-to-moderate breezes and, according to some, downwind. The syndicate had been tinkering with *Liberty* since bringing her to Newport in late spring. By the beginning of the June trials, Valentijn had shifted lead around in the keel, moving out most of the boat's internal ballast and putting it lower in the boat to improve upwind performance. Four feet was shaved from the stern to save weight, and the keel was moved forward. She became faster downwind, but she was still mushy in a breeze upwind.

Conner waited until the last minute before deciding which boat to enter in the June trials. Then he announced that it would be *Liberty*. Valentijn says the idea was to sail *Liberty* in June while they worked on *Freedom;* then sail *Freedom* in July so they could work on *Liberty*. In the Final Trials, they planned to race again with *Liberty*—and ultimately to win the right to defend the America's Cup with her. The plan seemed workable, but it exploded in their faces. In modifying *Freedom* during June, the syndicate overlooked a small change from 1980 in the international 12-Meter class rule. It changed the weight of a penalty so that it was no longer worthwhile to build a Twelve with a low freeboard. Thereafter, boats built with a low freeboard incurred a severe penalty in the rating formula. This new minus factor was severe enough to discourage any designer from considering it.

Freedom was built with a low freeboard before the rule changed. The boat was allowed to stay that way, since she was protected under a grandfather clause in the rule. The low freeboard turned out to be

Freedom's greatest asset. It lowered the boat's center of gravity and made her more stable, especially upwind in a breeze. Ironically, the freeboard part of the rule was changed to make 12 Meters safer in heavy weather.

In the rush to make *Freedom* perform better in light winds, Conner agreed to various structural changes in the boat. Valentijn modified the bow, moved the rudder and shifted lead in the keel. Once the work was finished, he called Mark Vinbury, the American measurer, to recertify *Freedom* as a 12 Meter. Vinbury refused to do so. "You made a mistake," Vinbury reportedly told Valentijn. "I can no longer give you credit for the freeboard." What Valentijn and Conner had overlooked was the fact that the grandfather clause is only in effect if there are no structural changes made to the yacht. That wasn't true anymore with *Freedom*.

Valentijn was upset that Vinbury hadn't reminded him of the change in the rule before the changes to the boat were made. Vinbury supposedly knew ahead of time what the syndicate planned. Vinbury apologized, reportedly saying that he had intended to call and inform the syndicate of the penalty, but he forgot.

Realization of what had happened came as a shock. The syndicate was embarrassed, especially Valentijn and Conner, for letting such a gross error occur. Instead of changing *Freedom* back to the way she was, they left her. But she no longer qualified under the rule as a legal Twelve. To make her conform to the rule, Valentijn would have had to remove 30–35 square feet of sail area. This would have slowed the boat down dramatically—too much to be competitive. As a result, they sailed her as a trial horse against *Liberty*, leaving the sail area intact. Valentijn says it was a mixed blessing. *Freedom* improved in light air; and, as such, she was a better trial horse for *Liberty*. But *Freedom* could no longer compete as a contender. She was out of the real racing entirely.

That was a fleeting crisis. Another one continued to nag Conner throughout the summer. It involved trouble in San Diego with his drapery business. Conner had said in 1980 that he had to give up his private life in order to compete for the America's Cup. But he maintained that his family and his business carried on perfectly well without him. "I have a lot of understanding customers," he said then. "I don't think my being gone affects the quality of our work. It might affect the quality of our romancing the customers, but the day-to-day operation of the business does fine without me."

This didn't appear to be true in 1983. The business reportedly was in the midst of a legal battle with Conner throughout the Cup summer. Conner reportedly received a subpoena to appear in court the day the June trial races began. When he returned to San Diego in September, the whole thing came to a head. A company known as Design for Living, which reportedly has management ties with Conner's firm—Vera's Draperies—charged that Conner unfairly collected his salary from October, 1982, to March, 1983, when he was occupied with practice racing for the America's Cup.

In addition, the company claimed in a suit filed on June 17 that Conner held on to equipment that wasn't rightfully his. Conner maintained that he had bought it from Alan Raffee, his original business partner, who died in a plane crash in December, 1979. Raffee supported Conner in his sailing pursuits while he was alive, and the two amicably split the business, leaving certain commitments between them intact. When Raffee died, Raffee's children became executives of the company.

Conner was forced to neglect his business for nearly two years. It was one more worry that added to the pressure Dennis Conner was under during the summer of 1983. He insisted all along that he was committed to taking his campaign for the Cup one day at a time, race by race. Once the trials were over, he was relieved, even though the Cup races themselves loomed ahead. But by then Dennis Conner had done all that he could.

And despite the allegations of improprieties within the Australian syndicate, Conner respected John Bertrand and looked forward to sailing against him in a boat race.

"Prince Andrew revives a feeling of romance, and I do believe a lot of us have become cynical. He does strike me as having an heroic image in this age of cynicism..."

—EILEEN SLOCUM, A LIFETIME NEWPORTER
AND LEADING MEMBER OF ITS WEALTHY SUMMER COLONY

CHAPTER 11
The Party Circuit

Sophie Trevor, a 9-year-old child who has seen the world's rich and famous come and go through the front door of her grandparents' mansion on Bellevue Avenue in Newport, left the British *Victory* Ball last summer starry-eyed. The family, Mr. and Mrs. John J. Slocum, children and grandchildren, were seated at a table close to Prince Andrew and his entourage. The 23-year-old prince was visiting Newport for five days to see the 12 Meters under sail and to represent his father, Prince Philip, the Duke of Edinburgh, who was honorary patron of the ball. Neither he nor Queen Elizabeth II could attend, although both had visited Newport before.

When it came time for dinner—a hot buffet—Andrew picked up his dinner plate and joined the line to be served like anyone else. Thirty or more people were already in the queue when the prince casually walked up. At his side stood Sophie and her seven-year-old sister, Irene. Both girls knew who the stranger beside them was, and both looked up. Andrew reached over, put his hand on Sophie's head and his arm around Irene, and said hello.

"What's your name," he said to Irene, who was nearly speechless.

"Irene."

"And yours?" he said to Sophie.

"Sophia," she said, hardly able to contain her ecstasy.

The line was moving along by then, and Prince Andrew told the girls he would talk to them later. But later never came. Andrew, who was unquestionably the beau of the ball, was whisked away by the hordes of people who, even in so rarefied a society as Newport's, make demands on a prince.

In the meantime, Sophie had gathered a small bouquet of flowers for

Andrew—a blossom from one vase, a leaf from another—to take to him later. When she went to present it to him, he was gone.

Prince Andrew dazzled Newport. He was everything a prince should be—charming, courteous, debonair. Missing in Newport was his Koo Stark side—the brash-playboy, man-about-town image presented in the British press. Andrew attended to duty, and he seemed to have fun doing it. But doing it wasn't easy. A security force made up of State Department personnel and Andrew's own bodyguards followed him everywhere. Irish nationalists kept the agents on their toes by staging a nonviolent demonstration in front of Beechwood, the Newport mansion where the *Victory* Ball was held the night of July 15. About 100 members of Irish Northern Aid—a group opposed to the British presence in Northern Ireland—gathered on the street. Guests in formal attire—black tie and tuxedos for the men and glittering floor-length gowns among the women—swept by without incident. The group sang Irish songs and chanted resistance slogans. A leaflet handed out to passersby quoted George Washington: "To bigotry, no sanction. To persecution, no assistance."

Their presence put a slight crimp in the evening, a night that Peter de Savary wanted to have remembered as the party of the season. He had planned a ball that would outdo even the traditional and highly extravagant America's Cup Ball that was to come later in the summer. Tickets to the *Victory* Ball were expensive—$150 per person. De Savary issued an edict early on that even his crew had to pay, that it was for the good of the syndicate and the English-Speaking Union, which was co-sponsoring the event. By the time all was said and done, estimates ran as high as a quarter of a million dollars for the cost of de Savary's gala. In the end, crew members and staff got a break in the ticket price. They paid $50 each.

Newport has its fair share of cynics, and a few of them felt that the party was a further attempt by Peter de Savary to impress Newport. And, more importantly, to impress his countrymen with his ability to draw royalty to his doorstep. A follow-up *Victory* Ball at summer's end drew other royals: Prince Michael, Duke of Kent and the cousin of Queen Elizabeth II, and his wife, Princess Michael. But those nearest to de Savary dismissed the rumors as sour grapes on the part of those who couldn't get in. De Savary himself disputed the ripest of the rumors—that he was desperate to win the America's Cup so that, like Sir James Hardy, the former America's Cup skipper from Australia, Peter de Savary would also be knighted.

"I'm just not interested," he said at the beginning of the summer. "If I wanted to do that, it would be much easier to spend a half-million pounds and be done with it."

"Eight million dollars—a peerage," added an associate who overheard de Savary's remark, implying that de Savary could buy knighthood if he chose to do so. The $8 million was the amount de Savary said he planned to spend on the 1983 British challenge for the Cup.

De Savary agreed. "I'm doing this because it's never been done before," he said then. "Everyone told me it couldn't be done." Others have to take him at his word, and believe that the America's Cup was a greater prize for the British businessman than a peerage. The only thing that seemed certain about Peter de Savary was that he knew how to throw a party, and damn the costs.

The *Victory* Ball lasted until 4 o'clock the next morning. Guests nibbled on an après-midnight champagne breakfast fit for an English lord: eggs, bacon, smoked fish, minced kidneys, sausages, toast, and fresh fruit. The meal followed a staggering fireworks display launched from a barge anchored just in front of the oceanfront estate. The home, once owned by the Astor family, had seen extravagant parties in its turn-of-the-century heyday. But few could have rivaled this one with its international cast of the famous and the fortunate. A few neighbors along the famous Cliff Walk, which edges Beechwood, complained among themselves about the aggravation of noise so late in the night. But others took advantage of the preparty publicity to invite friends to their homes for a front-yard fireworks display that rivaled the best of the Fourth of July spectaculars.

Guests danced to the music of one of the most renowned society bands in America—Peter Duchin. And the Sonatas Steel Band from Trinidad was on hand for the young at heart—and body. But little could compare with the grand entrance of the Regimental Band of the Irish Guards, one of several military bands that brings pageantry to the day's routine at Buckingham Palace. Close to midnight, the guards marched through a giant hedge gate that had been crafted for the evening at the far end of the property. As the makeshift gate swung open, 50 or more local youths could be seen gathered along the oceanside embankment to catch a glimpse of the goings-on inside the festive grounds. After the musicians marched through—a file of bearskin hats and jet-black uniforms with red tassels and trim—the gate swung closed again and the curious faces disappeared in the darkness. The party kicked off a social season that Newport had not seen since the days of the robber barons in the late 1800s—the days when dinner meant a footman for every guest at the dining table and fun was being handed a silver trowel with which to dig for precious stones in a sand mound at the center of the table.

"It was the greatest summer ever," says Eileen Slocum, of 1983. "I have lived here every summer of my life, off and on, for all but two of my 67 years. This year was an abundance. There were more interesting and attractive people than ever before, more glamorous boats, more wonderful parties, more tension, more suspense, and more intrigue."

Mrs. Slocum's summers in Newport are by no means ordinary. The wealthy who flock to Newport are among the most powerful families in America, many of whom come every summer to nurture friendships that rise and fall with the seasons as family fortunes have swung through successive generations. Eileen Slocum's guest lists include people like Mr. and Mrs. Hugh D. Auchincloss, Mr. and Mrs. F. Warrington Gillet, Ambassador and Mrs. Wiley T. Buchanan, Jr., Mr. and Mrs. Dillon Ripley, Senator and Mrs. Charles Percy, General and Mrs. William Westmoreland, Lady Rothermere, Mr. and Mrs. William Wood-Prince, Mr. and Mrs. Russell Aitken, Princess Tassilo von Fuerstenburg, and Mr. and Mrs. John R. Drexel.

The difference this summer was that parts of the outside world entered the inner sanctum. To enjoy a summer night in Newport dancing across a dew-soaked lawn, sipping champagne, and watching the moon rise over dark ocean swells involved a cast of thousands. One need not have been rich to feel like a millionaire in Newport.

Prince Andrew spent his time doing many of the things other tourists do—sailing, visiting one of the Preservation Society "cottages" now open to the public, going to church on Sunday, and dining out. The big difference was that he motored around town in a creamy beige Rolls-Royce accompanied by carloads of bodyguards. He spent one evening having dinner with members of the New York Yacht Club's America's Cup Committee aboard their motor yacht *Fox Hunter II*. He was affable and fun-loving, not at all stuffy as many Americans expect British royalty to be. In fact, whenever the telephone rang on *Fox Hunter II,* which was hooked into lines at its dock on Goat Island, Andrew picked up the phone and said hello. At one point, a friend of committee chairman Bob McCullough was on the calling end, asking if "Bob" was there. Andrew said yes, and asked the man to please hang on. Then he called McCullough to the phone.

"I didn't know you had a Brit working for you now," the friend chided McCullough.

"Oh, no. That was my friend Andy," McCullough replied amidst a cabinful of stifled laughs.

The social schedule was hectic among the crowd of jet-setters, yachtsmen, and local personalities tied into the party circuit that weekend. Perhaps one of the most relaxed and fun-loving times any of them had all summer was that Sunday afternoon at Beechwood. The British called for a cricket match and invited crewmen from other challenging America's Cup teams to play against a team from the *Victory* syndicate. The Australians and Canadians took up the challenge with gusto. Even Prince Andrew couldn't resist the call of his nation's favorite game.

The playing field—the "pitch"—was on the front lawn. The game, which is a cross between baseball and soccer (although the British like it to be compared to chess) involves batsmen, not batters, as in American baseball. Two batsmen are up at one time. They stand at opposite ends of the pitch, which is 22 yards long. If the first batsman hits the ball far enough, they both run. If he hits it out of the boundaries, it's six runs. If he hits a wicket, he's out.

The game was hilarious, mostly due to the behavior of the Aussie crewmen who insisted on spoofing proper British etiquette. It was like village cricket, described by one British onlooker as: "Slightly easygoing. Not too serious. Not too energetic, either. Quite nice for a hot summer's day. Cricket is a day-long party, you see. It's really very civilized."

It was questionable, however, how civilized was the "Dougy Walters Stand" at the far end of the field. The area, marked by a banner with the words "Dougy Walters Stand" across it, was a haven for a group of purposefully rowdy Australians who seemed to be having more fun than anyone else.

In Sydney, Dougy Walters is to cricket what Babe Ruth was to baseball. His fans sit on a hilltop away from the field, where they are notorious for carrying on the whole afternoon, drinking beer, shouting boisterously at opponents, and making as much of a nuisance of themselves as possible. A group of the Australians invited to the cricket match at Beechwood felt that cricket in Newport wouldn't be cricket without Dougy Walters, and they missed few appropriate moments in which to create havoc. When Phil Crebbin, skipper of the 12-Meter *Victory 83*, took his turn as batsman, the Dougy Walters fans dashed from their stand, came onto the field, grabbed Crebbin by the knees and chest, and ran off with him. This while the game was in play. One British observer, who had seen cricket played in Australia, "instructed" his friends that such behavior could be expected from the Dougy Walters fans; he pretended not to be amused.

Prince Andrew howled at the antics, and then, as if unable to stand being prince a moment longer, rolled up his shirt-sleeves and joined in the fun. Andrew, it turned out, was a reasonably good cricket player. He bowled (as opposed to pitched) a fast ball or two and even struck out an Aussie opponent. Security guards watching His Royal Highness went mad when it was his turn to play the backfield. It was a position far out of their reach. Little did the tourists who strolled down Cliff Walk that day know that the man only a few feet from them, waiting to catch the next ball, was Queen Elizabeth's son.

Beyond the playing field was an azure Atlantic, rolling placid and lovely under brilliant skies and a warm afternoon breeze. Many of the men who watched the game wore Panama hats, white shirts, and white slacks; the women were in pastel summer dresses, floppy straw hats with flowers, and white shoes. It was as if a Renoir painting had come to life. The traditional "tea interval" of British cricket drew guests to a linen table-cloth spread with fresh strawberries and cream, crumpets and jam, and finger sandwiches made with salmon paste and slivered cucumber. Tea was served in china cups.

The only real excitement that afternoon was when a helicopter that had been circling the estate suddenly lowered itself on a corner of the lawn, blades whirring. The guards protecting Andrew leaped into action, surrounding the mechanical bird within seconds. The "attack" turned out to be no more than a picture-hungry photographer dropping in for a better shot of Prince Andrew at play. The chopper was shooed away and the game resumed. The day was like that—slices of real life topped with royal pudding. Only in Newport, in the summer of 1983.

The Preservation Society of Newport, which owns and cares for eight mansions, had its hands full. The America's Cup Ball on August 20 was held in The Breakers, the largest and most lavish of all the turn-of-the-century estates. Built by Cornelius Vanderbilt in 1895, the opulent building is reserved for the America's Cup Ball only. Although the house and grounds are open to the public by day, it is closed at night. The other mansions under the Society's care, such as Marble House and Rosecliff, are available to private groups who rent them in the evening for parties. The Breakers is special, and so is the America's Cup Ball.

Few who had gone to the British *Victory* Ball could help comparing the two. There was no doubt that one tried to outclass the other. "Ours was a fund-raiser," quipped one America's Cup Ball organizer. "Theirs was more like a spectacle." In fact, the 2,400 people who danced the night away at the America's Cup Ball contributed $102,000 to each of the three American Cup-defense boats. The gift wasn't without its price. Tickets at $125 per person were Golden Eggs in a society that had whet its appetite earlier in the season with the British ball. Newport society had gone party crazy. More than $40,000 in ticket money was turned down because there wasn't any more room.

Scalpers with extra tickets reportedly stationed themselves outside one of the local dry cleaners the day of the ball, waiting for customers with tuxedos in their hands to walk out the door. As they did, they were offered tickets for friends, at substantially larger tariffs than the $125 they already had paid. For those lucky enough to get tickets when invitations were mailed in June, the evening offered the glitter and nostalgia of a bygone era. And for those astute enough to sense what the future held, it was, perhaps, the last chance to drink the wine of an America's Cup summer in Newport.

Fresh flowers from the Preservation Society gardens filled the great house to overflowing. Pink and white summer flowers and asparagus ferns filled huge urns that lined the driveway. Cars were parked by a team of valets lined up at the floodlit porte cochere, the magnificent gilded entrance to The Breakers. Inside, guests entered the Great Hall, where every available stairway, ledge and tabletop was festooned with flowers. Most of the guests had already been to sumptuous dinners before they arrived. In the receiving line was Countess Antony Szapary, whose grandfather was Cornelius Vanderbilt. At the end of the evening she was seen by guests skirting the winding marble staircase on her way to an upper floor, where she still maintains an apartment. "I live here," she said to a guest who seemed bewildered. "I have a few rooms on the third floor." Earlier that evening, Countess Szapary was caught up in dancing. The Roland Haas Orchestra, which played waltzes in the Great Hall, broke into a lively Hungarian piece. Countess Szapary, in her 60s, was reminded of the time she danced the *czardas* in that same hall in her youth. As if swept away by memories, she danced across the room with a grace that only someone brought up at The Breakers could bring to the moment.

The ball drew the cream of Newport society, international yachtsmen, crew members, syndicate officials, and out-of-town guests. A few society stalwarts fretted over the fact that several America's Cup yachtsmen showed up in syndicate blazers and ties rather than the formal dress specified in the invitation. But few others really cared. The younger set found its niche in the spinnaker tent on the front lawn, where Strike Force, a rock band, blasted the stillness of the summer night. The middle-aged preferred the main tent, a 240-foot-long canvas that sheltered Cliff Hall's Orchestra along with an eight-foot replica of the original yacht *America* that won the Cup from the British in 1851. "We looked around and felt that we, too, needed a star," said one organizer, referring to Prince Andrew's visit to the *Victory* Ball. "Of course, America doesn't have any royalty, so we wanted to have something special—something to represent the *America.*" Ben Smith, head of maintenance for the Preservation Society, went far beyond anyone's expectations on that score. In a matter of three weeks, he handcrafted an eight-foot wooden replica of the yacht with great detail. The model was hung from the main tent during the ball, tilted slightly to make it seem as if she were heeling under sail. Blue material was placed underneath to represent the water, and gold cloth was a summer sunset.

As in past America's Cup balls, everyone danced until nearly dawn. The night had offered perfect weather. As the last of the guests walked through the great front entrance, they carried with them little favors— America's Cup chocolates and small bottles of perfume and cologne. It was the end of another vintage party, and it was to be an end to an elegance that Newport claimed and the America's Cup series fostered—the last of an era.

The Italians set their own style in party-conscious Newport. The influence of the Aga Khan was evident in summer-night gatherings at Seaward, the oceanfront home rented by the Italian syndicate and temporarily renamed Casa Italia. The first get-together on June 16 was sponsored by SFIDA Italiana, the Italian America's Cup syndicate. It was an elegant reception attended by the Aga Khan, his wife, Salimah, and his half-sister, Princess Yasmin Aga Khan, daughter of actress Rita Hayworth and the Aga Khan's father, Prince Aly Khan. The home of beige stucco and Georgian-style columns was comfortably elegant compared to the massive opulence of The Breakers or Marble House. It may have been Casa Italia's easy style that made the Italian parties more lively and informal.

The governor of Rhode Island, J. Joseph Garrahy, arrived in an *Azzurra* helicopter. Unlike the fiasco at Beechwood a month later, his chopper was greeted with great fanfare. Members of the *Azzurra* crew, looking more Mediterranean than New England in their Italian-cut blazers, *Azzurra* ties, and tapered slacks, rushed down to meet their new guest. Gianfranco Alberini, syndicate chairman and commodore of the Yacht Club Costa Smeralda in Sardinia, meandered across the lawn as if he had lived there all his life.

At a party on July 23, sponsored by the Sardinian Department of Tourism and Handicrafts, Alitalia Airlines and the Yacht Club Costa Smeralda, a troupe of Sardinian folk dancers performed on the front lawn. By evening's end, guests had stopped watching and started dancing, too.

By the end of the summer, an invitation to an Italian party was one of the most precious commodities in Newport. Except that none were for sale. No one had to pay. And even though guests were asked to show their invitations at the door, the Italians never pressed the issue. More often than not, a car would pull up to the portico with six people inside and only two had been invited. Once a guest who had the good manners to call ahead and ask if she might bring two additional friends was told: "Ah well, what does it matter now? We are already too many. Yes, of course. Bring them." The Italians had some impromptu affairs as well. It wasn't unusual for them to telephone friends and acquaintances in town on a sunny afternoon and invite them for pizza at their information center at Bowen's Wharf. Most often, it was on a day when nothing else was happening; *Azzurra* had raced in the morning, and the crew was ashore that afternoon. People who had been to both styles of Italian gatherings swore that the little get-togethers were the best.

At the farewell party the night of August 26, more than 600 guests gathered under a green-and-white striped tent on the front lawn of Casa Italia sipping champagne and dancing. The after-dinner party began with fireworks at the far end of the lawn, followed by coffee and elaborate pastries and desserts under a tent nearby. At midnight, another table was set up with hors d'oeuvres and more drinks. Members of the New York Yacht Club mingled with Newport socialites, 12-Meter crewmen, politicians, an international press corps, and local townspeople. To the last, they lamented the fact that the Italians were going home. It seemed that no one had anything but good to say about the Italians. From their world-class effort on the water to their hospitality at parties, even jaded Newport was caught up in it. "They had the best parties in Newport," says Len Panaggio, America's Cup press coordinator. "People stayed late at their parties. You never felt like you were intruding. It was their first time in Newport, and they were very anxious to learn. They were curious about everything. They were the most gracious."

The other syndicates had parties as well, but they generally were more closed and less flamboyant. The French adopted a lower profile in 1983 than they had in previous Cup campaigns, mainly because the man behind previous French challenges, Baron Marcel Bich, had retired from the America's Cup wars. This summer he was enjoying the relative solitude of the Yacht Club d'Hyères on the south coast of France. During the Bich challenges from 1970 to 1980, the French threw lavish parties. But a greatly reduced budget in 1983 made life simpler. Yves Rousset-Rouard invited guests to a cocktail party August 9 at The French House, the crew's home on Gibbs Avenue. Rousset-Rouard already had invested in a substantial amount of the $1.5 million French syndicate budget. The party that night was thrown with the corporate largesse of Mumm Champagne, Barton & Guestier wines, Perrier, Cointreau and others.

Not that the French avoided a good time. On Bastille Day, July 14, they had a good excuse to party. They beat the 12-Meter *Advance* by three minutes, eight seconds on the race course, and made sure they celebrated in the best Gallic tradition—with plenty of good French champagne.

Louis Vuitton, the French leather-goods company that sponsored the challengers' trial race series, put on a clambake August 5 to beat all New England clambakes. It was "à la Française." That meant lobster cooked the long, slow way in a sandpit covered with seaweed. But it also meant linen tablecloths, fresh flowers, and a glorious setting at Hammersmith Farm, the childhood summer home of Jacqueline Bouvier Kennedy Onassis. Also on the menu were steamed brown bread, clams on the half shell, corn on the cob and melted butter. And there was the inevitable champagne, bottles of red and white wine at every table, crystal glasses, and dancing through dinner. There was even a traditional New England garden planted especially for the evening. And all for the gratification of the 600 fortunate Newport Sybarites who were lucky enough to be invited.

The Canadians ended the 1983 summer being remembered most for the breakfast and hockey game they hosted in midsummer. Crewmen from nearly every syndicate showed up to join the fun, and it didn't matter who you were as long as you were able to carry a hockey stick and run. The get-together, held on Ledge Road, a street that ends at the ocean, was a perfect backdrop for a morning of shenanigans in the middle of a lot of seriousness.

The Australians, too, enjoyed their share of frivolity, mostly at the end of every day. Although the crew of *Australia II* maintained a Spartan existence most of the summer, their fellow Australians made up for it by taking up their share of seats in local bars and restaurants. The night of August 31, the Australian syndicates chose the splendor of Rosecliff, the white limestone mansion on Bellevue Avenue where *The Great Gatsby* was filmed in the early 1970s. Special guest that evening was an Australian satirist, Campbell McComas, who was flown in for the occasion by Richard Pratt, chairman of the *Challenge 12* syndicate and party host. McComas' alias that night was Sir Winston Cholmondeley-Somers, a noted British naval architect. His round of chatter honed in on Keelgate with merciless one-liners that left few unscathed, particularly members of the New York Yacht Club. A few were in the audience. It was an Australian brand of humor that left some with aching sides and others with aching heads. Bus Mosbacher, American 12-Meter skipper in 1962 and 1967, walked out with his wife in the middle of McComas' comedy. The joke that precipitated their exit characterized Mosbacher as "that noted American skipper Bus Mosbacher, or, 'Must-bet-on-you'—as he probably did," referring to the American's belief that the only bet to make in the America's Cup series was on the defense. Other Cup figures were the butt of jokes as well. McComas described Alan Bond as "probably the most outstanding Australian businessman of the last 20 years. He told me so himself."

The American defense teams had a few extravaganzas, too. Several of the *Freedom* syndicate parties were held at Seaview, the Gothic-style estate where the crew and syndicate members lived throughout the summer. Crew dinners in the main dining room were given every evening. Larger get-togethers were every now and then. The *Defender/ Courageous* group had one of the first parties of the season, a fund-raiser at Belcourt Castle, a mansion owned by the Harold Tinney family on Bellevue Avenue. The $75 ticket was worth the price if you were: (a) a leftover Kingston Trio fan; (b) a museum buff who likes to party at home; or (c) you wanted to get Ted Turner's autograph. The June 12 bash featured that 1960s folk group, now middle-aged but still in tune, who happen to be managed by syndicate contributor Nick Heyl. The gilded mansion, the year-round home of the Tinney family, was so chock-full of artifacts and valuables that nearly a month later burglars broke into a downstairs room and stole $1 million worth of precious jewels and religious relics. And Ted Turner was there, gabbing nonstop and attracting attention like a latter-day Rhett Butler at Tara.

All in all, it was an unprecedented social summer on the lawns and in the mansion ballrooms of Newport, and it is a fair guess that nothing like it will ever happen again—unless the Cup returns someday to the city-by-the-sea. The possibility that the America's Cup would leave Newport was in the air all summer—on the water, on the docks, in the thronged streets, in the mansions of Bellevue Avenue—and that possibility may have enhanced the energy of the party circuit. "No one said anything aloud," Eileen Slocum remembers. "But we were all praying that it wouldn't be our last America's Cup Ball. No one ever thought at the time it could happen. Only Mrs. Winslow [Helen Winslow, co-chairman of the ball] said anything. She said over and over, 'I'm so afraid this is going to be our last America's Cup Ball. I want it to be so perfect.' Oh, yes, She said it very sadly, and she was right.''

"The boat was pretty silent then. Silent like a morgue. Then Dennis says, 'Does anyone here have any ideas?' When Dennis says that, you know you're in trouble."

—JOHN MARSHALL, DESCRIBING THE MOMENT THAT *AUSTRALIA II* PASSED *LIBERTY* ON THE DOWNWIND LEG OF THE FINAL RACE

CHAPTER 12
Seven Races in September

After a long, exhausting summer of racing, of words that ranged from gossip to angry exchanges, of parties, and of endless practice, it was time to get down to business. The America's Cup. Ten 12 Meters had come to Newport in the spring with the highest of hopes; the number was now down to two. The cream had risen. The defender was to be the ruby-red *Liberty*, driven by that taciturn Californian, Dennis Conner. The challenger was to be the controversial white *Australia II*, driven by a young, soft-spoken Melbourne sailmaker named John Bertrand. Behind both boats was the longest winning streak in the history of sport; before them, as it turned out, were seven races in September.

Early on the morning of September 14, *Liberty* left her dock pulled by her tender, the 53-foot Hatteras *Fire Three*. As she slowly moved away from the Williams & Manchester complex and into the crowded harbor, Dennis Conner's theme songs began to sound from her speakers. First it was the theme from *Chariots of Fire*, then it was the theme from *The Empire Strikes Back*. The harbor was filled with sound; it was an inspirational moment—the music more appropriate, more moving, than this nation's ponderous national anthem. The red boat, which seemed, at the beginning of the summer, to lack charisma, now represented "300 million Americans," as Dennis Conner promised it would, "when it comes down to the short strokes." America was now threatened by its most potent America's Cup challenger, and Americans rallied to the support of their defender.

Two docks down, at Newport Offshore, *Australia II* began to move slowly away from the other Twelves in residence: *Challenge 12, Azzurra,* and *France 3*. Pulled by her tender, *Black Swan,* named for Alan Bond's antipodal brewery, *Australia II* started her long, stately tow to the America's Cup buoy eight miles out in Rhode Island Sound. As she left the dock, her theme song, sung by Australia's hard-rocking Men At Work, sent these words over the waterfront: "I come from a land Down Under/ Where women glow and men plunder." *Australia II* looked ready to plunder.

"Leaving the dock, you get a tremendous shot of adrenaline," commented John Marshall, *Liberty*'s sailtrimmer. "You feel like you can break stones with your bare hands. You also have a sense of going out into combat and a sense of representing a lot of people—your personal friends, wives, sweethearts, the syndicate—and a very strong feeling of going out under the American flag."

This was Marshall's second America's Cup; he had sailed with Conner in 1980 aboard *Freedom*. In his understated way, Marshall is one of the sport's most articulate men. Now the president of North Sails, which he runs from his aerie in Addison, Maine, hard by the Canadian border, Marshall went to Harvard, where he decided that his life's calling was in research science. From there he went to Rockefeller Institute, now Rockefeller University in New York City, one of this country's most preeminent and prestigious scientific graduate schools. He planned on a Ph.D. in biochemistry and virus genetics; but he found that he couldn't get sailing out of his blood. He tried teaching until Lowell North, the now-worldwide sailmaker, called. Marshall answered. Whatever the loss has been to biochemistry and virus genetics, it has unquestionably been sailing's gain. Marshall's eye is keen and his words, if one listens closely, are like those of a brilliant professor—whether the subject is the aerodynamics of a sail, the hydrodynamics of Ben Lexcen's keel, or the dynamics of events on the race course.

The race committee on *Black Knight* set the course before noon. Twice the day before they had tried to start this first race, but the wind wouldn't settle down. This day it blew a fairly strong 18 knots and came from the compass bearing of 45 degrees. The America's Cup course of 24.3 miles consists of six legs with three of them (the first, fourth, and sixth) sailed into the wind. The committee boat set the course for the first mark directly into the wind at 45 degrees.

Marshall described the mood on *Liberty* going into that first race: "We had a pretty seasoned crew, so we didn't approach the first race with a do-or-die attitude. The attitude was more that it's just another sailboat race. You are able to go to an America's Cup starting line with that collective feeling that this is something you've done many, many times before—that is, going to a starting line against another 12 Meter and sailing a race. This is something that the crew is trained to do, is expert at doing, and they can probably do it with their eyes closed." Asked whether it felt different this time, what with the fearsome reputation of this contest's challenger, Marshall responded, "We had a more realistic appraisal of the other boat."

At noon the 10-minute warning gun roared from the cannon on the deck of *Black Knight*. Herded well away from the action by the Coast Guard were 800 spectator boats. Closer to the action were the 30 so-called "privileged" vessels, carrying ranking members of the New York Yacht Club, ranking members of the two competing syndicates, ranking members of the other eight syndicates, and members of the press. These privileged vessels were distinguished from the madding crowd by their red-and-yellow flags—"Oscar" or "O" in the International Code Flag scheme. It was an ultimate class system, and its sanctity was protected primarily by the U.S. Coast Guard, whose show of strength included one High Endurance Cutter, two Medium Endurance Cutters, a Navy destroyer, two Buoy Tenders, three 82-foot Patrol Boats, and 28 Utility Boats.

Things were no less complicated in the air. A Coast Guard HH-52-A helicopter hovered in unnerving fashion just above boats that tried to invade the course or the territory of the privileged fleet. The Goodyear blimp floated above the racing yachts—there to beam television images to the world, which, now that there seemed to be a race, appeared interested. A hundred feet above the blimp were the photographers' helicopters—nearly 20 of them—flying clockwise in half-mile circles above the two yachts and making their awful staccato noise. There was a war on the water as the red boat and the white boat circled warily during the 10-minute starting sequence, and there was a war in the air as the helicopter pilots—many of them veterans of Vietnam—fought one another to provide their passengers with the best vantages.

Another 500 feet above the helicopters were airplanes, streaming banners. Through this aerial medium, Cup spectators were given the message that the Boston *Globe* was there. At 1,500 feet were other, fixed-winged aircraft, flying counterclockwise, and carrying the less well-heeled photographers. (Helicopters went for $400 an hour, while the tariff for fixed-wing aircraft began at about $75.) It was like a scene from *Apocalypse Now,* and all it lacked was an out-of-control Robert Duvall and Wagner's *Ride of the Valkyries.*

At precisely three seconds after 12:10 on a cloudy Wednesday, *Australia II* crossed the starting line between *Black Knight* and the red America's Cup buoy. The America's Cup series had begun. Three seconds behind her came *Liberty.* "Both the start itself and the first leg were very much like boxers in an early round," commented John Marshall, who, like many world-class sailors, can seemingly remember every tack, every jibe, and every wind shift. "We were cautious rather than tentative. A major effort was made not to do anything that would put us out of touch with the opposition. To stay close, we passed up opportunities—perhaps good opportunities—to take the measure of the other guy."

Australia II appeared a little faster upwind, Marshall concluded, "but it was nothing too alarming." When both boats were about three-quarters of a mile from the first mark, *Liberty,* behind, initiated a tacking duel to see if the white boat was as fast in this maneuver as she was reputed to be. "In a half-dozen tacks it was obvious," said Marshall. "It was real and overwhelming, so we eliminated tacking duels from the repertoire."

The second and third legs of an America's Cup race are reaching legs, where the wind blows more or less perpendicular to the boats. *Liberty,* with a long waterline, should have been faster on these two legs, and she seemed to be; but *Liberty's* tacticians chose not to attack *Australia* on the first reaching leg because the spectator fleet, despite the Coast Guard's bests efforts, was playing havoc with the wind and water. "We had concluded that we were faster than *Australia II* at this point of sail," said Marshall, "but we had a feeling that her skipper, John Bertrand, didn't know that yet."

Rounding the orange wing mark at the end of the first reach, "we went into our full-attack mode," recalled Marshall. "We figured Bertrand was going to sail toward the next mark, figuring he's going to gain, and by the time he realizes that we're gaining, it may be too late to defend. That is indeed what happened." *Liberty* moved into the lead and held it through the next upwind leg as well.

On the fifth leg, which on the America's Cup course is downwind, something strange began to happen. *Australia II,* rumored to be so slow in this direction, started to charge. Commented Marshall, "That was bad news. We didn't know at that stage what was happening. Dennis [Conner] has a very sure intuition of when the other guy is faster and when he is not, so Dennis really was the first one to identify the fact that the other boat was faster on this leg. I think a number of us thought, well, hold on, Dennis, don't be a defeatist about this thing." But Conner was right; the white boat, supposedly so slow downwind, was sailing lower and faster— which normal boats aren't supposed to do. This, however, was no normal boat, and her clear superiority on this point of sail would be telling to the future events of this contest.

Australia II converged with *Liberty,* making up 29 seconds in the course of one leg. Then things happened quickly. Because of the rules specifying which boat has the right of way, *Australia II* was unable to attack. Sailors

RACE 1 DIAGRAM

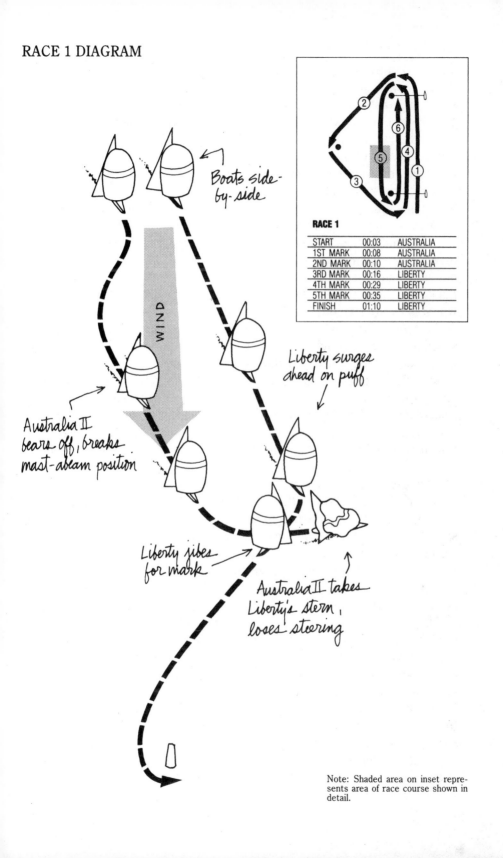

Boats side-
by-side

RACE 1

START	00:03	AUSTRALIA
1ST MARK	00:08	AUSTRALIA
2ND MARK	00:10	AUSTRALIA
3RD MARK	00:16	LIBERTY
4TH MARK	00:29	LIBERTY
5TH MARK	00:35	LIBERTY
FINISH	01:10	LIBERTY

WIND

Liberty surges
ahead on puff

Australia II
bears off, breaks
mast-abeam position

Liberty jibes
for mark

Australia II takes
Liberty's stern,
loses steering

Note: Shaded area on inset represents area of race course shown in
detail.

call the controlling position "mast-abeam." "We had mast-abeam on them," said Marshall. "But then something occurred that was very, very shocking. *Australia* simply bore off and sailed lower to the point where she opened up the necessary three boat-lengths between us. That effectively broke the overlap in the eyes of the rule. So much for mast-abeam. She reconverged with us . . . and had controlling position. That was a sign of great speed; I'd never seen that happen before. It seemed impossible."

The boats sailed side by side, with *Australia II* in control of *Liberty*, but biding her time as they neared the bottom mark. Then a puff hit and the American boat, with its longer waterline, accelerated slightly ahead. Conner jibed at that instant, onto starboard, catching *Australia II* unprepared. Since a starboard-tacked boat has right of way, the Australians had but an instant to respond, and they elected to take *Liberty*'s stern, rather than jibe to starboard. At that pivotal moment—as Bertrand swung the wheel hard—the steering gear collapsed and the boat spun into the wind out of control, narrowly missing the American yacht. Conner and company sailed one more leg and *Liberty* owned her first America's Cup race. The margin at the end was one minute and 10 seconds.

Alan Bond, chairman of the *Australia II* syndicate, was not disheartened. He blamed his yacht's failure this day on a mechanical problem. Asked how much time he thought his boat had lost during the breakdown, Bond replied, without missing a beat, "One minute, 11 seconds." He repeated a prediction he had made earlier that his yacht would win the series with a record of 4–2.

John Bertrand was asked if the easy time he had in the foreign trials contributed to his troubles this day. Bertrand, who looks like the nautical version of tennis's John Newcombe, complete with an imposing mustache, said, "We certainly weren't pushed that hard by the foreign boats. But we're good learners, and fast learners, and we'll come out better tomorrow." Dennis Conner said, "It's nice to get the first win under our belts; but one win doesn't make a series. We'd like to get three more before we get too excited about it."

They went at it again on Thursday. The wind had shifted very little—not in direction or speed—so the compass course to the first mark was 30 degrees. Six minutes before the start, the crew of *Liberty* noticed new mechanical troubles on *Australia II*. The car that carries the mainsail's headboard to the top of the mast broke, and *Australia*'s sail dropped 18 inches and ripped. "When I looked up and saw the problem, I thought there was very little chance they were going to be able to sail the course," said Marshall, who concluded that the crippled boat might try for a "knockout punch" during the 10-minute starting sequence. "I said, 'Dennis, don't foul out; that sail's going to fall down, and they're not going to be able to fix it.' We made a major effort not to foul them at the start.''

Conner didn't foul out, and he won the start by five seconds. It was apparent that, with their rival's injury, *Liberty* was faster, however slightly. Despite their troubles, the Australians found a big wind shift on the right side of the course, in what was turning out to be a dying northeasterly breeze, and passed in front of the Americans. The brain trust on *Liberty* was not overly troubled by the loss of the lead. Said Marshall, ''The feeling was that with the kind of speed advantage we had, all we needed to do was to stay close and eventually they'd drop back to us. They, on the other hand, came to the conclusion that if they didn't trim the mainsail harder, even if the sail ripped, they were going to lose this race. So they trimmed the sail, caution be damned. As soon as they sheeted it in, they started going. Maybe she wasn't 100 percent yet, but *Australia II* was substantially back to being a good, healthy boat. We had a boat race.''

Indeed. The injured but still potent *Australia* led at the first mark by an incredible 45 seconds. On the second leg, the Australians hoisted Colin Beashel 80 feet in the air to effect a repair as best he could. Eighty feet up is a long way to go, particularly in 17 knots of breeze and lumpy seas. The mast tip was making angry circles in the sky as Beashel was hoisted to a height not far below the Goodyear blimp. His journey must have been complicated by the knowledge that, a month before, fellow crew member Scott McAllister broke his arm and was rendered unconscious effecting a similar repair while racing the Canadians in the Semifinal Series.

During the two reaches *Liberty,* using all her waterline length, knocked 24 seconds from the Aussie lead. Said Marshall, ''The wind was going down, down, down. It was a real disappearing northerly, but there were patches of adequate sailing breeze, and there were patches of near calm. On the second beat we were simply able to get Bertrand hopelessly out of phase in very shifty wind conditions, and ultimately he sailed into a hole and we passed him.''

What was happening on Conner's boat during the second beat, or upwind leg, was interesting and perhaps a paradigm of his success in this arena. Marshall put it this way: ''The second beat of the second race was almost an ideal situation to optimize our strengths. To sail this type of race well, you have to have eyes well outside the boat to see patches of wind on the water and wind shifts at some distance. You also have to be sailing on the other guy's boat, which Dennis does superbly. In other words, you have to place yourself on the other boat, see his problems, figure how he is likely to respond to them, and at the same time keep your own boat in the groove.

''So what was happening then was that I was looking for patches of wind

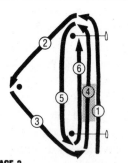

RACE 2

START	00:05	LIBERTY
1ST MARK	00:45	AUSTRALIA
2ND MARK	00:31	AUSTRALIA
3RD MARK	00:21	AUSTRALIA
4TH MARK	00:48	LIBERTY
5TH MARK	00:31	LIBERTY
FINISH	01:33	LIBERTY

Australia II is headed and sails into a hole.

Liberty catches lift

WIND

Liberty trails in dying breeze.

on the water—trying to identify the direction and strength of the wind 100, 200, or 300 yards away. Tom [Whidden] was concentrating on when we were headed or lifted, by shifts in the wind direction. Halsey [Herreshoff], the navigator, was concentrating on where we were relative to the mark. Dennis was watching the other boat, relative to us, and concentrating on when the other guy was clearly going to be out of phase with the wind if he made the conventional response. We kind of had the feeling that their tactician [Hugh Treharne] is going to be telling John Bertrand to do the conventional thing; that is, that he's not going to wander a lot from the conventional response because of the pressure not to.

"So what we tried to do on *Liberty* was to make his conventional response a wrong one, and that's what happened. He attempted to cover us carefully—just like the book says—and we maneuvered him from ahead to behind. That was an example of our afterguard working on a problem."

The Americans would win their second race by one minute and 33 seconds; but the Australians were flying a red protest flag, accusing the Americans of tacking too close to them on the second upwind leg.

Again Bond blamed his yacht's failure on mechanical difficulties. He was sure that the breakage had cost exactly one minute and 34 seconds. (Bond's pose—that this race, as the one before, had been *lost* by the Australians rather than *won* by the Americans—started to sound gratuitous and angered a few.) Bond also served warning that, although they lost this day on the race course, they would win the protest in the hearing room. Said the pugnacious leader of the *Australia II* campaign, "If there's any justice in racing, we should win the protest."

The next day the international jury, chaired by Livius Sherwood, a Canadian, saw things differently after discussing the matter for six hours. Upon losing the protest, Bond warned the world: "There is recourse."

Australia II was reputed to be a very under-rigged 12 Meter, and a boat subject to much breakage.* When we asked Bond if it was true that *Australia II* had been breaking down all summer, he denied it, and adamantly. Bond seemingly was hoping to perpetuate the myth that his yacht was not only a formidable but a reliable—and unbreakable—weapon.

Bruce Kirby, among others, had different memories of *Australia II*. The designer of the Canadian 12-Meter *Canada 1* said, in no uncertain

---

*In fact, all her sheets, halyards, and even the tails of her running rigging were made of Kevlar, a space-age synthetic material developed for tire cord. *Liberty,* on the other hand, was a very conservative 12 Meter; thus, she used wire for much of her sheets, halyards, and other running rigging. The difference in weight between Kevlar and wire saved *Australia II* 100 to 120 pounds aloft, where such weight is critical. This devotion to Kevlar was a first for America's Cup boats, and is further evidence of the aggressive philosophy of the challenger versus the conservative nature of the defender. This, too, would be telling in the seven races they sailed.

terms, "That's bull!" He then listed a number of major and minor injuries suffered by *Australia II* during the summer. "In a race against the Italians in midsummer, the Australians broke a halyard and a runner, and that cost them a race—the second race they lost. And the next race they lost was because of a broken jib halyard and a failure to the running backstays. Then they lost that race to us, which they couldn't sail because they broke a halyard lock, and while trying to fix the halyard lock, they broke their masthead crane, and then they broke that guy's arm. That was two different breakages—plus a broken arm—all in 15 minutes. They also broke a boom before a start one day; and they did a magnificent job of getting it ready and winning the race; but that was another breakage. They broke a jib halyard against *Challenge 12;* I saw the jib come down."

If Bond's statement at the press conference was murky, Conner's was salutary. Asked why he won, Conner, delivering his best line of the summer, said simply, "God smiled on us. The race could have gone either way. We were just fortunate today."

There was something familiar about this scene. The score was now 2–0 in favor of the Americans, and despite all of Alan Bond's braggadocio, all of his posturing, all of his railing at the New York Yacht Club, there were memories in the air of previous Australian defeats. Here was a man who had spent a reported $16 million to challenge for the America's Cup during the past decade and had only one thin race against the Americans to show for it. Bond's sole win in the America's Cup occurred on September 19, 1980, when *Australia I* and her bendy mast beat Dennis Conner, sailing *Freedom* on a light-air day. One victory for the Bond-sponsored Australians out of 15 meetings. Again, the Australians seemed about to roll over and play dead for the Americans. Their machine was breaking; the men were beaten. You could see it in Alan Bond; you could see it in John Bertrand. That sense of *déjà vu*, however, would prove fleeting.

If the Aussies seemed shell-shocked on Thursday, they served warning on Saturday, September 17, after a lay day. In winds under 10 knots and growing lighter on their way to nothing, *Liberty* trailed *Australia II* by 5 minutes and 57 seconds at the end of the downwind leg. Then, at 5:25 P.M., the time limit expired with *Australia II* less than two miles from the finish line. *Liberty,* a sailing light-year away, was out there somewhere, gasping for breath.

John Bertrand would later describe this aborted race as "the turning point." Although it added nothing to the win-loss column, it gave the Aussies confidence, he said, that they could do it. At the press conference, Dennis Conner seemed surprisingly relaxed. He claimed to have been receiving constant updates during the race from his navigator, Halsey Herreshoff, on the speed *Australia II* needed to finish on time.

"When it got to where they had to go about 1,000 miles per hour to make it, we knew they were in trouble." He seemed thankful for the reprieve and decided that this day, "God must be an American."

The scientist-turned-sailmaker John Marshall was dispassionate in his appraisal of this particular race. "I wasn't pessimistic at all until the spinnaker run," he said a month after the contest. "Their capability to blow a race open on the square run was something we had not anticipated. Well, it turned out to be the ultimate weapon, because if you look at the time charts you'll see that we were remarkably effective in neutralizing their upwind advantage; but those square runs put things out of reach. It should be remembered that *Australia II* sailed poorly downwind all summer against the foreign competition. We don't know whether they were able to get their spinnaker inventory up to American standards, or whether they were purposely sailing their boat slowly so as not to tip us off about what a potent weapon they had in that direction."

Liberty had a hole card to play, however, which Marshall found cheering even on this otherwise dismal day. As they had discovered during the multiple-certificate experiments in July, the ballast of *Liberty* could be changed to stay in harmony with various wind strengths. "All the way on that endless spinnaker run," said Marshall, "it looked like maybe we'd be able to get close to their performance if we went to our light-air configuration. That was what was going through my mind. First of all, it seemed obvious we'd never win a race in those conditions again; but if it looked like we'd have to sail in such conditions another time, and had a lay day—which would give us sufficient time to make the ballast change and get the yacht remeasured—maybe it'd be close."

What was seen on Saturday was confirmed on Sunday in a zephyrous seven knots of breeze. Conner won the start by eight seconds; but while crossing the line he had to turn into the wind to avoid hitting *Black Knight*'s anchor rode. That maneuver pretty much stopped the red boat, and she seemed stopped for the rest of the afternoon. *Australia* led at the first mark by one minute and 14 seconds. On the two reaching legs, *Liberty* reduced that to a more manageable 42 seconds. Upwind, the Australian boat gained another 33 seconds; but then on the downwind leg it was, as they say in Newport, "Adios." *Australia II* more than doubled her lead to 2 minutes and 47 seconds. At the finish, the challenger had bested the defender by 3 minutes and 14 seconds—a record margin. The previous record belonged to Britain's *Endeavour*, which beat *Rainbow* by 2 minutes and 9 seconds in 1934. The record established by *Australia II* would not last as long.

At the press conference, John Bertrand was asked whether *Australia II* was capable of winning the America's Cup. A much relieved Bertrand,

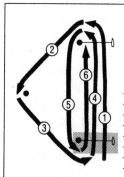

RACE 3

START	00:08	LIBERTY
1ST MARK	01:14	AUSTRALIA
2ND MARK	00:52	AUSTRALIA
3RD MARK	00:42	AUSTRALIA
4TH MARK	01:15	AUSTRALIA
5TH MARK	02:47	AUSTRALIA
FINISH	03:14	AUSTRALIA

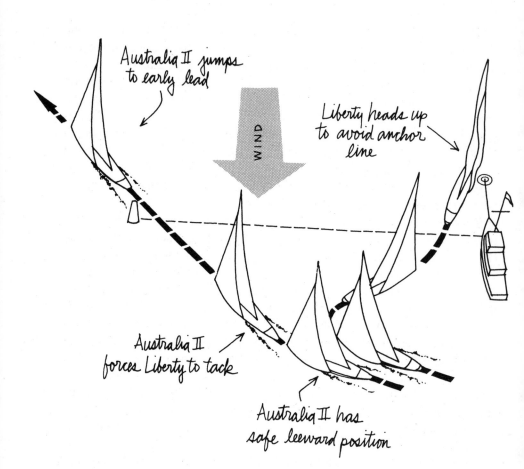

Australia II jumps to early lead

Liberty heads up to avoid anchor line

WIND

Australia II forces Liberty to tack

Australia II has safe leeward position

having shed the worry that only days before seemed etched on his face, said, "I've always maintained that we can win the America's Cup. We've got the people, got the expertise, got the boat, and we have the equipment. It is just up to us. I think we're good enough to do it, and I think we will do it." Bertrand claimed to feel "very strong about the future."

An Australian reporter posed this question to Dennis Conner: "I believe yesterday you claimed God was an American. Does He have Sunday off?" "No!" replied Conner. "But even He couldn't cope with *Australia II* today."

Another reporter asked, "In the last couple of days, *Australia II* has been awesome downwind. Do you think she was sandbagging in the trials?" Conner handled that one quite well—he'd had practice. "I found out recently that sandbagging is something you do at the beach," he said. "I'll never discuss that again in regard to a sailboat race."

Two other interesting statements were made at this press conference. Dennis Conner—as if he needed reminding—was reminded by a reporter that *Australia II* had proven herself to be a very formidable boat. "Are you worried about losing the Cup?" asked the reporter. Said Conner, "Well, I'm certainly aware that that's a possibility." Then, sounding his theme song, he continued, "But I don't believe in dwelling on the negatives. We're just going to do everything we can to work on the positive things and hope things go better. We're no worse than we were yesterday. We only have to win two races."

Conner was also asked this day his opinion of the winged keel on *Australia II*. "The 12-Meter class has always been a development class," he said, "and it has done a lot for yachting over the years by allowing development . . . There may be places for winged keels on a lot of boats that might improve their performance, so I'd have to think about that . . . I haven't carefully thought this through. I think, however, it would be a shame to outdate—if it turns out that *Australia II* is indeed a breakthrough—I think it would be a shame to outdate 20 or 25 existing 12 Meters; but *Intrepid* basically did that in 1967."

Conner asked for a lay day in order to wait for more wind. Asked how much wind he wanted, Conner, who was beginning to show a sense of humor, said, "about 40 knots."

The fourth race, on Tuesday, September 20, showed the world the perfect Dennis Conner. Part of Conner's brilliance, it is said, has to do with his extraordinary sense of speed and distance. His admirers say that "he knows where he's going and how long it will take him to get there better than anyone in the world." Marshall put it this way: "I've been driving in a car with him, and Dennis will casually say, 'In seconds, how far away do you think that bridge is?' I'll say, 'Thirty seconds.' Dennis says, 'I think 20 seconds—want to bet a buck on it?' I lost once or twice, but then I began to realize that this is a game he plays to win, so I stopped betting with him unless I was sure. Dennis does that a lot. In many, many situations he's thinking about time and distance; that is an essential element in starting a 12 Meter. He's better at it than anyone.

"A lot of the trick maneuvers at the start of a match race—the circling and starting and stopping—turn out to be a standoff, because with two good boats, both well sailed, both equally maneuverable, it's rare for one of them to box in the other. So most of that ends up in a standoff, and then the trick is who is going to go for the line first, with what speed, and from what distance. Dennis very often takes mediocre starts and turns them into clear wins by simply hitting the mark precisely on time and at full speed."

The most basic rule of yacht racing is that a starboard-tacked boat has right of way over a port-tacked boat. So if you're sailing on port tack and you're trying to cross ahead of a starboard-tacked boat, you had better make sure that your speed-distance calculations are correct. Otherwise, as they say about a collision at sea, "It can ruin your whole day." On this day, Dennis Conner port-tacked *Australia II,* not once but twice, and sailed perhaps the finest race in America's Cup history.

Marshall described the first of these crossings, which occurred at the start of the fourth race: "If anyone is ever going to write about what was the most audacious move in the America's Cup, this was it. It was not a move of bravado, mind you, but a calculated, known, brilliant move. Keep in mind that when Dennis made the decision to port-tack *Australia,* both boats were reaching at each other. And the rules permit the starboard-tacked boat to turn toward the line at any time. So Dennis, by knowing in his mind how much he was going to head up [for the line] and looking at the other boat and judging what her course would be when she turned for the line, concluded that we could cross her bow. Dennis was the one person out of 11 on our boat who said with surety, 'We will cross their bow!' He said that. He looked at her and said calmly, 'We're going to cross their bow.' "

Marshall, asked what were his thoughts at that moment, said, "I thought, I hope to God he's right, otherwise this is going to be a short afternoon."

Liberty port-tacked *Australia II* and won the start by six huge seconds. Then they sailed up the weather leg. Nearing the mark, Conner needed to tack to port; but again the speedy *Australia II,* on starboard tack and in the controlling position, blocked her way. Remembered Marshall, "Dennis looks back and says, 'I think we can tack and cross their bow.' I looked

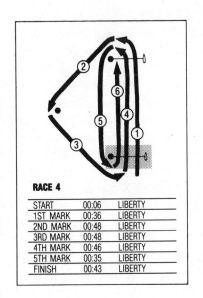

RACE 4

START	00:06	LIBERTY
1ST MARK	00:36	LIBERTY
2ND MARK	00:48	LIBERTY
3RD MARK	00:48	LIBERTY
4TH MARK	00:46	LIBERTY
5TH MARK	00:35	LIBERTY
FINISH	00:43	LIBERTY

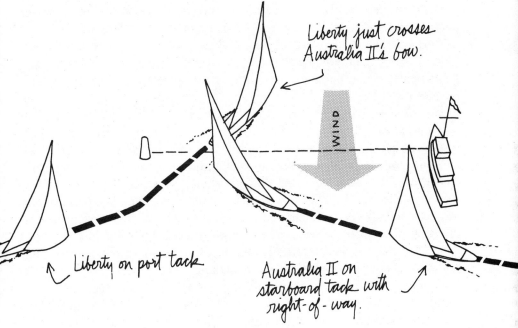

Liberty just crosses Australia II's bow.

WIND

Liberty on port tack

Australia II on starboard tack with right-of-way.

back and said, 'Dennis, don't try to take me into the protest room if you tack now.' I was confident that if we tacked we were going to foul out of the race. We kept going for another 15 or 20 seconds, and he looks back again and says, 'I think we've got to try it.' Dennis felt that if we didn't round the first mark ahead, we weren't going to win the race. That is part of the psychology or reality of racing against a faster boat—you have to take risks. But we kept going, and then in another 30 seconds or so we got a little wind shift—a header—and we tacked to port and crossed them. That was another heart-stopper.''

Liberty led at the first mark by 36 seconds. This was the first time (in five races, including the aborted third race) that she was ahead at the first mark. That was it. As she crossed the finish line to lead in the series 3–1, Bob McCullough, head of the New York Yacht Club's America's Cup Committee, raised a fist of victory into the air, from his perch on the commanding *Fox Hunter II,* which for this series carried the NYYC's America's Cup Committee.

Asked if that was the finest 12-Meter race he'd ever witnessed or been part of, Marshall said that it was. ''I mean, you can take away all the ones that you might think were perfect, when you were sailing against an inferior boat, and you beat them by several minutes. That's pretty meaningless. What's really perfect was to sail against a faster boat and sail perfectly and beat them.''

But despite Conner's and *Liberty*'s brilliance this hazy last day of summer, a darker truth had been confirmed. *Liberty* had sailed flawlessly for more than 26 miles, and yet the margin of victory was a razor-thin 43 seconds. Marshall was asked if this realization was frightening. He answered, ''I'm sure we all felt that we had to sail perfectly, or very, very close to it, to win. I don't think Dennis carries something like that around as a particular burden. I think he puts himself under the personal pressure of sailing to his own standards all the time he is out there. I didn't have the sense that this conclusion rattled him; but I was very aware of it—a feeling that on this boat we couldn't make mistakes.''

Despite the fact that the Americans needed only one more victory, Bond elected to race the next day, saying, ''We really can't dial up God to give us the wind we need.'' He seemed little troubled by the fact that with the score 3–1 the Australians were running out of room. Said Bond, ''We had our backs to the wall at the battle of Gallipoli, and we won that one. So, you don't want to count us out now.'' A reporter reminded Bond that, during this World War I battle, the Turks slaughtered the Australians. Bond, untroubled by his flawed history, said he used the reference as a parable, not as an historical truth. The outcome aside, said Bond, the battle was proof positive that Australians don't give up.

On Wednesday, September 21, *Liberty*, after sailing her perfect race, returned to the real world with a bang. With less than an hour to go to the noon warning gun, *Liberty* experienced a rigging failure—her first significant mechanical breakdown of the summer. The weather was troubled this day: there was 18 knots of breeze and the sea was lumpy and confused.

While sail-testing before the start, the piston that tensions the port jumper exploded. The jumper gives support to the top of the mast. "The reaction was what the hell are we going to do now?" recalled Marshall. "We made the immediate decision to start the race and to make a maximum effort to fix the broken piston." A spare part was ashore, so the high-speed chase boat *Rhonda* was sent for it. Commodore McCullough, much concerned, radioed from *Fox Hunter*. "What's the problem?" Back came the response: "We have urgent need for a part. It's on its way out with *Rhonda*. Must have that part."

Meanwhile two crew members, Tom Rich at the top spreader and Scott Vogel just below him, worked aloft. Said Marshall, "Those guys were taking a terrible pounding. The only direction that was relatively easy on them was downwind, but that was taking us away from the starting line, and taking us away from it at about nine knots. We tried beam-reaching back and forth, but we were just punishing those guys up the mast. Ultimately, we came to the solution of running downwind, with the mainsail trimmed in all the way, and the trim tab set in one direction and the rudder in the other. That slowed us considerably. When it got to the point where we began to worry about our distance away, we turned toward the line and the guys would hold on as best they could." Somehow they managed to make the repair, but the replacement part, it turned out, was two inches longer than the original and likely to break. But there wasn't time to worry about that—yet.

The two yachts began the 10-minute war dance prior to the 12:10 start. At the noon warning gun, *Liberty* didn't even have a headsail on. Bertrand engaged her and both boats turned downwind. The foredeck crew of *Liberty* tried to set a headsail; but, by doing it with the boat heading downwind, the luff tape ripped from the sail. Down went that suddenly obsolete $10,000 worth of Kevlar/Mylar, and up came its replacement. Conner, in the meantime, kept his mind on the business at hand: John Bertrand. The ever-aggressive Conner drove Bertrand down to the leeward end of the line. Bertrand ended up being over the line early by perhaps two feet. By the time the Australian skipper sorted himself out, *Liberty* owned a commanding 37-second lead.

Both boats sailed to the right side of the course. Four minutes into the race, the new piston on *Liberty* failed—as expected—and the top of the mast sagged off ominously. Numerous adjustments had to be made to the

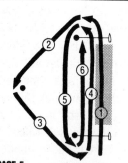

RACE 5

START	00:37	LIBERTY
1ST MARK	00:23	AUSTRALIA
2ND MARK	00:23	AUSTRALIA
3RD MARK	00:18	AUSTRALIA
4TH MARK	01:11	AUSTRALIA
5TH MARK	00:52	AUSTRALIA
FINISH	01:47	AUSTRALIA

Using superior speed, Australia II is ahead when boats converge. No significant wind shifts.

WIND

Australia II tacks to clear wind

Liberty elects to stay on port tack, hoping for favorable wind shift.

Liberty leads with broken mast ram

mast to counteract the failed rigging and the sudden softness of the mast tip. As *Australia II* gained on her crippled competitor, she sailed into *Liberty*'s backwind and tacked off to the left side of the course. Conner let *Australia II* go her own way for an agonizing 10 minutes. For this he would later be criticized, but Marshall explained the thinking on the boat quite lucidly. "At this point, Dennis said very explicitly, 'We have to round this first mark with a substantial lead or we're going to lose the race.' Even though we were ahead by three or four boat lengths when Bertrand tacked away, Dennis already in effect had decided that he was behind and that the right-hand side of the course would be favored. It was, in effect, a move you would make in the late stages of a race when you are losing, but Dennis had applied that thinking to the early stages. I think Dennis's analysis was right. Had we rounded that first mark ahead, we had a chance to win the race, but behind, we had none . . . ''

Liberty sailed alone to the right, looking and hoping for a wind shift in that direction that never arrived. *Liberty* trailed at the first mark by 23 seconds and *Australia* won the race by one minute and 47 seconds. The score was now 3–2, and the Australians, with their backs against the wall, as at Gallipoli, were not about to give up.

Conner again won the start of the sixth race by seven seconds on a glorious Indian-summer day. The conditions seemed perfect for a sailboat race: the wind was blowing from the northwest at an honest 15 knots. Shortly after the start, *Australia II* tacked to starboard for the left side of the race course. *Liberty* tacked to cover. *Australia II* tacked again and *Liberty* covered—placing herself directly in front of her rival, just like the book on match racing says. Both boats got a large port-tack lift, and *Australia II* tacked, presumably to clear her air. Tacking on a lift is not considered good match-racing tactics; but sailing in dirty air from another boat isn't either, so *Australia II* seemingly opted to solve the latter problem. When *Australia II* got upwind of *Liberty,* she again joined her on port tack heading for the right side of the course.

Then the "hands of God," as Marshall would put it, entered the contest. God, who just days before had seemed undeniably American, turned to embrace the other side. "What happened," said Marshall, "was that *Australia* put her nose into an entirely new wind. And this was not a light-air day; I'm talking about a day when it was blowing 15 or 18 knots true. A really good, fresh sailing breeze it was. But then *Australia* gets her own private breeze, which is several knots more in strength, and 15 or 18 degrees closer to the mark." The white boat from Down Under made a hard left-hand turn for the mark, in what was the beginning of a most rare 100-degree wind shift, and she was gone. She led at the first mark by a full 2 minutes and 29 seconds, and at the finish by 3 minutes and 25 seconds—

RACE 6 DIAGRAM

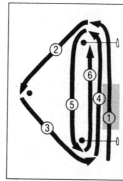

RACE 6

START	00:07	LIBERTY
1ST MARK	02:29	AUSTRALIA
2ND MARK	02:48	AUSTRALIA
3RD MARK	03:46	AUSTRALIA
4TH MARK	03:22	AUSTRALIA
5TH MARK	04:08	AUSTRALIA
FINISH	03:25	AUSTRALIA

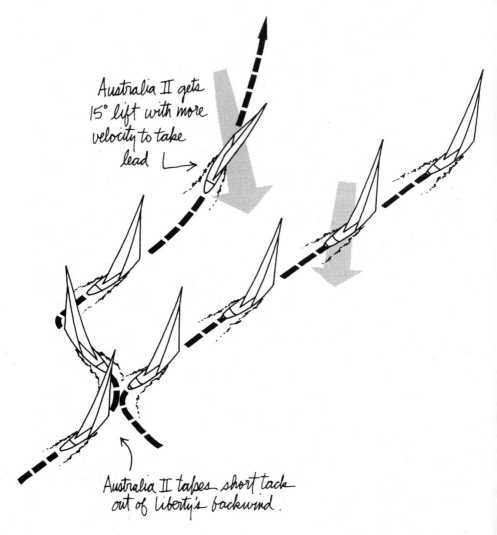

Australia II gets 15° lift with more velocity to take lead

Australia II takes short tack out of Liberty's backwind.

a new record for a victory by a challenging yacht. More important than records, however, was the fact that *Australia II* had tied the series at three wins. To put that into perspective, between 1958—when this competition began to be sailed in 12 Meters—and 1980, there have been 35 America's Cup races. In those eight challenges over 22 years, foreign yachts have won only three races. In 1983, *Australia II* owned three races.

Australia II called for a lay day, which surprised many. She had her opponent on the ropes and then let her off. This was perplexing, and one wondered if Bond wanted to savor this historic moment. Would the Australians be content with winning three races—something never done before? Did they have the character to cross the line from a worthy challenger to a winner? That is such a huge step, and Conner took pains to point it out to them. He said at the press conference, "It made me feel better when Alan Bond called for a lay day so he could savor the fact that he has tied the series after six races."

Bond, at the press conference, explained the lay day this way: "To allow us to check the boat from stem to stern. There were quite strong winds out there, and the boat took quite a bashing. And to give our crew some relaxation after two very testing days. They've been under a lot of pressure to come from behind."

Bertrand was asked if he was surprised when Conner didn't cover him on the first leg. "We were happy going to the left," he said, "just from what we could see on the water. I think we were surprised, but I don't know what Dennis was thinking." Moments later, he would explain it further: "It was a little bit like lake sailing out there; a good friend of mine, Buddy Melges,* has spoken many times to me and to other people about sailing on lakes and looking at the wind on the water. That was really the key to today's racing . . ."

Bertrand expected the seventh and deciding race, scheduled for Saturday, "to be very tough . . . It couldn't be better for the scriptwriters. I expect it to be a very dramatic race . . . A great finale for the summer."

Conner was asked why he didn't cover Bertrand when his boat sailed left. He denied making any such error, and reporters had the sense—as they did on more than one occasion with Conner—that they had witnessed two separate races. In the wake of that confusion, Conner was asked, "John Bertrand has admitted making some mistakes in this series. In your own estimation have you made any errors today?" Conner answered with

---

*Bertrand met Buddy Melges when he joined North Sails and was sent for training to the Pewaukee, Wisconsin, loft. John Kolius, skipper of *Courageous*, also holds Melges—a deservedly famous one-design sailor from Zenda, Wisconsin—in high regard, but with decidedly less awe. See Chapter Four.

some ire: "I'd like to see the sailor yet that has never made a mistake. I don't think it [not making mistakes] happens very often. Most people can certainly think of something they'd do differently in every race they've sailed, so the answer to your question is yes. We've made mistakes, but I think relative to the potential of our yacht, we've gotten a fair bit out of it in the series, and we're pleased."*

Conner was asked how it felt to be the first man in 132 years to have to sail a seventh race. He answered, "Well, it's going to be very exciting to be involved in the race of the century. At this point we're hoping we can find a way to prevail like we have in the last 132 years. I think we have an awful lot of tradition going for us; we have a very courageous crew, and somehow I think we'll pull it out on Saturday."

It was time for the American boat to play its last card. The forecast for Saturday's "race of the century" was for light winds. Thus they towed *Liberty* to Cove Haven Marina on the lay day and reballasted the boat into her light-air configuration. It was reported that 924 pounds of lead ballast were removed; but even a month after the contest the figure remained a secret. Not only did *Liberty* weigh less, but sail area was added. As they moved the mast back two feet, five genoas had to be rebuilt. "That's a major amount of sailmaking work to insert pieces into the luff of those genoas," said Marshall. While the sailmakers and crew were busy reconfiguring the red yacht, Conner, who is not famous for his mechanical aptitude, played golf at Newport Country Club with Bus Mosbacher, who defended the America's Cup with *Weatherly* in 1962 and with *Intrepid* in 1967.

To keep his crew happy on the lay day—and presumably away from Newport's deservedly famous watering holes—Bond bought the cable-TV rights for the finals of something called Australian Rules Football. He paid a reported $46,000 for the pleasure of having the Newport exclusive on this great moment in sports, and his crew watched TV on the lay day.

Marshall discussed the reballasting strategy: "It was written in the newspapers that reballasting and remeasuring the boat was a desperation move, but quite the contrary; the boat had been in those various configurations at various times, and it had been tested extensively. The line of

---

*A month later Marshall explained the circumstance. He said that, to his way of thinking, Bertrand didn't go left because he saw wind; instead, he went left to clear his air. Marshall thinks the Australians got lucky, and anything else is revisionist history. "Possibly we could have tacked over and maybe gotten the same lift, but only very momentarily was that option available, because this was a tremendous lift. It was obvious that if we were in the same breeze *Australia* was, we were behind . . . Bertrand at the press conference said something like he was happy to be left; but I think also, once you first taste the honey on the left, then you know left, left, left. You can hardly give anyone credit for protecting the honey pot . . . He didn't sail the race as if he knew it was going to be better over there; he sailed the race as if he knew he was in trouble, and he was going to minimize our lead."

rating is an absolute continuum, an absolutely continuous line of different ballast and sail area configurations that all add up to 12 Meters. For simplicity's sake—I mean, how precisely can you call your weather—we set the boat up in A, B, and C configurations.''

Since the boat had to be remeasured—a time-consuming process, which includes the weighing of the yacht—this change could only be made on a lay day. Marshall was surprised when Bond gave them the opportunity to do that. Asked whether he thought Bond anticipated the ballast change, Marshall responded, "I'd be surprised if he didn't because of the to-do of the summer when we were working on the thing, and the *Defender/ Courageous* people made it a public issue. It was obvious that to take that to the newspapers was not in the best interests of the defense of the Cup, but that's another story.''

With the eyes of the world upon those two gladiators—including ABC, which supposedly brought a contingent of 317 journalists and technicians, followed only by CBS, who felt 180 were sufficient for the job—the Cup Committee tried to sail "the race of the century" on Saturday. It was a glorious day, warm and sunny. But in a repeat of September 13, the wind proved too unsettled. With two and a half minutes to go before the start, the red-and-white postponement pennant was hoisted on *Black Knight*. It would not come down this day, and at 1:50 the committee abandoned the race. One journalist, unfamiliar with the strange ways of yachting, commented, "This is the only sport where they cancel the competition on a beautiful day.''

Dennis Conner called for a lay day on the heels of this postponement. With stronger winds forecast for Monday, he wanted to reballast his boat. Bond was not pleased, nor presumably were the television networks, who now knew their weekend sports spectacular would be moved to Monday. At half time during the Notre Dame–Miami game, Brent Musburger, host of *The NCAA Today,* informed his partner Ara Parseghian and the television audience about the ballast change to *Liberty*. With a confused smile, Parseghian, a former Notre Dame coach himself, said, "Anything you say.''

At a press conference that Saturday afternoon, Bond made his point clearly: "We came here to race one boat, not three yachts." He threatened a protest because of the ballast change. Then, casting an aspersion apparently at the manliness of his American competitors, Bond requested this favor in a voice dripping in innuendo: "Perhaps they would be so kind as to paint [their boat] . . . pink." This way, he said, the Aussies might know whom they were racing.

Liberty stayed light, however, for the Monday race, as the earlier predictions of heavy winds changed back to more familiar 5- to 15-knot southerlies. On September 26, they met in the seventh and deciding race;

but there would be yet another anticlimax before the plot would work itself out. With two minutes to go before the start, the red-and-white answering pennant was hoisted on *Black Knight,* signaling another postponement. They tried a second start at 1:05 P.M., and it was even: *Liberty* crossed the line ahead by eight seconds, but *Australia II*'s end of the line was a bit closer to the first mark. *Liberty* wanted the right-hand side of the course, so Conner was willing to give the Australians the favored left end of the line. Marshall says the crew was confident this day, confident with their boatspeed and confident with their tactics. They had every right to be sure of their tactics.

According to plan, *Liberty* sailed to the right side of the course, and *Australia II* to the left. The Australians tacked first, and then *Liberty* tacked at them "to check in," said Marshall. As they came together *Australia II* got a good port-tack lift. It was obvious that the white boat was once again ahead. "Then our bow started to drop," recalled Marshall. "We began to get headed. We decided to see if we could get Bertrand to go into a conservative mode of reflexive tacking. We waited until we got a pretty good lift, and tacked. Sure enough, Bertrand followed us, despite the fact that what we were doing was wrong. We tacked right back, even before we were up to speed. You had a sense that Bertrand couldn't quite figure out what we were doing. The next time we came together, we had gained substantially . . . Bertrand made a mistake. He simply covered us without thinking. The Aussies hadn't been in many close races all summer, and when they were they had the advantage of being able to out-tack and out-boatspeed the opponent every time. In some of the subtle stuff—the chess moves—Dennis was superior, just plain superior. This was an example."

The Americans gained but still weren't ahead. Both boats sailed together on a long starboard tack to the left side of the course. The Australian boat was ahead and slightly upwind. In that formation, said Marshall, "Bertrand is vulnerable if both boats get headed, and also if we have a little speed advantage. We had a little bit of both. We had a very slight performance edge this day, and we sailed into a header. We took a quick look back, closed our eyes and tacked." Once again Conner port-tacked *Australia II,* and once again he survived this often dangerous maneuver. *Liberty* was ahead by 29 seconds at the first mark. And for minutes the boat horns roared on Rhode Island Sound.

On the first spinnaker reach, the Americans stretched their lead to 45 seconds. But the wind had gone left. This meant that the next leg was going to be more downwind—like the fifth leg, in which *Liberty* had been so vulnerable. Sure enough, the white boat cut the lead to 23 seconds. A good weather leg saw *Liberty* take back all of that time, and at the fourth mark she led by 57 seconds. Only once before had she led the white boat by more than that. To spectators, at least, the Cup seemed safe.

"I don't think anyone said it," recalled Marshall, "but each of us had a feeling that we had to round the fourth mark some distance ahead. Whether that number was a minute, a minute and a half, I don't know. I was thinking we needed a minute and a quarter, if we were to withstand her charge downwind. I thought, if we can only get another 15 or 20 seconds here, we're home free. We rounded 57 seconds ahead."

Both boats bore off on starboard tack and hoisted spinnakers. Marshall continued, "Halsey is taking ranges and *Australia II* is gaining. It doesn't take Dennis too long to figure out what proportion of the leg is gone and how many boat lengths they've gained. The answer was they were going to be ahead at the leeward mark." So Conner jibed to port, on what he thought was a slight lifting wind shift; he also intended to be the inside boat at the turning mark, which has rounding rights. The Australians continued toward the right side of the course, toward the spectator boats, and toward their destiny. Both boats jibed, and when they reconverged the Australian boat had demolished *Liberty*'s 57-second advantage.

Then Conner jibed again straight in front of *Australia II*. Said Marshall, "Then the really discouraging stuff started to happen. *Australia* simply sailed lower and faster . . . I think at that point everyone knew on our boat that there was a very good chance we were going to lose that race. She was gaining and doing it in a way that there is no defense. We initially tried to match her sailing angle in order to keep our windshadow close to her so that she'd have to sail through this area of disturbed wind. That proved futile; she simply sailed lower and gained more.

"The boat was pretty silent then. Silent like a morgue. Then Dennis says, 'Does anyone here have any ideas?' When Dennis says that, you know you're in trouble." *Australia II* rounded the bottom mark with a 21-second lead.

With few options left, *Liberty* started tacking on the final leg of the final race of the America's Cup. Conventional tacking wasn't working, so *Liberty* invented something new. "Dennis simply held the boat head to wind in the midst of the tack. *Australia* matched us. It seemed she was having more trouble hooking up after the tack than we were. We repeated the process two or three times. It was essentially a tack with a very long hold in the center. It's not the right way to tack, but conceivably it was something they'd never done, and it seemed to be causing them more difficulty than it cost us." But even after 47 tacks, it was not enough.

At 5:20, *Australia* crossed the finish line to end the longest winning streak in sports. Forty-one seconds later came *Liberty*. Asked his thoughts at that moment, Marshall said, "I don't think I had any terribly

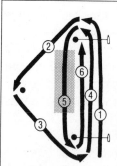

RACE 7

START	00:08	LIBERTY
1ST MARK	00:29	LIBERTY
2ND MARK	00:45	LIBERTY
3RD MARK	00:23	LIBERTY
4TH MARK	00:57	LIBERTY
5TH MARK	00:21	AUSTRALIA
FINISH	00:41	AUSTRALIA

Liberty rounds 52 seconds ahead

Australia II goes right and picks up fresher breeze

WIND

Liberty jibes on small shift

Australia II bears off and pulls ahead

verbal thoughts at that point. It was more an enormous emotional letdown, a really profound sadness. It really hurt.''

For a time no one spoke on *Liberty*. Continued Marshall, ''Dennis very shortly thereafter made a point that all the guys really understood and really respected. He said that he felt they'd sailed superbly and that no one had anything to be ashamed of. We'd done everything we could to win this regatta. But it was not to be.''

At the press conference, Conner was red-eyed and on the edge of control. This man who seemed so emotionless, this man who wanted no excuse to lose, spoke about his loss with difficulty, yet with dignity: ''Today, *Australia II* was just a better boat. And they beat us. And we have no excuses. So I'd like to at this point congratulate Alan Bond and *Australia II* on their superb effort over the summer. They proved that they were an outstanding boat, and today was their day.''

He pressed on even as his voice began to lose its way. ''However, I'd like to point out that our guys did a great job of hanging in there in conditions that in the past have proven to be awfully good for *Australia II*, so I'm very proud of them. And I'd like to thank all of you for your support over the summer.'' He ended by saying America had nothing to be ashamed of. Then Dennis Conner got up slowly and with his wife, Judy, disappeared into the Newport night.

Warren Jones, manager of the *Australia II* syndicate, did the best job of summarizing the Australian victory that night. Said Jones at the press conference, ''All I can say is 'Mate!' That is the very finest Australian saying. And all summer it's been 'Check' to the New York Yacht Club, to the British, to Dennis, or whatever it was. We were playing chess with them. 'Check, check, check, check.' And today we say 'Mate!' ''

"It's the end of a great era; but we knew it would end sometime. At least now it has ended with such wonderful racing. It was so close..."
—SOHEI HOHRI, LIBRARIAN OF THE NEW YORK YACHT CLUB
FOR THE PAST 25 YEARS

CHAPTER 13
Kiss the Cup Goodbye

It was a tearful farewell. Grown men, in fact, do cry. Members of the New York Yacht Club had a wrenching day on September 26, 1983, the day the America's Cup was lost. Gone was the icon of U.S. yacht racing history and the 132 years of American match-racing supremacy it represented.

The ornate silver pitcher, made by Garrard's of London, was not particularly beautiful. It had a bit of a chink in the middle, as if it had been dropped once by an errant child and put back where it belonged without anyone else seeing. No such thing could have happened. Children were not allowed to touch the America's Cup. Neither were adults. The Cup knew the touch of human hands only once a year, when the NYYC closed down for three weeks in the summer. Then the 134-ounce ewer was placed carefully in its three-quarter-inch black plywood box, and secured among the club's other treasures in the basement wine cellar. In August, when the six-story granite building was reopened to members, the revered trophy was put back on its pedestal, bolted down and covered like a pheasant under glass. This summer, however, the club remained open, so it missed its short journey to the wine cellar. It would make a longer one in the fall to Perth, Western Australia.

The Cup might as well have been a living thing, given the adoration it received. To some members it was the club's reason for being. To most it was a source of great pride. And to the outside world it was a mysterious relic.

The first shock waves began to ripple through the West 44th Street clubhouse at about 4 o'clock the afternoon of Monday, September 26. *Liberty* was ahead in that final race, but she seemed to be falling back, even losing her lead to *Australia II*. Members kept tuned to a radio in the club's office on the main floor. There wasn't a television in the place. One man sat at a switchboard nearby to handle a barrage of phone calls that kept pouring in. Rounding times at each mark were scribbled on a tally sheet mounted on a bulletin board in the club's lobby. This was the vital race, and more than 50 members had gathered by mid-afternoon. Most spent their time near the bar; a few sat down to a late lunch in the club dining room. Others meandered among the memorabilia in the upstairs Model Room, or sat comfortably in one of the leather chairs reading a newspaper.

The realization set in at 4:22. That was when *Liberty* rounded the fifth mark 21 seconds behind *Australia II*. With only one leg to go in the race, this group of seasoned yachtsmen knew that doomsday was at hand, that there was little chance now for the red boat from America to overtake the white boat from Australia.

As if not wanting to believe other reports, members waited for the official call from Lois Muessel, director of the America's Cup office in Newport, to report the race's times. There was a delay. The switchboard was overloaded. When word finally came, the bad news was posted on the board. It was an emotional moment, a moment in which more than a few eyes dampened.

The original plan, devised less than a week before, was that the America's Cup would be presented to the Australians at a ceremony in New York later that week, possibly Wednesday. These were last-minute arrangements, because it wasn't until the Australians won their third race that the NYYC actually came to grips with the reality of possibly losing the Cup. The NYYC House Committee asked Bud Fullerton, head of promotion and marketing for the club, to work out a plan. He appeared before the committee Friday, just three days before the final race. His scheme involved a pool system for journalists and photographers in order to limit the size of the crowd inside the club. It was going to be tight, considering all the people who would be invited, but the plan seemed viable. On Sunday, a day before the final race, a "contingency" plan was devised that only a select few knew about. That plan was to ship the America's Cup immediately to Newport should the Australians win. The presentation would be the next day.

"It's a little like having your tooth pulled," Fritz Jewett explained later. "The sooner you do it, the better."

The morning of the race, few knew whether the contingency plan would go into effect. Bill Foulk, chairman of the House Committee, who was working out the logistics with William H. Dyer Jones, chairman of the Race Committee, mentioned the plan to Lois Muessel. "They talked about it as if I knew what it was all about, but I didn't," she says. "I had to ask. Even then, they didn't tell me very much." Foulk left the America's Cup office that morning with the understanding that a decision was yet to be made, but that the club wanted Mrs. Muessel to make additional hotel reservations in Newport for the next day.

When *Australia II* won, members at the New York clubhouse were unsure what to do with the Cup. John Reid, ranking member at the time, telephoned Mrs. Muessel, informing her that he was unwilling to let the Cup go unless he got confirmation from the Race Committee that Foulk would be there to accept it. Knowing that a VHF radio call to the committee boat, *Black Knight,* can be monitored by the public, Muessel decided to ask the question in code. "Will Mr. Foulk keep his appointment tomorrow?" she asked *Black Knight* on Channel 74. "I believe he will," was the answer back. Lois Muessel knew what that meant. She telephoned Reid, and told him that he had the confirmation he needed.

The Brinks truck pulled up outside the yacht club at about 7:50 in the evening. By that time, word had spread to the 100 or so members and their guests who had gathered there. There was to be an ad hoc ceremony, but it was taking on the ambience of a deathbed vigil. The group collected in the Trophy Room, where the glass casing was removed. Members began making small spontaneous speeches, some of which were more moving than others. One, in particular, about how the Cup had at least been won by a deserving team, brought tears. Two of the members sobbed openly.

In the midst of the orations a bottle of Korbel champagne—made in America, of course—appeared from the downstairs bar. A member proceeded to pour it inside the mighty Cup with the wish that Neptunus Rex would see that the Cup was returned to West 44th Street. With any other vessel, the libation would have been gallant and symbolic. In this instance, it was almost ludicrous. The America's Cup has no bottom. The stream of champagne spewed from the base of the trophy, spilling onto the table, off the sides and onto the floor. "It was a very emotional period," says one observer. "But it was also a little irregular. Parts of it were rather messy. The symbolism was nice, but it was sloppy. One of the kitchen staff came out and tried to wipe it up with an apron. But everything was a mess."

Next, a member stood and dictated a document, which basically stated that the club was duly turning the Cup over to the Royal Perth Yacht Club. As it was dictated, another member transcribed the words on club stationery. Members were asked to sign the document as it was passed around. Others signed it as well—wives, friends—until it totaled 70-odd signatures. The group, which by now had drifted past the Model Room door and down the marble staircase, gathered near the front door. It was decided that only members should put the Cup in its case, so two stepped from the crowd and placed it inside. As the front door was opened, a crowd of more than 50 people waiting on the street broke into a rendition of "Waltzing Matilda," a song that was being sung at the same time up and down the streets of Newport. By now it was 8:20 P.M. The Brinks guard loaded the black box into the truck and drove into the night.

Sohei Hohri, who still had the 40-inch bolt that secured the Cup to the tabletop, followed by car an hour later. He and Peter Wawra, NYYC manager, decided to drive to Newport. When they arrived about 1 A.M. at the yacht *Black Knight,* the Cup still had not arrived. They were anxious, but were persuaded to check into their room at the Viking Hotel. When the Cup arrived, they would be called. An hour later the Brinks truck drove up to Goat Island in Newport, where the Cup was transferred to a station wagon and driven to the summer home of William H. Dyer Jones, who had agreed to care for the world's most esteemed yachting prize until morning. He was not alone. In addition to Jones, his wife, and Bill Foulk, there was a Newport policeman. The box containing the Cup was soaked in champagne, and when they opened it the full bouquet of the stale wine greeted them. The policeman said, "Phew! It *smells* like it's 132 years old." He sat up through the night with the Cup, while the Jones's boxer slept at his feet, snoring gently.

Early the next morning four police cars arrived at the Jones house. The officers came to the door to fetch the Cup, wearing bulletproof vests. When they opened the door, the boxer, now fully rested and ready to go, escaped from the house. Forgetting their mission for a moment, they chased after the runaway dog.

Finally the Cup was delivered to Marble House, the Newport mansion once owned by America's Cup sailor and patron Mike Vanderbilt. The NYYC planned to present it at noon to the Australians. When the box was opened, the Cup inside looked like the relic of a New Year's Eve bash—smeared and sticky with American champagne. Members of Newport's Preservation Society, which was preparing Marble House for the pending ceremonies, were faced with the unpleasant task of restoring the Cup. They had to wipe out the black box and lay it in the sun to dry. The Cup itself had to be cleaned several times with silver polish to bring up its luster.

When guests arrived an hour later, the America's Cup looked dazzling on its pedestal on the outdoor veranda. It was a spectacular day—crystalline skies and balmy temperatures. "[The Cup] seems to sparkle more here," remarked Bud Fullerton, as he viewed it in the light of day. "I don't remember it sparkling so much when we had it inside."

The sad scene on West 44th Street the night before was like a tea party compared to the evening madness of Newport. When *Australia II* crossed the finish line at 5:20 P.M. on Monday, the city-by-the-sea burst open at the seams. The madness started on the water, where a fleet of more than 1,000 spectator boats blasted their horns, blew sirens, and revved engines for the sheer joy of it and for a closer look at the winning crew. *Australia II* was awash in a sea of powerboats, sailboats, dinghies, and tour boats. Green and yellow balloons floated skyward over an energized mass of humanity afloat. The heavies of the *Australia II* syndicate—Ben Lexcen, Alan Bond, and Warren Jones—jumped from an inflatable outboard to the deck of *Australia II,* where the crew hugged and kissed each other in a tangle of flailing arms.

John Bertrand passed the helm over to Ben Lexcen, who steered the boat into shore. The crew had dropped the sails, a departure from their usual method of doing things, win or lose. Normally, they sail in and are towed when they near the harbor entrance. On this triumphant evening, the towline was attached immediately, and the mainsail dropped to the deck like a fallen butterfly. The crew, who by this time were beside themselves with joy, shoved the pile of sailcloth under the boom with their hands and feet, not even bothering to fold it over the boom. "Who cares? What the hell! We won!"

The tension of that last leg of the race had been profound. John Longley, who was grinding winches, said the crew was concentrating 110 percent, afraid that the slightest slip-up would deprive them of the victory they ached for. In the final moments, when *Australia II* cracked off for the finish line, Longley remembers being the first one to speak up.

"I was in the position of port grinder," he says. "I got up, poked my head around the forestay, looked out, and then said quietly to Brian Richardson, 'I think we're going to win the America's Cup.' All of a sudden about four guys yelled, 'Shut up, Chink [Longley's nickname]! It's not over 'til we get to the line!' I really got my head snapped off. Boy-oh-boy. And that was only within 40 seconds of the finish.

"A few seconds later, I said, 'Stuff you all. I could swim the boat that far.' And then all went a bit quiet until we rounded up across the line."

It was night by the time *Australia II* made her way into Newport harbor. Strains of "Waltzing Matilda" and words from the Australian rock group Men At Work—"I come from a land Down Under/Where women glow and men plunder..."—drifted over the water. The Coast Guard, which by now had become expert at moving large numbers of boats around, continually shooed spectator craft from the Australian tender and its towed Twelve. But there was nowhere to go.

The crowd along the docks had swelled to thousands. Every possible vantage point was occupied—boat hoists, travel lifts, buildings, porches, truck tops. The boat basin at Newport Offshore Ltd., where *Australia II* was kept, was a sea of bumping boats—inflatables, dinghies, speedboats, even a kayak. All were waiting for the victorious crew. ABC television had mounted a large scaffold at the end of a pier, and its floodlights spread nightlight in all directions. Fireworks and flares added to the visual effects.

To the crowd's surprise, an entourage from the *Freedom* syndicate appeared first. The 12-Meters *Freedom* and *Liberty,* rafted up to each side of their tender, *Fire Three,* appeared before the guests of honor. The midnight-blue *Freedom,* with her red and white stripes down each side, and the ruby-red *Liberty,* unadorned but colorful, both flew oversized American flags from their masts. Aboard *Fire Three,* "The Stars and Stripes Forever" played loudly. Coast Guard boats turned their searchlights on the billowing flags as Dennis Conner and his crew stood on the foredeck of the tender. Norman Rockwell would have lunged for his paintbrush had he seen it.

"I mean, that was worth everything," says Ed du Moulin, who orchestrated the scene. "I just don't ever recall in any of the other 12-Meter events that I know, where you had such a surge of patriotism and proud feelings. So it can't be a downer; it had been such a horrendous contest."

Australia II emerged from the night minutes later. Conner and a few of his crewmen jumped aboard the Australian 12 Meter in a display of good sportsmanship. From there, they hopped aboard *Black Swan* with Bond, Bertrand, Lexcen, and the rest of the *Australia II* crowd. It became an awkward scene, a handful of red jackets intermixed with the green-and-yellow rugby shirts of the Australians, a dash of losers among winners. *Liberty* tactician Tom Whidden was the first to bolt. As *Black Swan* eased in to the dock, a shower of champagne and cheering voices filled the boat basin. Whidden scrambled to the foredeck, looking lost and confused until he found his way over a heap of sailbags and finally to a place where he could disappear into the dockside crowd.

Finding an escape route was not so easy for the more conspicuous Conner and his wife, Judy. Conner hung back on the stern of *Black Swan,* trying to block his tears with a handkerchief. In stark contrast to the Australian heroes, he and Judy edged their way to the waterside rail and jumped into a dinghy below. They found themselves in a maze of small craft, not knowing which boat to hop into next. One to the other, they made their way through the mini fleet in search of a way out. Finally there was nothing but more water. Seeing their dilemma, a man on a nearby float grabbed a line and hauled in the dinghy with the Conners aboard. From there, the Conners disappeared under the *France 3* boat hoist, up a ladder, and into the darkness.

The Australians, meanwhile, were celebrating in a big way. The crewmen had congregated on *Australia II* as the boat slipped into position beneath its hoist. A cluster of friends and fans dumped champagne on their heads from the adjacent lift, which cradled *Challenge 12* in its slings. Bruno Troublé, the skipper of *France 3,* who had stayed on in Newport to watch the final races, yanked a line from the water with his own special bottle of French champagne nicely cooled at the end.

Chants of "Let's see the keel! Let's see the keel!" erupted from the dockside crowd. Several *Australia II* crewmen encouraged them, waving their arms up high as if leading a symphony orchestra. Alan Bond finally acquiesced. It had been a secret too long, and not a particularly well-kept secret at that. Lexcen himself was on board as the hoist slowly lifted *Australia II* out of the water. The green-and-blue camouflage drapes that covered the fins all summer hung like wilted petals at each side of the hull. The minute the boat was exposed, the crowd roared. The flotilla of dinghies scuttled underneath for a closer look. Scores of news cameramen and amateur photographers scrambled for the best angle.

At the same time that the famous keel was being shown, Dennis Conner was speaking to a jammed press conference at the Armory. Conner's speech was to the point. He spoke with honesty and determination, but the slight crack to his voice and a watery look in his eyes hinted that he was on the edge of control. When he was finished recapping the race, he got up and left. No questions were asked.

"There was no question that he was in complete shock," his longtime sailing friend and alternate helmsman, Jack Sutphen, says. "But I've never known Dennis to go into any regatta without thinking he was going to win. He has a great ego and great confidence . . . We felt Dennis was the better skipper, and that we had as good, or better, crew. We were very concerned about the speed of the boat. But, like any team sailing together so long, we thought we could do it. We thought Dennis was invincible."

Conner left the press conference with his wife. The two were dogged by a crushing mix of sympathizers and journalists. They walked down Thames Street on their way back to the *Liberty* docks, and Conner looked neither to right or left. People shouted encouragement. Conner thanked them quietly as he strode along. Suddenly, the mass came to a dead halt. Conner turned, looked slightly puzzled, and asked what street it was. He was lost. A voice in the crowd set him straight and he was off again. It was a path he had taken a hundred times before. By the time he made it to the docks a few minutes later, only one reporter was in his wake. "Where are you going next?" Doug Riggs, of the Providence *Journal,* asked. "Home," said Conner.

The Australians had to fight their way to the press center. Newport police had blocked traffic from Thames Street. This waterfront street runs past the 12-Meter docks, the press center in the Armory, and local bars and restaurants. Hundreds of people jammed the entrance to the Armory, vying for a better view of who walked in and out. Only media people with credentials and syndicate members were allowed inside. When Bond, Bertrand, and Jones arrived, there was what police later described as a "mini riot" at the door. Most of the police department were on duty that night, in addition to 10 officers from nearby Middletown. They were barely enough. One of the policemen was nearly "crushed" at the door, and another reportedly was punched in the face. Eileen Bond, Alan Bond's wife, had her $50,000 gold and diamond-studded Cartier watch ripped off her arm as she tried to plunge through the crowd to get inside; the watch was later recovered.

The Australians celebrated that night in their homeland as well. It was 5:20 on the morning of September 27 when live broadcasts to Australia announced that the Cup was won. The continent of six million inhabitants went wild. Prime Minister Bob Hawke declared a national holiday, adding that "any boss who sacks anyone for not turning up today is a bum. It's Australia's Cup now." A breakfast party at the Royal Perth Yacht Club drew more than 2,000 well-wishers for a champagne celebration. A month later, an even bigger celebration was held as the crew of *Australia II* gathered for the first time since being back home.

The day after the race, Dennis and Judy Conner were packing their bags to go home. Their two daughters, aged 11 and 13, already were back in school in San Diego. Judy, who is a school teacher and had missed the start of classes to stay with her husband, was anxious to return. Conner, who had mountains of work to attend to after the lengthy absence from his drapery business, also wanted to leave. Beyond that, he was in no mood to deal with Newport as the man who lost the Cup. Even in 1980, however, when Conner won the Cup series with ease, he left town almost immediately. No one said anything that year. This time he was criticized for it.

On Tuesday morning, word came to the *Freedom/Liberty* crew house at Seaview that the Cup presentation ceremony would be at noon that day at Marble House, rather than later in the week in New York. Conner was in the midst of packing his bags—he ended up with 35 suitcases and boxes— and neither Ed du Moulin nor Fritz Jewett had the heart to pressure him to stay. When they discussed with him whether or not he should attend the ceremony, they agreed it wasn't necessary.

"The man was physically beside himself trying to get ready," du Moulin says. "This was a man who had given so much of himself to this that there was no way I could criticize him. He was trying to do the right thing, but he had no time to himself. Just to get his gear off was a terrible rat race.

"All I know is that with anyone who would be critical of him, I'd be very disappointed. This man had given everything. Fritz and I both agreed there were some things you just couldn't ask him to do.''

More than 500 people gathered at Marble House that afternoon. Earlier in the day, members of the NYYC met with Peter Dalziell, commodore of the Royal Perth Yacht Club, and his attorney, to sign the Deed of Gift. The deed is a document, agreed upon in the 19th century between the original owners of the America's Cup and the NYYC, on how the race should be governed. Thankfully, the meeting went off without a hitch.

By 11:30 A.M., the guests started arriving. The *Australia II* crew was dressed for the occasion in sports jackets with *Australia II* insignias, dress shirts and ties, gray slacks, and matching gray laced shoes. Officials and invited guests stood on the upper veranda next to the America's Cup. Scattered around it were potted yellow hibiscus trees in full bloom and tables covered with white linen in preparation for the champagne that was to follow. Behind the America's Cup stood the men of *Australia II*. The public stood on a patio five steps below the veranda. Most of the *Liberty* and *Freedom* crewmen were there as well. Word of the presentation was so scattered that few of the crewmen knew whether they should dress up for the occasion, or where they should stand. As it turned out, they melded with the crowd and went almost unnoticed.

Commodore Stone represented the NYYC. Commodore McCullough, the head of the America's Cup Committee who had stirred so much controversy throughout the summer, never appeared. Jewett was one of many who thought that, of all people, McCullough should have been there. As soon as the race was over, McCullough went to New York, and then was off two days later for Europe, where he stayed for nearly a month. Several people within the *Freedom/Liberty* syndicate, including Jewett and du Moulin, were critical of McCullough for not stopping by the house after the race, and never calling Conner to say, at least, that the NYYC was grateful for his efforts.

"He had been calling Dennis every time he lost a race, telling him what he was doing wrong," another syndicate member says. "But on the day of the last race, McCullough disappeared and never said a word. I think that was rude."

The presentation ceremony lent a bit of serenity to what had been a fitful night before. The America's Cup was having its day in the sun. Local and state officials were reflecting in its glory, including Mayor Paul Gaines, who lamented the fact that he had said earlier in the summer that the Cup would never be lost while he was mayor.

Commodore Stone added a much needed touch of humor and warmth to the occasion, presenting designer Ben Lexcen with a battered Plymouth hubcap. The bit of scrap metal was a joke inspired by a comment made earlier in the summer by Lexcen that, if they won, the Australians planned to flatten the America's Cup with a steamroller and turn it into the America's Plate. The hubcap, Stone said, was a memento of the American heritage and its connection with Plymouth (referring to the first settlers who landed at Plymouth, Massachusetts).

"We hope they will maintain this Cup as we have," said Rhode Island's governor J. Joseph Garrahy. "But for a very short period of time." When it came to the Cup, the Australians got silly. Warren Jones kissed it. Alan Bond held it over his head like Bjorn Borg at Wimbledon. And Ben Lexcen simply grinned at it.

That same day, both the American and the Australian syndicates received a phone call from the White House. President Reagan had invited them to Washington, D.C., the next afternoon. Du Moulin was able to contact almost everyone except Halsey Herreshoff, *Liberty*'s navigator, who was on his way to Greece, and Dennis Conner, who was at Green Airport in Warwick, Rhode Island, waiting to catch a plane to New York, and then another to San Diego. Again, Conner's absence would seem unfortunate and conspicuous.

"It was just completely impractical for him [Conner] to change his course in midstream and go down to Washington," du Moulin says. "And I didn't want to push him, because I knew he was under pressure . . . He was way overdue in getting back there and handling certain things that had come up. The series [being] delayed . . . made it even tougher for him.

"In the meantime, I thought he did a marvelous job with the crew the night we lost. He had gone over to *Australia*, and to his press conference, and to the party that night at the house."

Conner had talked to Reagan by telephone after the race. The call came in after he had finished the evening press conference. Conner joked with Reagan about the loss and told him that he and the crew were going to take up horseback riding from now on. Reagan, as one might expect, could relate to that. When the *Liberty* crew got to Washington, the remark from Conner would be the first thing the President mentioned.

"I've been through the *Enterprise* loss, and I've been through the *Freedom* victory, and I've been through this," du Moulin commented. "This, without question, was the proudest moment of my life. I was so proud of what we did and how we did it. It wasn't the happiest day of my life; but it certainly was a greater day than the day we won with *Freedom* [in 1980], because the effort was tremendous and the odds were heavily stacked against us. I believe the guys feel that way, too.

"On top of that, we were never invited to the White House when we won the America's Cup. We were invited there after we made what I would call a fantastic defense of it."

The syndicate reserved 14 seats on US Air Flight 267, leaving the Providence airport for Washington at 11:50 A.M. Wednesday. Tom Whidden was one of two members of the afterguard who made it. Eight other crewmen went, including John Marshall, who flew in from his home in Addison, Maine, and Jon Wright, who met them in Washington after a flight from Philadelphia.

The Australians chartered their own plane. Bond and his wife Eileen went along with Ben Lexcen, Warren Jones, John Bertrand, three members of the crew, and Peter Dalziell, commodore of the Royal Perth Yacht Club.

Ironically, the two planes were heading into the Washington airport at the same time. The US Air pilot spoke over the cabin loudspeaker and announced that 6,000 feet beneath them was the plane taking the Australian crew to Washington. The pilot said he had spoken to the tower at National Airport and was assured that the US Air flight would land first. "*Liberty* will beat the Australians this time," the pilot promised.

The *Liberty* crew rendezvoused with Commodore Stone at the Sans Souci in downtown Washington. The restaurant, which is a famous watering hole for the capital city's political élite, offered a free lunch to the team. Its owner, who happens to be an avid Lightning-class sailor, had heard of the pending visit and asked the White House to extend the invitation.

The crews met in the White House Rose Garden. President Reagan appeared only briefly—no more than 15 minutes—to say hello and to extend his best wishes to both teams. The Americans gave Reagan a photograph of *Liberty* racing *Australia II; Liberty,* of course, was ahead. The Australians presented him with a book. Later, the Americans forwarded a box to Reagan with a *Liberty* poster inside signed by the crew and with *Liberty* T-shirts and ties.

Vice-President George Bush joined the group in the Rose Garden and stayed on after the President left. The crews were treated to a private tour of the White House which, for the Australians, was cut short because their chartered plane was scheduled to leave. The Americans, whose plane wasn't leaving until 7:10 P.M., took additional tours of the Senate and House of Representatives, both of which were in session.

By the time the two groups went their separate ways, it was clear that they'd all been touched in some way by the day's events. Altogether, it had been an extraordinary two weeks.

*"So if I were Alan Bond and someone
asked me, 'Well, Mr. Bond, would
you paddle during a race?' I would
say, 'No, that's cheating.' On the
other hand, if someone asked, 'Mr.
Bond, if you had a little opportunity
to get help from someone in designing
the boat, who wasn't Australian,
would you accept it?' I might say,
'Well, if there is no one there to keep
me from doing it, of course.' "*

—JOHN MARSHALL, DISCUSSING WHO DESIGNED *AUSTRALIA II*

CHAPTER 14
From the Perfect Perspective of Hindsight

It seemed fitting that Ben Lexcen, the designer of *Australia II,* was the
first Australian to speak at the press conference that followed *Australia
II*'s victory. Fitting because, in the final analysis, the history of the
1983 America's Cup series was written by the yacht designers. And
especially by Ben Lexcen. Lexcen, who had invested so much of his
creative energy in 12 Meters, said that he was "stunned" by the
Australian triumph. "I just had no confidence," he explained. "We were
pushing to beat Dennis Conner; I tell you . . . I was worried about Dennis
Conner. Dennis saved the Cup last time, and he deserves a lot of credit for
trying to save the Cup this time."

A reporter asked Lexcen, "You mean that, even though you had the
faster boat, you were afraid that somehow [Conner] might pull it out?"

Lexcen responded, "He's a tricky little devil."

In America—and probably the world—nobody sails Twelves better than
Dennis Conner. Not Tom Blackaller, not Gary Jobson, not Ted Turner,
not John Kolius; and if you are measuring man against man, not even
Australia's John Bertrand is better. If nobody does it better, why did
America lose the America's Cup? From the presumably perfect perspec-
tive of hindsight, we explore that question.

First—and foremost—America lost the America's Cup because our technology was found wanting. *Liberty* was a good 12 Meter, perhaps a great Twelve of her lineage, but she was a refinement of a theme that dates back to 1967. *Liberty* was a small step taken at a time when, on the other side of the world, Ben Lexcen was taking giant steps in yacht design. *Liberty* was conservative, perhaps an appropriate approach to a boat that would defend the longest winning streak in sport; but *Australia II* was radical, which seems philosophically correct for a boat challenging that record. It seems so simple from this perspective: if the Australians could make the radical boat right (no simple proposition, considering that there have been only two breakthrough 12 Meters—*Intrepid* in 1967 and *Australia II* in 1983), they could win the America's Cup.

John Bertrand, the skipper of *Australia II,* works for John Marshall, the sailtrimmer on *Liberty* and the president of North Sails. In 1980, after a competitive *Australia I* lost 4–1 to Dennis Conner's Americans, the boat was unceremoniously sold to the British. Marshall remembers being surprised by that, because he considered *Australia I* a very good Twelve. "I said to Bertrand, who had just been named skipper, 'What are you doing?' He responded, 'There is no way we can beat Dennis Conner in a conventional 12 Meter in Newport. We're going to have to break new ground. We can't win this thing sailing the same equipment because, no matter how good we are, we will at best be equal, and someplace in the chain of necessity we'll be weaker—whether it's in starting skills, tactics, or crew work, or tacking, or sails, or meteorology.' "

Marshall has not forgotten that judgment.

What Ben Lexcen wrought, following that mandate, was perhaps the largest step ever taken in designing boats to the 12-Meter rule. What Dennis Conner had in comparison was an obsolete Twelve that he had to drag around the course on the strength of his talent and the force of his character. When one compares equipment, it is less surprising that Conner lost the America's Cup than that he won three races.

Liberty was, concludes Marshall, a "creative failure." To Marshall's way of thinking, the fault does not lie specifically with Dennis Conner or Johan Valentijn. "It's more of an endemic American problem of not reaching far enough, not taking large enough risks, and not having the structure to permit or encourage that," he says. "The Australians won the America's Cup because they had a more creative design, a radical design—a risk-taking design, but a successful one.

"We lost the America's Cup for want of the right ideas in yacht design. Maybe for want of an environment that lets bright young designers focus on 12-Meter design, make it their life's work, and come up with the right answers. Johan, Langan, Dave Pedrick are undoubtedly very, very skilled, very excellent designers, but finally, it was an illusive thing they were seeking: an improvement on *Freedom*. Certainly anyone who designed a conventional boat—anyone trying to come up with a better all-around boat than *Freedom*—must have been very frustrated with how very difficult that was.

"If that small amount of improvement is very hard to find, the breakthroughs and the inspiration—the real dawning of a new age in 12-Meter design—are exceptionally hard to find. I think simply having more bright young guys working on the problem and attacking it from different areas might have helped. But so many of the good designers are so involved with their IOR [International Offshore Rule] yacht careers and with the necessity of running an ongoing business, rather than a once-every-three-years business, they simply couldn't do it. Maybe they weren't given the opportunity; but, on the other hand, they hadn't sought the opportunity.

"In this particular instance, Lexcen has been virtually committed to little else but designing 12 Meters, and he did have the inspiration. That ultimately was the story."

But could some responsibility for that lack of vision, lack of inspiration, belong to Dennis Conner? Bill Langan, of Sparkman & Stephens, commented that after *Magic* and *Spirit of America* proved unsuccessful, Dennis Conner decided he would design the boats. In light of that statement, Marshall was asked who designed *Liberty*. "It was Johan's boat in the sense that there was no one else in our program with the technical expertise to design a 12 Meter," he said, "but what Dennis contributed to the design was a numerical guideline. After sailing *Freedom*, and knowing her numbers, sailing *Enterprise*, and knowing her numbers, and modifying both boats . . . we had a good feel for the changes."

When neither boat proved capable of beating *Freedom*, it was decided to build another boat. "I think it was clear in Dennis's mind," continued Marshall, "that it would have to be a conservative shot. We couldn't risk another radical effort, like *Magic*, because the probability of success would be small . . . So what this all boiled down to was that after consulting with Halsey [Herreshoff] and other people, including myself, Dennis largely prescribed to Johan some leading parameters for *Liberty*: a displacement, a length, almost therefore a sail area, and the lateral plane. He also had some input into more detailed things, such as the sectional shapes in the boat—that sort of thing."

Designer Bruce Kirby, though impressed with Conner the sailor, is less impressed with Conner the yacht designer. Said Kirby, "I've talked to Dennis a lot over the years, and his knowledge of design is really pretty limited. He talks about things in very simplistic terms. The same is true of Blackaller. I talked to Blackaller about the changes they were making to

Defender, and I couldn't believe how simplistic he was about it. Obviously, they made a major step backwards on that boat, at Pedrick's expense.''

For Bruce Kirby, one factor in the lack of imagination on the U.S. side of the America's Cup design wars may have been the competition between the syndicate's designers. Said Kirby, ''There was that terrible political thing with S&S, Johan Valentijn, and the syndicate. I think that may have cost them more heavily than we realize, because I know a lot of people who still think that *Freedom* [an S&S design] was probably the faster boat. But after S&S bowed out—in murky circumstances—Conner wouldn't choose it. (Then, after they modified it, the rules made it unattractive for them to choose it.) On the other hand, I can't imagine Dennis not choosing the faster boat; but it's really hard to know, even if someone as objective as he usually is could perhaps be influenced, subconsciously, by those machinations . . . I've talked to guys on their crew afterwards, who nearly all seem to think that *Freedom* would have been a better choice. They also said that, throughout the summer, *Liberty* was slow downwind.''

But because of a mistake, Dennis couldn't choose *Freedom* even if he wanted to. The changes made to the boat in June, which canceled the grandfather clause, saw to that. This is why *Freedom* didn't sail in the trials in July, as planned, and why she may never be a competitive Twelve again. In retrospect, those structural changes in the boat had to be one of the bigger blunders of the summer.

Marshall disagrees that *Liberty* was a slower boat than *Freedom,* but he does question the syndicate's decision to have two designers in competition. Marshall is not convinced that the creative process flourishes under competitive pressure. ''A competitive and nonexclusive relationship is very tough on creative people,'' said Marshall. ''Creative people don't necessarily strive in that environment. You don't take two sculptors or two painters and put them in opposite ends of the room and tell them that one or the other is going to hang in the Louvre.''

Marshall had firsthand knowledge of this problem, as he shared the cockpit and the sailmaking responsibilities in the *Freedom* camp with Tom Whidden, the president of Sobstad Sails. That particular competitive relationship dates back to 1980 with *Freedom.* Asked if it was hard to work so closely with a business rival, Marshall said, ''It is hard to work with a competitor in any environment, particularly in a creative one, because a creative person needs a certain amount of room and a certain amount of freedom from intense pressure to flourish . . . The North organization has been leading the way in high-technology sails for some time, particularly in 12 Meters, and there is always a sense that another sailmaker involved in the program is piggybacking technology that you had to develop from scratch and very much the hard way . . . You have the feeling that the other guy comes into the program, and finds it a little easier. The other side of it, however, is that Tom contributed a great deal to the program as tactician and as a leader among the crew. And the sailmaking that he did was also creative and constructive, so I've always respected his contribution on a personal level, and we were able to work together, ultimately, very effectively.''

The S&S-Valentijn–*Freedom* syndicate battles ultimately seemed very costly in three areas: time, money, and creativity. Valuable weeks were spent sailing *Magic* and *Spirit* against each other before the syndicate learned the awful truth that neither was faster than the 1980 boat, *Freedom*. Why, one wonders, did the syndicate wait so long to commission *Freedom*? Once they found that neither new boat was faster, they had to design and build a third boat, *Liberty,* and rebuild *Spirit*. That was costly in terms of resources and time. And after Dennis Conner had built *Liberty,* the third new boat, he almost had to choose it. (How could he build three new Twelves—at a cost of at least $300,000 apiece—and then decide that he liked the 1980 *Freedom* best?) Also, when the radical *Magic* failed, it was obvious that the boat that followed (*Liberty*) would be a conservative boat. That was costly in terms of creativity. And, finally, a related question must also be asked: how costly was the effort to end the design competition—a monster decidedly of the syndicate's making? Breaking the agreement with Sparkman & Stephens must have cost heavily in terms of psychic energy, not to mention in the area of public relations. You don't ''fire'' the dean of naval architecture—and then try to hold his firm to an exclusivity clause—without some psychic injury to both parties.

There were other reasons for America's loss of the Cup. In his autobiography, *No Excuse to Lose,* written with John Rousmaniere, Dennis Conner makes this interesting statement: ''I have sailed with and against the best in 12 Meters, ocean racers, and small boats, and I think I have learned something from each person. What is interesting is that, although each is especially good at one particular thing—leadership, boat preparation, helmsmanship—they all have this in common: when they get up in the morning and look at themselves in the mirror, they all have the self-confidence to be able to say realistically, 'I am the best.' ''

In July, however, people weren't saying that Dennis Conner and *Liberty* were the best; they were saying that John Bertrand and *Australia II* were the best. And perhaps more damaging for Dennis Conner, the comments were coming from within. Wrote Halsey Herreshoff, yacht designer and Conner's navigator, in June: ''If the closely guarded peculiar keel design of *Australia II* is allowed to remain in competition, or is allowed to continue to be rated without penalty, the yacht will likely win the foreign trials and will likely win the America's Cup in September.''

That was part of the 34-page missive that officially launched Keelgate, and this battle, concluded many, exploded in the Americans' faces.

Said Bruce Kirby, "In my opinion, they did the keel program in order to harass the enemy, but it backfired. They thought that by bringing up this keel thing—I'm not sure they ever thought they'd win it—but they thought it would be harassment of a sort that might discourage the Aussies and get them thinking about other things besides winning the America's Cup. I think, rather, it got the Americans concentrating on the keel and worrying about it. And when it all fell through—which it was bound to do—where were they? Having said this thing is a breakthrough, having said it is going to win the America's Cup and so on, they were struck with having to race against it. They nailed themselves to the wall."

Conner approached the Cup races in September without his requisite self-confidence. One wondered what he thought about when he looked in his mirror. He had an excuse to lose—the other boat was faster—and he lost.

"No matter what you heard at the press conferences, no matter what Dennis Conner and John Bertrand said to various reporters, the fact of the matter is that, for the first time, the defender was the underdog—in his own mind," said Bruce Kirby. "I think that cost them more than the speed of *Australia II*. [Conner] didn't think he was going to win. If you look at Dennis's book, you realize his psyche has to be in really good shape to win. He admits that; he even admits that he's not the world's greatest sailor; but he tries harder, and he gets himself worked up to the point where he almost can't lose. He went in there knowing he could lose. I think that made more difference than anything else. And because he was running scared the whole time, he blew it."

Even his first two victories in the first two races could not have been cheering to Dennis Conner. This motivated man, who will outwork you, outspend you, outsmart you, outsail you, could barely beat a crippled *Australia II*. And his third win was much the same; Conner had sailed perfectly for 24.3 miles and yet his margin of victory was a scant 43 seconds. The conclusion was plain: Conner needed perfection, luck, or a miracle to successfully defend the America's Cup. He went to that well three times, but finally, he couldn't find it for a fourth win.

In the brilliance of *Australia II*, one tends to overlook the other pieces, which fit perfectly. Kirby put it this way: "Everything was right on that boat. *Australia II* had eight guys who had sailed in the America's Cup before and five who had been here three times. They had very, very excellent sail development. The whole thing was right. Then they had this unusual keel and hull. That is what usually happens: if a guy puts up enough effort to come up with something like *Australia II*, he is also putting up the effort in all the other areas.''

Kirby's opinion of John Bertrand? ''He is technically excellent as a sailtrimmer and as a guy who will make the boat go as fast as possible in any wave or sea condition. I think that he is a very, very good helmsman; he gets the most out of the boat. I'm sure his ability to maneuver the boat was as good as anyone's, including Dennis's. Mind you, his boat was set up to be tacked and maneuvered. He seemed to have starting-line problems. Even in the foreign trials, that problem was there; but he didn't need the expertise then. His timing of a start seemed faulty, but Dennis is a master at timing. Dennis spends all his waking hours timing things with a stopwatch . . .''

Finally, we must address the question that seemed cardinal to the New York Yacht Club: did Ben Lexcen design *Australia II* or did the Dutch? A strong case could be made that this was a group effort. Lexcen says as much: ''They [the staff of the Netherlands Ship Model Basin] were just doing what I told them. Sometimes they'd tell me things back. How the hell can you stop them from telling you things? It's like in a jury—'Well, disregard that remark . . . ' You can't disregard that remark. If someone says, 'I think this could be a good idea,' you can't say, 'Well, I didn't hear that.'

''The situation at the tank puts you almost under conditions that would contravene the spirit of the bloody ruling of the New York Yacht Club. But as far as I'm concerned, if you can use the tank, then you can talk to the people at the tank.* The only time they [the NYYC] brought it up was after the boat was good. But they never would have brought it up if the boat had been a turkey.''

A dispassionate view is that *Australia II* wasn't created in a vacuum. Marshall, who studied to be a research scientist, describes the typical creative process in such a situation: ''I can only comment that as a person who has been through university and a research-laboratory environment, I know the way these things happen. It's a creative ferment. Everyone gets involved; you can't keep people out of it. The more radical, the more interesting the idea, the more people want to be involved. So the concept of national independence, in a multinational research environment, is absolutely antithetical. My personal opinion is that Lexcen in a vacuum could have conceived of *Australia II*, but I don't think he did.''

---

*As there is no test tank in Australia, the New York Yacht Club gave the Australians permission to use the Dutch tank. Victor Romagna, secretary of the NYYC's America's Cup Committee, set these conditions in a letter of June 11, 1982. '' . . . Officially your tank tests in the Netherlands Ship Model Basin are entirely within the rules if: (1) They were under the sole supervision of Australian nationals; (2) The designs were from the drawing board of Australian nationals; and (3) The results are used in the design of that Australian challenger only.''

Then there is the fact that Lexcen, like nature, seems to abhor a vacuum. He is, to put it simply, a sociable fellow. The fact that Dr. Peter van Oossanen, of the Netherlands Ship Model Basin, supposedly called him "a friend" is not surprising. Lexcen is an eminently likable man. He lived in Holland for four months while designing *Australia II*; he presumably made friends there; and it is certainly conceivable that, occasionally, he and his friends talked about work they were doing both formally and socially.

Marshall was asked: Isn't it naïve to think that there would be no cross-pollination in such a relationship? "That's right," he said. "I think that in the most simpleminded case, a designer could take a model to a facility, the technicians could subject it to tests, and present the designer with an envelope of the results. That would be the total interaction. But the practical reality is that the Stephens tank [in New Jersey] and the Hydronautics tank [in Maryland], which U.S. designers are familar with, have always taken some interest in the process of design and have always sat down with the designers, looked at the results, helped interpret them, and helped the design to advance. But here vastly more was going on than that. Here was an ongoing situation with the designer in residence for a number of months, so I think Halsey and Dennis and the other people felt that the reality was that there was quite a lot of input into the boat which was not Australian..."

But, finally, was it cheating? The Deed of Gift is vague: its country-of-origin rule reads "... the designers of the yacht's hull, rig, and sails shall be nationals of that country...." The three-page affidavit that the New York Yacht Club presented to the Australians was specific—like a bullet [see Appendix A]. In its whereases and wherefores is the line, "*Australia II* was designed solely and exclusively by Ben Lexcen, a national of Australia, and no 'foreign consultants' and no 'foreign designer—however he is designated' assisted or participated in the design of *Australia II*'s keel, hull...."

It seemed indeed to be a case of rewriting the Constitution to fit the circumstances, and thus it is not surprising that Bond, Lexcen, Jones, and Dalziell refused to sign the NYYC affidavit. There was a penalty of perjury.

"When rules are unenforceable," says John Marshall, "then they are not in any degree rules. If I were Warren Jones or Alan Bond, I would think that the objective was to win the Cup, to seek all available avenues, and that the enemy was the New York Yacht Club. And if the enemy left a door open—the fact that the enemy had written a proscription and said that wasn't a valid avenue is irrelevant. I would not consider myself unethical for taking that approach. I would say that is the enemy's rule, and if he's not prepared to defend that rule, it is no rule. So if I were Alan Bond and someone asked me, 'Well, Mr. Bond, would you paddle during a race?' I would say, 'No, that's cheating.' On the other hand, if someone asked, 'Mr. Bond, if you had a little opportunity to get help from someone in designing the boat, who wasn't Australian, would you accept it?' I might say, 'Well, if there is no one there to keep me from doing it, of course.' "

But didn't the New York Yacht Club effectively fight to enforce this rule? Fight?—yes. Effectively?—no. To only touch on the New York Yacht Club's pursuit of Keelgate, the club made no effort to find out about *Australia II* until she started winning. The NYYC missed the measurement date of the boat, which could have dismissed all the secrecy. When they finally got around to attacking the design, they had no standing in the matter. And while they were attacking the legality of the design, the leading syndicate was attempting to secure information in order to equip one of their boats with a similar keel. They tried to impugn the reputation of Ben Lexcen, on a vague legal point, without sufficient evidence.

Bruce Kirby put it this way: "I think the NYYC's America's Cup Committee was very, very late. It was a case of too little too late. They thought about copying it; but then they realized they couldn't copy it in the time they had. And having decided they couldn't copy it, they decided it was illegal. It was ludicrous. Like everyone else, they knew about the keel early in the game. I've been told on very good authority that they had pictures of it before the boat ever got to the U.S. They certainly had sketches of the thing. I know they talked to Jerry Milgram [of M.I.T.] quite early in the summer about working on a similar idea. But they didn't do anything. Everybody sat around saying, 'Let's see how it works.' And then when it started to work pretty damn well, they said, 'Maybe that boat would be winning anyway; after all, they have the best crew, the best sails, they've all been here before, so maybe that's not why they are winning.' By the time they realized that the boat was in fact exceptional, and that the keel must have something to do with it, they were too late to do anything about it."

Marshall, too, wondered what the New York Yacht Club was up to. "There were a lot of rumors about the keel going back to December or January. Stuff like that the boat had wings, that the boat was or wasn't as fast as *Challenge 12*, which, of course, was an unknown quantity. The Australians did a good job of confusing any casual observer to what was going on. But the really shocking and surprising thing was that there was no serious observer around; that none of the syndicates felt it necessary to have any serious observers there; and that the New York Yacht Club incredibly didn't feel it was necessary or saw any need to look into the thing seriously themselves. A dispassionate observer would have to feel that Australia, of all the countries involved, was most likely to mount a very serious challenge. So where would the threat come from? From the Australians, who have the skill to sail a radical boat. Yet nobody made any serious effort to find out about the boat. In fact, never in any real serious way was any attempt made to find out about that boat.''

The New York Yacht Club was not wrong in pursuing the matter of the Australian keel—its questions were legitimate—but sensitivity to public relations, to gentlemanly behavior, to good sportsmanship was sorely lacking in its heavyhanded attempt to discover the parentage of the keel.

Alan Bond drafted and perfectly executed his master plan. He built the best 12 Meter ever. He manned it with a brilliant skipper and an experienced crew. He kept the crew far removed from the politics of Keelgate. And, perhaps most important to his successful campaign for the America's Cup, Alan Bond knew how to fight and how to win. He met the New York Yacht Club at every turn, anticipated its every move, and flexed his muscles when he had to. Through it all, he had the world persuaded that he was the victim of these men who would do anything to keep the America's Cup. That may not have been the case, but it was definitely savvy public relations.

From the perfect perspective of hindsight, is it so surprising that Alan Bond managed to take away the America's Cup? Take it away from these men who had become so accustomed to winning over 132 years that they had forgotten how to fight to win?

*"I guess we'll have to put an
America's Cup buoy out there
like you do . . ."*
—JOHN LONGLEY, MANAGER FOR THE
1987 AMERICA'S CUP CAMPAIGN IN PERTH, AUSTRALIA

CHAPTER 15
The Cup in Western Australia

Peter de Savary decided that he wasn't going to miss the final America's Cup Race no matter what. He had flown back to London two days before to attend to pressing business—much of which had been neglected all summer in favor of his *Victory* challenge. Even his friendship and business dealings with Alan Bond, his Australian counterpart, weren't enough to keep de Savary in Newport a day longer. At least not until the Australian team won its third race. Things were getting serious. De Savary hopped on a Concorde with three friends the morning of September 24, had breakfast on the plane, landed at JFK airport in New York, jumped aboard de Savary's twin-engine seaplane, flew to Newport and boarded de Savary's Magnum 53 for a 40-knot ride to the race course. Only the wind failed to show that day, so two hours later the foursome zoomed back to the *Victory* syndicate docks aboard the million-dollar speedboat, retraced their tracks to New York and were back on the Concorde in time for supper.

The America's Cup may not be that convenient for the jet-set moves of Peter de Savary when the 1987 series is held in Perth, or for corporate sponsors who count on selling their products to a lucrative market. Western Australia has about one million inhabitants. It also has an almost equal number of square miles to spread them around. The likes of de Savary, who use an America's Cup campaign to meld business and play, duty and fun, may find that the land Down Under, for all its dreamland countryside, may be a nightmare for those who live in the world of commerce.

The uncertainty of keeping American, European, and Middle East deals alive from a temporary headquarters in Perth has left de Savary hedging on whether he will challenge another time. "If it had been Newport, he'd have come back in a shot," says Angus Melrose, a *Victory* syndicate sail designer. "As it stands, he's the kind of guy who jumps on things by

197

instinct. He's interested in going, but he must level down from this attempt first." Despite the wait-and-see stance of the British team, its challenging club in 1983 has already taken the plunge. The Royal Burnham Yacht Club filed a formal application to challenge within a week of the last 1983 race. No one in de Savary's camp would say categorically that their bald-headed, cigar-chomping leader was behind the move. But when asked who else it could be, the reply was clear. "There is nobody else."

Maybe not in Great Britain. But the rest of the yachting world seems eager. The French, Italians, and Canadians will be giving the Cup another go. The Italians, in fact, are so serious that they bought *Freedom*, still one of the most competitive 12 Meters in existence, for $450,000. The boat will no doubt become a trial horse for a new Italian 12 Meter, for which *Freedom* will be a fine benchmark for tuning-up sessions on the water. The Swedes, who challenged for the Cup in 1977 and 1980, but stayed away in 1983, are planning on Perth. Newcomers from Germany and Japan seem serious. And inquiries from New Zealand, Spain, Finland, and the Netherlands look promising. The Germans already have a good start. A team of designers from Hamburg, Judel-Vrolijk, penned two winners in the 1983 Admiral's Cup international yacht-racing regatta in England. The only problem was that these boats were designed to a different set of rules from America's Cup 12 Meters. In fact, the German group has never designed a Twelve. Given the German reputation for efficiency and ingenuity, however, this may not be a problem. "We will try very hard to make this a professional effort," says Rolf Vrolijk. "We will come to win, no matter what the cost."

The Australians expect to hold the next challenge in 1987 as a prelude to the nation's bicentennial in 1988. Alan Bond plans to return—this time a defender. And new challenges are expected from Sydney's Royal Sydney Yacht Squadron, which challenged in 1983 with *Advance,* and from the *Challenge 12* syndicate, representing the Royal Yacht Club of Victoria in Melbourne.

The twist in 1987 is that the traditional defenders—the American boats—will now be challengers. And the Australians, of course, will be defenders of the America's Cup. In the past, the word "defender" was synonymous with the likes of *Liberty, Courageous, Freedom, Defender, Clipper,* and all the other red, white, and blue hulls that have fought so hard for the right to keep the America's Cup. Cino Ricci, skipper of the Italian 12-Meter *Azzurra,* doesn't like the idea of having the U.S. teams on the challenge side of the Cup equation. In the end, he figures it means tougher competition for him.

"I want Dennis Conner to win," he said just before the 1983 Cup races. "If he does not win, then the Americans will be challengers next time.

Then I must go out and sail each day against American skippers—against John Kolius and Tom Blackaller and Dennis Conner. I only want to meet the Americans on the race course once—when they are the defenders, and I am the challenger."

Unfortunately for Ricci, he's not about to have his way. The Americans are going to try—and try with a vengeance—to win the America's Cup back. Several syndicates are in the formative stages already. Within them, Dennis Conner will surely return as the perennial rose in a garden of wildflowers. In fact, the idea had taken root within a week of the final 1983 race. "Are you set to go to Australia?" Conner asked his alternate helmsman, Jack Sutphen, in a coast-to-coast telephone conversation. "Are you ready to line up your team yet?" was Sutphen's direct reply.

Although it may be too early for Conner to say unequivocally that he's going, those who know him best believe that he'll take up the challenge. "Sailing is his life," says Ed du Moulin. "I think if we had an organization he could be satisfied with, he'd go for it again."

Du Moulin himself, who has managed 12-Meter syndicates through three campaigns—1977, 1980, and 1983—says he won't do it again. He will be 73 in 1987 and would rather spend the time between now and then relaxing, visiting the three new grandchildren he has acquired since the 1980 campaign, and even doing a bit of sailing on his own. "I'll do what I can to get a new campaign off and running," he says. "But I'd rather let someone younger than me run the thing." He appeared at the final press conference after the 1983 series, confirming his plans to meet with the Fort Schuyler Foundation on October 19 to ask for its support in 1987. "We would like to retain *Liberty* as a benchmark for 1987 and then go for it again," he said. The foundation has agreed to lend its support.

The *Freedom/Liberty* group isn't the only one interested. Once the America's Cup bug bites, the fever lasts. Gary Jobson was bitten in 1977 and he, of all people, has been unable to shake it. He planned to visit Perth within two months of the 1983 series to scout out the America's Cup's new territory with *Defender/Courageous* backers Nick and Jane Heyl. The syndicate has split, leaving John Kolius siding with Chuck Kirsch, the *Defender/Courageous* project manager, for another try, perhaps from a club with Texas blood. The New York Yacht Club is sure to fly its burgee again, but it will not have the dominance it once had in Cup campaigns.

Although the stage is set for 1987, finding corporations to kick in money for campaigns won't be easy for either challengers or defenders. Australia, for all its sunshine and clean waters, has fewer than six million people, most of whom are clustered in Sydney, Perth, and Melbourne. The Germans, for example, found Porsche, BMW, and Lufthansa eager to back a 1987 challenge—in America. Now that the Cup has been lost, sponsorship must be reevaluated by all the syndicates. Selling a Porsche in Perth is not the same as promoting a fast car in Newport, where wealth is a 40-room house overlooking the Atlantic, and the New York metropolitan area—a market for sure—is a three-hour drive away. Perth, by contrast, is relatively isolated, homogeneous, and middle-class. This is not to say that a market for everything from Porsches to boat shoes is nonexistent. But selling it to the all-important sponsors may take some doing.

Filling syndicate coffers is an uphill battle when it comes to the America's Cup, corinthian as the sport still is. Nearly every syndicate has its godfather who kicks in a major percentage of the cash up front. But syndicate budgets that now average $4–$5 million must tap numerous other sources as well. One insider put it this way: "One of the ways we get money from some of these people is that they like to come to Newport; they like to feel they're important when they come here, and that they're treated well. Going out on one of the syndicate boats to watch the races is a big deal for them. I don't think having the Cup in Perth will have the same appeal. There's something much greater involved when you have to think about getting on board an airplane to go to Australia." Obviously, the insider is American. But the problem is international. Even the Australians got something out of the American market that they won't be able to squeeze out of their own economy. The only salvation may be that the magic of the America's Cup is enough to keep the cash outlays flowing, regardless of where the America's Cup buoy is anchored.

The Australians are sure to like the change. No more $2,000 round-trip airfares to Newport. No more letters home. No more living out of suitcases. No more New England clambakes in place of Australian barbecues. No more "insipid" American beer at Newport's otherworldly prices. Newport locals joked about having to learn to talk "Strine" just to get along with the "racer-chasers." One conversation, overheard by a Providence *Journal* reporter in a downtown pizza parlor, was a case in point:

"What's your name?" said the waitress to the man who had just ordered a pizza. "I'll call you when it's ready."

"Wine," he said.

"W-I," she began tentatively.

"No," he said, looking confused. "Wine."

They looked at each other for a few seconds. Then he reached for the order pad and wrote his name.

"Oh," she said, biting back a laugh. "Wayne."

The tables will be turned on Americans in Perth, especially if *Australia II*'s skipper John Bertrand is any indication. During one of the press conferences in late summer, Bertrand was asked a question by a broadcast journalist from Atlanta. A puzzled look came over Bertrand's usually placid face as he listened, and then he asked the woman if she would kindly repeat the question. "I'm sorry," he said, "but I can't understand your accent." The press room crowd roared, especially the Americans who had been straining all summer to understand the nuances of Australian English, as opposed to American English. Speakers of "English" English seemed to have the least trouble; in a scrape, they would volunteer to interpret.

Aside from language problems, the most difficult challenge facing the Americans who go to Perth is their lack of familiarity with Australian waters. So, too, the French, Swedes, Canadians, and Italians, who have spent more than one summer in Newport divining local sailing conditions. In Perth they will have to start over. For openers, Newport has too much fog; Perth has none. "On the rare occasion when we have something that looks like fog, it disappears in an hour and makes headlines in all the newspapers," says John Longley, a resident of nearby Fremantle, and an experienced crewman and team manager for *Australia II.*

The 1987 race course most likely will be about eight miles offshore and west of Fremantle, which is a city considerably smaller than Perth and about 11 miles downriver. The Royal Perth Yacht Club is located outside Perth's city limits on the Swan River, a wide, undulating body of water that hosts a good number of small-boat races. In life's tangled skein, it was here, on the Swan River, that Alan Bond, a 13-year-old boy from England, first stepped ashore to embrace his new home.

Ocean racing is relegated to waters offshore. The America's Cup buoy would be behind a small island chain and reefs below Rottnest Island, which is about 13 miles west of Fremantle. The land masses and coral reefs protect the area from open-sea swells that roll in across the Indian Ocean on a prevailing southwest breeze. Newport is notorious for the swell conditions that build up on the tail end of a hearty sea breeze. That, combined with a changeable northerly, creates confused seas that run in opposite directions and make sailing a 12 Meter off Brenton Reef more like riding a bronco.

Fremantle, on the other hand, is protected from the open sea's prevailing winds, and an afternoon chop is about as bad as it gets. When the wind is up, it's 15–25 knots. When it's down, there is less than six knots. "The windsurfing conditions are sensational," says John Longley, an avid boardsailor. "You get flat water, which is really good for high-speed stuff. In the afternoon, when the sea breeze comes in, you get a wave, and you can go up by the reefs. If you're a really good windsurfer, you can get up in the morning and windsurf to Rottnest Island on the easterly, have a couple of beers, hang around, and when the sea breeze comes in, you get a rocket ride home.

"All the coastline north of Fremantle is a series of beaches—beautiful beaches—unlike any I've seen anywhere else in the world. Dazzling white sand—not fine so it gets into everything, but coarse-grained and white— and a very clean, beautiful sea."

Perth is a big city of 800,000; but it is also the most remote big city in Australia—a continent nearly as large as the United States. The next closest city of any size—Adelaide—is 1,300 miles away by the Indian-Pacific Railroad. The road system is not high-speed and air service is scattered. Perth has a skyline dominated by high-rises and modern office buildings, and here and there stand remnants of what it once was—a 19th-century town destined to ride the wave of 20th-century progress. Fremantle, on the other hand, with its population of 10,000, somehow missed the boom years and remains as Perth was in Queen Victoria's time.

"Perth is the most beautiful city in the world," says Ben Lexcen wistfully. "It's clean; it's modern; it has a beautiful waterfront and harbor. It doesn't know much about poverty." Lexcen says he would treasure living in Perth, but yacht designing requires that he live in Sydney instead. Longley, on the other hand, prefers Fremantle because it retains its last-century character. Longley lives in a house near the beach, where he likes to hang out with the fishermen as well as the yachties. He belongs to the Fremantle Sailing Club at Success Harbor, a new state-supported marina complex that has berths for 500 boats. The Sailing Club and the Royal Perth Yacht Club will be the centers for the America's Cup in 1987. Both groups are considering annexes. Hotels in Perth were bombarded with reservations for 1987 within 10 days of the last Cup race, and local entrepreneurs were having daydreams that Perth could become the Costa del Sol of Down Under.

The Australians want to hold the America's Cup series in the winter of 1987, which is summer in the Southern Hemisphere. Trial racing most likely would begin in January, and the Cup races themselves would be held in March. The temperature is always warm in Perth. With a latitude of about 33 degrees south, the area has a Mediterranean climate similar to that of Majorca, or of Cape Town, South Africa. Even in the dead of winter, Perth is rarely chilly. In summer, it gets hot. Heat-wave conditions are about 110 degrees Fahrenheit. But, as in Arizona, the climate is extremely dry, and the effects are less severe than they are on Australia's East Coast, where heat of 110 degrees in Sydney is unbearable.

Easterly low-pressure systems scoot across the continent during the winter months. But in Perth's summer, the shifting, easterly gradient gives way to steady sea breezes from the southwest, which build in strength and reliability as the summer wears on. The wind direction rarely shifts as it does so often in Newport. Several races were abandoned in

Newport last summer as exasperated race committee members tried unsuccessfully to set a course that would stay fair in the flukey breezes offshore.

"The whole weather forecasting situation is terribly simple," says Longley about the Perth/Fremantle area. "You've got a coastline, and you've got 3,000 miles of fetch across to Africa. With satellite forecasting, you get these systems coming across the Indian Ocean, and by the time they get there you know exactly what's going to happen."

Reports just after the 1983 Cup series that the current crop of 12 Meters would never withstand the high winds off Western Australia's coast led to rumors that the fleet would have to be scrapped and replaced by sturdier boats. Not so, says Longley, who spent the months of June through December, 1982, sail-testing and tuning with *Australia II* off Perth. Winds rarely go above 30 knots. Fifteen to 25 knots is usual.

Tides are about the same as at Newport—two to three feet. But currents are practically nonexistent. Five-tenths of a knot is not much. To the average tourist, these details are unimportant; but to a 12-Meter sailor who must take wind direction and velocity, tidal patterns, and currents into account in order to win a race, the offshore conditions in Western Australia are crucial.

Jack Sutphen, who has sailed with Conner since the 1974 America's Cup series, says he's uncomfortable about sailing in unfamiliar waters. It's a gripe that the Australians have made for years, and one that is a major concern to challenging clubs. The "local knowledge" advantage was as sacred among the defense crews as the desire to take the Cup away was a holy quest for challengers.

"I think it's even more of a challenge for us to go to Australia," says Sutphen. "We know this area [Newport]. That's one of the things that's disturbing about losing the Cup. We just feel that these are our home waters here. I feel so badly about leaving Newport. It's not going to be easy going to some foreign land where we don't know what to expect." Sutphen, a ruddy-faced outdoorsman with a lifetime of yachting experience behind him, is a team player—loyal, hard-working, capable, and selfless. If Dennis Conner goes to Australia, there's little doubt that Sutphen will be there, too.

The thought that the America's Cup was actually taken halfway round the world seemed, at first, absurd. Disbelievers scoffed that it wouldn't stay there long, that Alan Bond and entourage would realize the folly of trying to duplicate Newport, and would announce, after winning the Cup, that they would bring it back to Newport in 1987 for the next series. Realization of the way things really are came in late September, veiled in the sweet talk that Bond can deliver so well when there's good reason.

"This isn't goodbye to Newport," he said the night of the last press conference. "It's an open invitation to come to Perth and try and win the Cup back."

It was at least a week before the shock waves subsided in Newport. Residents seemed dazed. Some appeared genuinely pleased. Others were depressed. Newport has enjoyed a love-hate relationship with the America's Cup over 12 campaigns. Few Newporters remembered the America's Cup summers of the 1930s, but a fair share had tales to tell of the Cup racing that resumed in 1958 after a 21-year hiatus. Many had been rooting for the Australians for a variety of reasons, some of them so that Newport could have a breather from runaway development and that recent phenomenon of the street—"gridlock." The only certainty was that the revered silver trophy that filled Newport's coffers had been snatched away to a land most Americans knew only through pictures of leaping kangaroos and adorable koalas. Newport was left holding the postcards.

The loss of the America's Cup will certainly change the city-by-the-sea. The Newport Chamber of Commerce estimated that 4.5 million people would visit the resort town in 1983. The number was twice that of 1982. Business was booming; hotels were going up like castles in the sand; and it seemed that condominiums were dropped by helicopter overnight. Newport was steadily growing as a great mecca for tourists. A lovely coastline, attractive architecture, superb summer weather, and a diverse population made Newport a desirable place to visit. But by the time the last race in the final series of the last big day of summer was held, Newport's America's Cup had runneth over. The streets were packed with people; the restaurants were overbooked days ahead; traffic stood at a standstill. Six days later, the Viking Hotel had rooms available; you could get a seat at Cafe Zelda; the taxicabs were back in their Washington Square stand; the tour boat *Amazing Grace* could back out of her slip; and the Wharf Deli help actually smiled.

Down at the Island Omelette Shop, Mike was still flipping bacon on the grill. Gay and Carol were still running cups of hot, black coffee between tables. And Jack, the local recluse, was still shuffling his way to a seat at the far end of the Formica counter. The CBS cameramen who had found their way to this watering hole every day during the last two weeks of the America's Cup series were gone. And the visitor from Atlanta who came to show his wife "one of them 'Merican's Cup boats" had pulled out of town.

"I'm waiting for the Cup to come back so I'll get busy again," Mike said to the customer on his way out the door. "I mean, this is nice. I need a week of it. But then that's enough."

APPENDIX A

CERTIFICATION OF COMPLIANCE WITH THE CONDITIONS
GOVERNING THE RACES FOR THE AMERICA'S CUP 1983

Whereas: AUSTRALIA II, representing the Royal Perth Yacht Club, has won the elimination races held between the several challenging yachts, and

Whereas: the Royal Perth Yacht Club and the America's Cup Challenge 1983, Limited, (herein the "AUSTRALIA II Syndicate") desire to obtain the agreement of the New York Yacht Club to the substitution of the Royal Perth Yacht Club as the Challenging Club and the acceptance of AUSTRALIA II as the Challenger; and

Whereas: such agreement and acceptance by the New York Yacht Club are conditioned upon assurances satisfactory to it that the substituted challenging club and substituted challenger have heretofore complied, and will in the future comply, in all respects with the Conditions Governing the Races for the America's Cup 1983, as required by Section 16 thereof; and

Whereas: Section 12 of said conditions provides that AUSTRALIA II shall comply in every respect with the requirements regarding construction, sails and equipment in the Deed of Gift of the America's Cup, dated October 24, 1887, the 1958 Resolution, the 1980 Resolutions, the Footnotes in Amplification thereof and the Further Amplification of the 1980 Resolution, dated January 30, 1981, (copies of each of which are attached hereto) applying to national origin of design and construction; and

Whereas: information available to the New York Yacht Club has raised certain questions regarding AUSTRALIA II's compliance with said Section 12, as to which the Royal Perth Yacht Club, the AUSTRALIA II Syndicate and the designer of AUSTRALIA II desire to provide such clarifications and assurances as will insure that the New York Yacht Club has fulfilled its obligation, as trustee under the Deed of Gift, to wit, "that it will faithfully and fully see that the foregoing conditions are fully observed and complied with by any contestant for the said Cup."

NOW THEREFORE, the undersigned Peter R. Dalziell, Commodore, for and on behalf of the Royal Perth Yacht Club; Alan Bond, Chairman, and Warren Jones, Executive Director, each for and on behalf of the AUSTRALIA II Syndicate; and Ben Lexcen, designer of AUSTRALIA II, in order to provide such clarifications and assurances and to gain the aforesaid agreement and acceptance by the New York Yacht Club, do hereby jointly and severally, make the following representations, certifications and warranties to the New York Yacht Club:

1. AUSTRALIA II was designed solely and exclusively by Ben Lexcen, a national of Australia, and no "foreign consultants" and no "foreign designer—however he is designated" assisted or participated in the design of AUSTRALIA II's keel, hull, rig or sails.

2. All tank tests leading to the design of AUSTRALIA II, conducted in the Netherlands Ship Model Basin, were under the sole supervision of Australian nationals and the designs were from the drawing board of Australian nationals, in accordance with the letter of June 11, 1982 from the America's Cup Committee to the AUSTRALIA II Syndicate, a copy of which is attached hereto.

3. Neither the AUSTRALIA II Syndicate nor Ben Lexcen contracted with or retained the Netherlands Ship Model Basin to perform consulting and research services to assist in the design of AUSTRALIA II. Neither the Netherlands Ship Model Basin nor the Netherlands National Aerospace Laboratory, or any employee or representative of either of said organizations, contributed any inventions or design concepts which led to or were incorporated in the design of the keel, hull and/or rig of AUSTRALIA II.

4. The only computer programs employed at the Netherlands Ship Model Basin, in connection with the design of AUSTRALIA II, were standard computer programs used at that facility to evaluate the results of tank tests of models from the drawing board of Australian nationals. No proprietary or confidential computer programs were developed for or made available to Ben Lexcen or the AUSTRALIA II Syndicate for use in developing by computer the design of the keel, hull and/or rig of AUSTRALIA II.

5. The keel design of AUSTRALIA II, on which Ben Lexcen filed on February 5, 1982 patent application number 8200457 with the Netherlands Patent Office, was totally and solely conceived by Ben Lexcen, and neither the Netherlands Ship Model Basin nor the Netherlands National Aerospace Laboratory, or any employee or representative of either of said organizations, participated in or contributed to the invention.

6. The hull of AUSTRALIA II was constructed and built entirely in Australia, including the lofting and the fabrication and assembling of all framing and plating.

7. The spars of AUSTRALIA II were manufactured in the United States using standard extrusions; however, all the engineering and design details of the taper and scarf splice, as well as all other fittings, shroud positions, spreader details, etc., were provided by Ben Lexcen, in accordance with the America's Cup Committee's letter of January 13, 1983 to all Challengers, a copy of which is attached hereto.

8. Any computers or other electronic equipment carried aboard AUSTRALIA II to monitor her performance were either designed and manufactured by Australian nationals or are standard "shelf items" generally available; and no such equipment was either custom designed or custom built by other than nationals of Australia.

9. AUSTRALIA II, the AUSTRALIA II Syndicate and the Royal Perth Yacht Club have, and each of them has, complied, and will in the future comply, in all respects with the Conditions Governing the Races for the America's Cup 1983.

10. Each of the undersigned further declares, under penalty of perjury, that each of the foregoing representations, certifications and warranties is true and correct.

Dated: at Newport, Rhode Island, September _____, 1983.

Peter R. Dalziell, Commodore, for and on behalf of the Royal Perth Yacht Club

Warren Jones, Executive Director, for and on behalf of the America's Cup Challenge 1983, Limited (AUSTRALIA II Syndicate)

Alan Bond, Chairman, for and on behalf of the America's Cup Challenge 1983 Limited (AUSTRALIA II Syndicate)

Ben Lexcen, Designer of AUSTRALIA II

APPENDIX B
Record of the America's Cup Matches

Date	Name	Rating	Course	Allowance	Elapsed Time	Corrected Time	Wins by
		†Tons		M.S.	H.M.S.	H.M.S.	M.S.
Aug. 22, 1851	America	170.	Cowes, around the Isle of Wight	—	10.37.00	10.37.00	8.00
	Aurora	47.	(Second)	—	10.45.00	10.45.00	
		†No time allowance.					
		Waterline Area					
Aug. 8, 1870	Magic	1680.0	NYYC course 35.1 miles	12.14.7	4.07.54	3.58.21.2	39.17.7
	Cambria	2105.8	(Tenth)	—	4.34.57	4.37.38.9	
		Displacement					
Oct. 16, 1871	Columbia	1694.	NYYC course. 35.1 miles	1.46	6.17.42	6.19.41	27.04
	Livonia	1881.		—	6.43.00	6.46.45	
Oct. 18, 1871	Columbia	1694.	20 miles to windward from	5.17¾	3.01.33½	3.07.41¾	10.33¾
	Livonia	1881.	Sandy Hook Lightship and return. 40 miles. Distance approximate; yachts reached round the course.	—	3.06.49½	3.18.15½	
Oct. 19, 1871	Livonia	1694.	NYYC course. 35.1 miles	—	3.53.05	4.02.25	15.10
	Columbia	1881.	(Partially disabled)	4.23	4.12.38	4.17.35	
Oct. 21, 1871	Sappho	1957.	20 miles to windward from	—	5.33.24	5.39.02	30.21
	Livonia	1881.	Sandy Hook Lightship and return. 40 miles	.53	6.04.38	6.09.23	
Oct. 23, 1871	Sappho	1957.	NYYC course. 40 miles	1.09	4.38.05	4.46.17	25.27
	Livonia	1881.		—	5.04.41	5.11.44	
		Cubical Contents					
Aug. 11, 1876	Madeleine	8499.17	NYYC course. 32.6 miles	1.01	5.24.55	5.23.54	10.59
	Countess of Dufferin	9028.40		—	5.34.53	5.34.53	
Aug. 12, 1876	Madeleine	8499.17	20 miles to windward from	1.01	7.19.47	7.18.46	27.14
	Countess of Dufferin	9028.40	Sandy Hook Lightship and return. 40 miles.	—	7.46.00	7.46.00	
		Cubical Contents					
Nov. 9, 1881	Mischief	3931.90	NYYC course. 32.6 miles	—	4.17.09	4.17.09	28.30¼
	Atalanta	3567.60		2.45	4.48.24½	4.45.39¼	
Nov. 10, 1881	Mischief	3931.90	16 miles to leeward from	—	4.54.53	4.54.53	38.54
	Atalanta	3567.60	Buoy 5 off Sandy Hook and return. 32 miles	2.45	5.36.32	5.33.47	
		Length & Sail Area					
Sept. 14, 1885	Puritan	83.85	NYYC course. 32.6 miles	—	6.06.05	6.06.05	16.19
	Genesta	83.05		0.28	6.22.52	6.22.24	
Sept. 16, 1885	Puritan	83.85	20 miles to leeward from	—	5.03.14	5.03.14	1.38
	Genesta	83.05	Sandy Hook Lightship and return. 40 miles	0.31	5.05.23	5.04.52	
Sept. 7, 1886	Mayflower	87.99	NYYC course. 32.6 miles	—	5.26.41	5.26.41	12.02
	Galatea	86.87		0.38	5.39.21	5.38.43	
Sept. 11, 1886	Mayflower	87.99	20 miles to leeward from	—	6.49.00	6.49.00	29.09
	Galatea	86.87	Sandy Hook Lightship and return. 40 miles	0.39	7.18.48	7.18.09	
Sept. 27, 1887	Volunteer	89.10	NYYC course. 32.6 miles	—	4.53.18	4.53.18	19.23¾
	Thistle	88.46		0.05	5.12.46¾	5.12.41¾	
Sept. 30, 1887	Volunteer	89.10	20 miles to windward from	. —	5.42.56¼	5.42.56¼	11.48¾
	Thistle	88.46	Sandy Hook Lightship and return. 40 miles	0.06	5.54.51	5.54.45	
Oct. 7, 1893	Vigilant	96.78	15 miles to leeward from	—	4.05.47	4.05.47	5.48
	Valkyrie II	93.11	Sandy Hook Lightship and return. 30 miles	1.48	4.13.23	4.11.35	
Oct. 9, 1893	Vigilant	96.78	Equilateral triangle, from	—	3.25.01	3.25.01	10.35
	Valkyrie II	93.11	Sandy Hook Lightship. 30 miles	1.48	3.37.24	3.35.36	
Oct. 13, 1893	Vigilant	96.78	15 miles to windward from	—	3.24.39	3.24.39	.40
	Valkyrie II	*93.57	Sandy Hook Lightship and return. 30 miles	1.33	3.26.52	3.25.19	
Sept. 7, 1895	Defender	100.36	15 miles from mark, 3 miles	0.29	5.00.24	4.59.55	8.49
	Valkyrie III	100.49	N.E. of Seabright, N.J., and return. 30 miles	—	5.08.44	5.08.44	

Date	Name	Rating	Course	Allowance	Elapsed Time	Corrected Time	Wins by
		†Tons		M.S.	H.M.S.	H.M.S.	M.S.
Sept. 10, 1895	†*Valkyrie III*	100.49	Equilateral triangle from	—	3.55.09	3.55.09	
	Defender	100.36	Sandy Hook Lightship. 30 miles	0.29	3.56.25	3.55.56	
	†Disqualified for fouling *Defender*.						
Sept. 12, 1895	*Defender*	100.36	15 miles to windward from	0.29	4.44.12	4.43.43	
	‡*Valkyrie III*	100.49	Sandy Hook Lightship and return. 30 miles	—	Did not finish		
	‡Withdrew on crossing the line.						
Oct. 16, 1899	*Columbia*	102.135	15 miles to windward from	—	4.53.53	4.53.53	10.08
	Shamrock	101.092	Sandy Hook Lightship and return. 30 miles	0.06	5.04.07	5.04.01	
Oct. 17, 1899	*Columbia*	102.135	Equilateral triangle from	—	3.37.00	3.37.00	
	°*Shamrock*	101.092	Sandy Hook Lightship. 30 miles	0.06	Did not finish		
	°Carried away topmast and withdrew.						
Oct. 20, 1899	*Columbia*	102.135	15 miles to windward from	0.16	3.38.25	3.38.09	6.34
	Shamrock	*102.565	Sandy Hook Lightship and return. 30 miles	—	3.44.43	3.44.43	•
Sept. 28, 1901	*Columbia*	102.355	15 miles to windward from	0.43	4.31.07	4.30.24	1.20
	Shamrock II	103.79	Sandy Hook Lightship and return. 30 miles	—	4.31.44	4.31.44	
Oct. 3, 1901	*Columbia*	102.355	Equilateral triangle from	0.43	3.13.18	3.12.35	3.35
	Shamrock II	103.79	Sandy Hook Lightship. 30 miles	—	3.16.10	3.16.10	
Oct. 4, 1901	*Columbia*	102.355	15 miles to leeward from	0.43	4.33.40	4.32.57	.41
	Shamrock II	103.79	Sandy Hook Lightship and return. 30 miles	—	4.33.38	4.33.38	
Aug. 22, 1903	*Reliance*	108.41	15 miles to windward from	—	3.32.17	3.32.17	7.03
	Shamrock III	104.37	Sandy Hook Lightship and return. 30 miles	1.57	3.41.17	3.39.20	
Aug. 25, 1903	*Reliance*	108.41	Equilateral triangle from	—	3.14.54	3.14.54	1.19
	Shamrock III	104.37	Sandy Hook Lightship. 30 miles	1.57	3.18.10	3.16.13	
Sept. 3, 1903	*Reliance*	108.41	15 miles to windward from	—	4.28.06	4.28.06	
	Shamrock III	104.37	Sandy Hook Lightship and return. 30 miles	1.57	Did not finish		
		Sail Area: Limits & Penalties					
July 15, 1920	*Shamrock IV*	93.8	15 miles to windward from	—	4.24.58	4.24.58	
	†*Resolute*	83.5	Ambrose Channel Lightship and return. 30 miles	6.40	Did not finish		
	†Throat halyard rendered on winch drum—withdrew.						
July 20, 1920	*Shamrock IV*	*94.4	Equilateral triangle from	—	5.22.18	5.22.18	2.26
	Resolute	83.5	Ambrose Channel Lightship. 30 miles	7.01	5.31.45	5.24.44	
July 21, 1920	*Resolute*	83.5	15 miles to windward from	7.01	4.03.06	3.56.05	7.01
	Shamrock IV	94.4	Ambrose Channel Lightship and return. 30 miles	—	4.03.06	4.03.06	
July 23, 1920	*Resolute*	83.5	Equilateral triangle from	6.40	3.37.52	3.31.12	9.58
	Shamrock IV	*93.8	Ambrose Channel Lightship. 30 miles	—	3.41.10	3.41.10	
July 27, 1920	*Resolute*	83.5	15 miles to windward from	6.40	5.35.15	5.28.35	19.45
	Shamrock IV	93.8	Ambrose Channel Lightship and return. 30 miles.	—	5.48.20	5.48.20	
	*Remeasured						

Races of 1930, 1934 and 1937 started and finished at a mark anchored nine nautical miles S.E. (Magnetic) from Brenton Reef Lightship.

Date	Name	Rating	Course	Allowance	Elapsed Time	Corrected Time	Wins by
Sept. 13, 1930	*Enterprise*	*76.	15 miles to leeward and	—	4.03.48		2.52
	Shamrock V	"	return. 30 miles	—	4.06.40		
	*Built to Rating: no allowance.						
Sept. 15, 1930	*Enterprise*	"	Equilateral triangle. 30 miles	—	4.00.44		9.34
	Shamrock V	"		—	4.10.18		
Sept. 17, 1930	*Enterprise*	"	15 miles to windward and	—	3.54.16		
	‡*Shamrock V*	"	return. 30 miles	—	Did not finish		
	‡Parted main halyard at masthead sheave: withdrew.						
Sept. 18, 1930	*Enterprise*	"	Equilateral triangle. 30 miles	—	3.10.13		5.44
	Shamrock V	"		—	3.15.57		

Date	Name	Rating	Course	Allowance	Elapsed Time	Wins by
Sept. 17, 1934	*Endeavour*	"	15 miles to windward and	—	3.43.44	2.09
	Rainbow	"	return. 30 miles	—	3.45.53	
Sept. 18, 1934	*Endeavour*	"	Equilateral triangle. 30 miles	—	3.09.01	.51
	Rainbow	"		—	3.09.52	
Sept. 20, 1934	*Rainbow*	"	15 miles to leeward and	—	4.35.34	3.26
	Endeavour	"	return. 30 miles	—	4.39.00	
Sept. 22, 1934	*Rainbow*	"	Equilateral triangle. 30 miles	—	3.15.38	1.15
	Endeavour	"		—	3.16.53	
Sept. 24, 1934	*Rainbow*	"	15 miles to leeward and	—	3.54.05	4.01
	Endeavour	"	return. 30 miles	—	3.58.06	
Sept. 25, 1934	*Rainbow*	"	Equilateral triangle. 30 miles	—	3.40.05	.55
	Endeavour	"		—	3.41.00	
July 31, 1937	*Ranger*	"	15 miles to windward and	—	4.41.15	17.05
	Endeavour II	"	return. 30 miles	—	4.58.20	
Aug. 2, 1937	*Ranger*	"	Equilateral triangle. 30 miles	—	3.41.33	18.32
	Endeavour II	"		—	4.00.05	
Aug.4, 1937	*Ranger*	"	15 miles to windward and	—	3.54.30	4.27
	Endeavour II	"	return. 30 miles	—	3.58.57	
Aug. 5, 1937	*Ranger*	"	Equilateral triangle. 30 miles	—	3.07.49	3.37
	Endeavour II	"		—	3.11.26	

RESUMPTION OF AMERICA'S CUP RACES IN 12-METER CLASS

Date	Name	Course	Wind	Time of Start Each Boat	Time of Finish Each Boat
Sept. 20, 1958	*Columbia*	Windward-leeward twice	N½E	12.30.10	17.43.56
	Sceptre	around. 24 miles	8 mph	12.30.11	17.51.40
Sept. 22, 1958	*Columbia*	Triangular. 24 miles	N½E	12.21.32	Time limit
	Sceptre		7 mph	12.21.34	expired No race
Sept. 24, 1958	*Columbia*	Triangular. 24 miles	SW½W	12.20.03	15.37.43
	Sceptre		8 to 10 mph	12.20.05	15.49.25
Sept. 25, 1958	*Sceptre*	Windward-leeward twice	SWxW¼W	12.10.04	15.27.27
	Columbia	around. 24 miles	15 to 20 mph	12.10.05	15.19.07
Sept. 26, 1958	*Columbia*	Triangular. 24 miles	SWxW	12.10.10	15.14.22
	Sceptre		12 to 17 mph	12.10.23	15.21.27
Sept. 15, 1962	*Weatherly*	Windward-leeward, twice	WNW	13.10.12	16.23.57
	Gretel	around. 24 miles	12 mph	13.10.26	16.27.43
Sept. 18, 1962	*Gretel*	Triangular Course. 24 miles	WxN	12.20.11	15.06.58
	Weatherly		22 to 28 mph	12.20.17	15.07.45
Sept. 20, 1962	*Gretel*	Windward-leeward, twice	NxE	12.50.21	17.19.56
	Weatherly	around. 24 miles	10 to 11 mph	12.51.24	17.11.16
Sept. 22, 1962	*Weatherly*	Triangular Course. 24 miles	S½E	13.05.19	16.27.28
	Gretel		9 to 11 mph	13.05.23	16.27.54
Sept. 25, 1962	*Gretel*	Windward-leeward, twice	WSW	13.10.09	16.29.57
	Weatherly	around. 24 miles	9 to 11 mph	13.10.13	16.26.17
Sept. 15, 1964	*Constellation*	1964 America's Cup Course	WxS	12.35.08	16.05.41
	Sovereign	24.3 nautical miles	7 to 9 mph	12.35.10	16.11.15
Sept. 17, 1964	*Constellation*	1964 America's Cup Course	SSW	12.10.21	15.56.48
	Sovereign	24.3 nautical miles	17 to 20 mph	12.10.23	16.17.12
Sept. 19, 1964	*Constellation*	1964 America's Cup Course	E½N	12.10.03	15.48.07
	Sovereign	24.3 nautical miles	15 to 17 mph	12.10.43	15.54.40
Sept. 21, 1964	*Constellation*	1964 America's Cup Course	ExN	12.10.11	16.22.27
	Sovereign	24.3 nautical miles	21 mph	12.10.02	16.38.07
Sept. 12, 1967	*Intrepid*	America's Cup Course 24.3	ExN¼N	12.30.16	15.55.03
	Dame Pattie	nautical miles	17 to 21 mph	12.30.06	16.01.01
Sept. 13, 1967	*Intrepid*	America's Cup Course 24.3	ExN¼N	12.35.15	16.04.21
	Dame Pattie	nautical miles	8 to 16 mph	12.35.14	16.07.57
Sept. 14, 1967	*Intrepid*	America's Cup Course 24.3	NExE	12.20.07	15.40.14
	Dame Pattie	nautical miles	14 to 18 mph	12.20.06	15.44.55
Sept. 18, 1967	*Intrepid*	America's Cup Course 24.3	SW	14.00.04	17.27.39
	Dame Pattie	nautical miles	9 to 14 mph	14.00.01	17.31.14
Sept. 15, 1970	*Intrepid*	America's Cup Course 24.3	ESE	12.10.06	15.36.03
	Gretel II	nautical miles	14 to 18 mph	12.10.08	15.41.55

Date	Name	Course	Wind	Time of Start Each Boat	Time of Finish Each Boat
Sept. 18, 1970	*Intrepid*	America's Cup Course 24.3	SSW	12.30.11	Race abandoned
	Gretel II	nautical miles	11 mph	12.30.08	due to fog
Sept. 20, 1970	*Intrepid*	America's Cup Course 24.3	SW½W	14.00.00	18.38.10
	**Gretel II*	nautical miles	7 to 11 mph	14.00.00	18.37.03
	**Disqualified for fouling *Defender*.				
Sept. 22, 1970	*Intrepid*	America's Cup Course 24.3	SWxW	12.10.09	15.34.43
	Gretel II	nautical miles	12 to 21 mph	12.10.14	15.36.01
Sept. 24, 1970	*Gretel II*	America's Cup Course 24.3	ExS	12.10.21	15.33.59
	Intrepid	nautical miles	5 to 12 mph	12.10.13	15.35.01
Sept. 28, 1970	*Intrepid*	America's Cup Course 24.3	NNE	12.10.11	16.39.03
	Gretel II	nautical miles	6 to 11 mph	12.10.10	16.40.47
Sept. 10, 1974	*Courageous*	America's Cup Course 24.3	SW¾S	14.10.06	18.22.03
	Southern Cross	nautical miles	7 to 11 mph	14.10.08	18.26.57
Sept. 12, 1974	*Southern Cross*	America's Cup Course 24.3	SWxW	12.10.08	15.43.48
	Courageous	nautical miles	11 to 16 mph	12.10.09	15.42.37
Sept. 16, 1974	*Courageous*	America's Cup Course 24.3	NW¾W	12.11.01	15.43.02
	Southern Cross	nautical miles	11 to 12 mph	12.11.17	15.48.29
Sept. 17, 1974	*Courageous*	America's Cup Course 24.3	SSW	12.10.07	15.42.25
	Southern Cross	nautical miles	12 mph	12.10.27	15.49.44
Sept. 13, 1977	*Courageous*	America's Cup Course 24.3	SW	12.10.24	*Courageous*
	Australia	nautical miles	12 to 17 K	12.10.12	by 01.48
Sept. 15, 1977	*Courageous*	America's Cup Course 24.3	NE½E 10K	12.10.07	Time limit
	Australia	nautical miles	to SExE 3 K	12.10.06	expired
Sept. 16, 1977	*Courageous*	America's Cup Course 24.3	SxW¼W	12.10.02	15.54.07
	Australia	nautical miles	to SxE¾E	12.10.03	15.55.10
			11 to 15 K		
Sept. 17, 1977	*Courageous*	America's Cup Course 24.3	SWxW to	12.10.15	16.33.23
	Australia	nautical miles	NW½W 8 K	12.10.21	16.35.55
Sept. 18, 1977	*Courageous*	America's Cup Course 24.3	W½S	12.10.09	15.42.31
	Australia	nautical miles	14 to 9 K	12.10.09	15.44.56
Sept. 16, 1980	*Freedom*	America's Cup Course 24.3	E½S 10 K to	12.10.29	15.58.32
	Australia	nautical miles	SExS 12 K	12.10.24	16.00.24
Sept. 18, 1980	*Freedom*	America's Cup Course 24.3	NxW¼W 6 K to	12.25.06	Time limit
	Australia	nautical miles	SWxW¼W 2 K	12.25.16	expired
Sept. 19, 1980	*Australia*	America's Cup Course 24.3	WxS¾S 6 K to	14.10.14	19.16.42
	Freedom	nautical miles	SWxW¾W 8 K	14.10.09	19.17.10
Sept. 21, 1980	*Freedom*	America's Cup Course 24.3	WxS¾S 12 K to	12.10.02	15.45.07
	Australia	nautical miles	SW½W 16 K	12.10.05	15.46.00
Sept. 23, 1980	*Freedom*	America's Cup Course 24.3	W 12 K to	12.10.08	15.51.20
	Australia	nautical miles	NW½N 12 K	12.10.21	15.55.08
Sept. 25, 1980	*Freedom*	America's Cup Course 24.3	SExE¾E 17 K	12.10.08	15.38.00
	Australia	nautical miles	to ExS¾S 14 K	12.10.15	14.41.38
Sept. 14, 1983	*Liberty*	America's Cup Course 24.3	NE to NE½E	12.10.08	15.35.50
	Australia II	nautical miles	18 K	12.10.05	15.37.00
Sept. 15, 1983	*Liberty*	America's Cup Course 24.3	NNE¾E 17 K	12.10.08	15.58.14
	Australia II	nautical miles	to NE¾E 10–13 K	12.10.13	15.59.47
Sept. 17, 1983	*Liberty*	America's Cup Course 24.3	SSE¼E 10 K	12.10.14	Time limit
	Australia II	nautical miles	to SSW¾W 7 K	12.10.03	expired
Sept. 18, 1983	*Australia II*	America's Cup Course 24.3	SW 7 K to	14.00.10	17.50.34
	Liberty	nautical miles	SW½W 10 K	14.00.02	17.53.48
Sept. 20, 1983	*Liberty*	America's Cup Course 24.3	SW¾W	12.10.07	15.39.24
	Australia II	nautical miles	10 K to 15 K	12.10.13	15.40.07
Sept. 21, 1983	*Australia II*	America's Cup Course 24.3	SxW 18 K	12.10.43	15.39.56
	Liberty	nautical miles	to S½W 16 K	12.10.06	15.41.43
Sept. 22, 1983	*Australia II*	America's Cup Course 24.3	NxW¾W 12 K	12.10.21	15.41.36
	Liberty	nautical miles	to WNW 16–19 K	12.10.14	15.45.01
Sept. 26, 1983	*Australia II*	America's Cup Course 24.3	SSW¼W to	13.05.16	17.20.45
	Liberty	nautical miles	SxW¾W 8 K	13.05.08	17.21.26

FREE AMERICA'S CUP POSTER

WITH YOUR PAID SUBSCRIPTION TO **NAUTICAL QUARTERLY**

The editors of NAUTICAL QUARTERLY hope you have enjoyed *UPSET: Australia Wins the America's Cup* and invite you to subscribe to the world's most exciting and beautiful yachting magazine.

Since NAUTICAL QUARTERLY's first issue in 1977 (a dazzling display of America's Cup history), we have won a unique place in yachting journalism—exploring the excellence of boats and personalities that make this sport unlike any other. We tackle subjects other magazines ignore or can't handle, and present them with often jazzy, always in-depth reportage . NAUTICAL QUARTERLY has won the National Magazine Award for design, among other prestigious graphics awards. Our colorful pages (bound within a seaworthy hard cover) include boat surveys, photo essays, and close-ups of people who design, build, race, cruise, live aboard, make their livelihood with—or just dream about—boats. Whether the subject is sloops or schooners, dinks or dories, cutters or catboats or cruisers, NAUTICAL QUARTERLY consistently publishes the finest journalism in the nautical world.

We invite the readers of this NAUTICAL QUARTERLY book to join the thousands of discriminating yachtsmen who enjoy each issue of NAUTICAL QUARTERLY magazine.

Although yearly subscriptions are normally $60, you may use the coupon below (or a facsimile) to subscribe for only $49.50. We guarantee that you'll find each issue an extraordinary experience, or we'll refund your payment for any unmailed copies. PLUS, if you send your check or credit card instructions now, we'll send you our handsome commemorative America's Cup poster as a thank-you, with the same refund guarantee.

Whether as a gift for yourself or for shipmates who share your passion for the sea, NAUTICAL QUARTERLY is designed to please. We look forward to welcoming you aboard.

To: **NAUTICAL QUARTERLY**
Subscription Dept.
373 Park Avenue South
New York, NY 10016

Please send me one year (4 gorgeous issues) of NAUTICAL QUARTERLY at the special price of only $49.50 (usually $60). Also, if I enclose payment now, please send me your handsome America's Cup poster, mine to keep whether or not I choose to continue my subscription.

☐ Payment Enclosed
☐ Charge my credit card:
    ___MasterCard
    ___VISA
    ___American Express
☐ Bill me later (no poster included in special offer)

NAME _____

ADDRESS _____

CITY _____ STATE _____ ZIP _____

ACCOUNT # _____ EXP. DATE _____

S3BUPCA